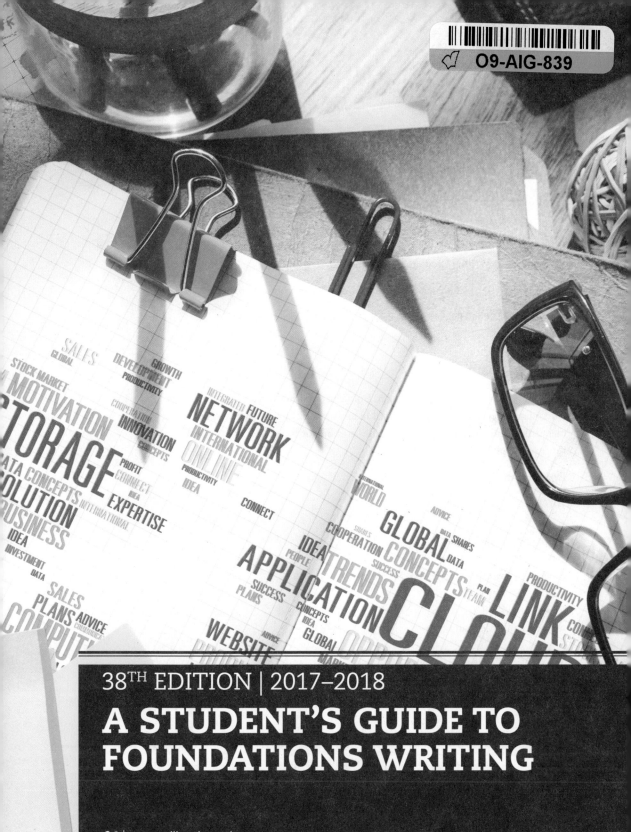

38TH EDITION | 2017–2018

A STUDENT'S GUIDE TO FOUNDATIONS WRITING

macmillan learning
curriculum solutions

printed on 100% recycled paper

ISBN 978-0-7380-9228-7

Macmillan Learning Curriculum Solutions
14903 Pilot Drive
Plymouth, MI 48170
www.macmillanlearning.com

Miller-CochranS 9228-7 F17

macmillan learning
curriculum solutions

Sustainability
Hayden-McNeil's standard paper stock uses a minimum of 30% post-consumer waste. We offer higher % options by request, including a 100% recycled stock. Additionally, Hayden-McNeil Custom Digital provides authors with the opportunity to convert print products to a digital format. Hayden-McNeil is part of a larger sustainability initiative through Macmillan Learning. Visit http://sustainability.macmillan.com to learn more.

bedford/st. martin's • hayden-mcneil
w.h. freeman • worth publishers

Acknowledgements

Writing is a social act, and this book would not be possible without the collaboration of UA faculty, graduate students, and foundations writing students. Now in its 38th edition, *A Student's Guide to Foundations Writing* is more than just a guide to writing—it is a reflection of over three decades of conversations about writing in the university and in the world. We wish to thank all of the contributors to these pages over the years and those who have offered constructive feedback in meetings, surveys, emails, and hallway chats. These ongoing conversations help this text remain relevant as the work of writing evolves.

We would like to begin the 38th edition by thanking our Writing Program Director, Dr. Susan Miller-Cochran, and our Writing Program Associate Directors, Dr. Christine Tardy and Dr. Aimee Mapes, for their administrative guidance, constant support, and continued efforts to improve the University of Arizona's Writing Program and its curriculum.

We also extend our thanks to the Writing Program's exceptional faculty, course directors, and staff. We are especially grateful to our adviser, Dr. Shelley Rodrigo, whose support was vital in conceptualizing this new edition and seeing it to fruition. In addition, we are indebted to all of the members of the Writing Program Action Curriculum and Assessment Committee, who offered valuable suggestions at various stages in this process and generated important content for this edition:

Dev Bose	D.R. Ransdell
Sean Bottai	Kara Reed
Rachel Buck	Jamey Rogers
Jeremy Godfrey	Maribeth Slagle
Keith Harms	Stefan Vogel
Joey Nardinelli	Erin Whittig
Carol Nowotny-Young	Victoria Wilson

Additionally, we would like to thank the talented Writing Program staff who manage everything behind the scenes. Thank you, Monica Vega, Maribeth Slagle, Anne Sheperd, and Sara Vickery, for everything you do.

Acknowledgements

We also owe many thanks to our publisher Hayden-McNeil and especially to our outstanding editor Lisa Wess and our layout designers Christine Victor and Amanda Humphrey. Thank you so much, Lisa, Christine, and Amanda, for always answering our emails, offering insightful ideas, and helping guide us to the completion of this project. We also wish to acknowledge Hayden-McNeil's financial support of our annual essay contest: We could not recognize the excellent work by the writers in our program without your gracious contributions.

Your 38th edition editors,
Eric House and Christopher Brown

Table of Contents

Table of Contents

Table of Contents

Chapter 9: Using Evidence to Make Arguments 145

PART IV: REFLECTION AND REVISION 165

Chapter 10: Introducing Reflection and Revision 167

Table of Contents

Table of Contents

PART I: INTRODUCTION TO FOUNDATIONS WRITING

Introduction to Foundations Writing

CHAPTER

1

1.1 Overview of Writing at the University of Arizona

Welcome to the University of Arizona! By enrolling in your foundations writing courses, you are taking the first step in your journey toward becoming a stronger, more confident writer.

The **bold** terms you'll find throughout this book are glossary terms. See the glossary near the end of the book for definitions.

Being a writer means different things in different writing situations. The strategies offered in this textbook will help you to prepare for these situations by thinking about your writing as a series of choices that you, as the **author**, will make based on several factors. One of these factors is your **purpose**: the reason you are writing and what you hope to accomplish with your writing. Another factor is your **audience**. You might ask yourself, "Who is going to read my writing?" As a writer, you must make choices that correspond to your purpose and audience. Your purpose and audience will become more specific as you evaluate the individual **context** of your piece of writing. Understanding the **conventions** of the **genre** or type of writing that you seek to produce may help you determine a broad idea of purpose and audience. A particular genre of writing may already have guidelines and conventions that will help you make choices regarding **voice** and **form**. For example, a reporter for the *Arizona Daily Star* will use a distinctly different writing **style** from the author of a history textbook. Even if these two writers were recounting the same events, the **texts** would look quite different because the writers are writing for different genres and, therefore, have different purposes and audiences in mind as they write and revise. Your foundations writing courses are designed to guide you to evaluate **rhetorical situations** (purpose, audience, and context), practice critical **analysis**, and respond accordingly.

Foundations writing classes, also known as composition classes, are usually much smaller than your other general education classes. In addition, many instructors make use of full-class and small-group discussion, so you will have more of an opportunity to get to know your classmates and instructor. In this setting, your responsibilities as an individual student will be more clearly defined. We find UA student Ray Hum's advice especially pertinent here:

> "The true value of an English composition class depends largely on the student. If the student approaches the class with high motivation, then the class will certainly be enjoyable and valuable. If, on the other hand, the student approaches the class with an uninterested attitude, then the class will inevitably be a waste of time."

While the small size of your foundations writing class may mean that your instructor has high expectations for your participation and work, there are many benefits to this smaller group. Some of these benefits include the opportunity to receive feedback and assistance from your instructor and your peers. UA student Chris Clark provides the following advice to fellow students:

> "The most important thing all freshmen should know in order to succeed is that you have to go to class. English is probably the most common course at UA, and success later starts in the beginning. You will find that the majority of students taking first-year writing are freshmen just like yourself, and going through the same things you are. It's a good chance for you to make friends while starting college out on the right foot. First-year writing instructors are also well aware that you are going through a big adjustment and are sensitive to that. Not only have I found that the English instructors go out of their way to help accommodate new students, but they also act as advisors if you need help."

UA's foundations writing courses seek to provide you with practical writing and critical thinking skills that can be applied to diverse writing situations at the university and in your personal and professional lives. Attending your foundations writing class, doing the work, and applying it elsewhere will set you up for a successful career at the UA.

1.2 A Guide to the *Guide*

1.2.1 Content and Organization of the *Guide*

The Student's Guide offers useful information specific to the University of Arizona's foundations writing program. The *Guide* is organized into five parts, which reflect the Writing Program's **Goals** and **Student Learning Outcomes**. Each part focuses on knowledge or an ability that you will learn through your experience in foundations writing.

Part I (Chapters 1–2), Introduction to Foundations Writing, gives an overview of foundations writing at the UA. This first chapter is a general introduction and examines some basic assumptions of college writing. It also discusses grades, provides an overview of the kinds of assignments you can expect to encounter in the foundations writing sequence, and directs you to additional resources. The second chapter introduces you to writing studies as a field and discusses how writing and learning work. Chapter 2 will also introduce you to the Writing Program's Student Learning Outcomes.

Part II (Chapters 3–5), Rhetorical Awareness, introduces you to reading and writing strategies. It guides you to think critically about texts that you consume as a reader and produce as a writer through the lens of the **rhetorical situation**. In these chapters, you will learn how a text's purpose, audience, and context help to shape its meaning for readers. You will also explore how writers use their knowledge of these and other variables to create texts that are rhetorically effective.

Part III (Chapters 6–9), Critical Thinking and Composing, explains how to apply the strategies discussed in Part II for purposes of research, problem solving, and participation in written conversations. In these chapters you will learn how to employ different methods of research, incorporate ideas from other authors into your writing, and compose persuasive researched arguments.

Part IV (Chapters 10–12) describes the importance of **reflection** and **revision** to the writing process. Writing is a collaborative process that requires you to be willing to give and accept feedback. It is also a reflective process that requires you to focus on your own goals and practices as a writer. These chapters guide you in responding to peer and instructor feedback, suggesting useful revisions to other writers, and reflecting on your progress as a student in foundations writing.

Part V (Chapter 13) explains the role of conventions, such as **grammar**, **mechanics**, and **citation** practices, in the writing process. This section will prompt you to use *Writer's Help 2.0* to understand and follow the conventions appropriate for your audience, purpose, and context.

Throughout the *Guide*, you will notice references to *Writer's Help 2.0* in the margins and within the text. All of these materials will guide you through your foundations writing courses and can be used as references throughout your academic career.

1.2.2 Using the *Guide*

The *Guide* is organized into five parts, parts II–V representing one of the Writing Program's Learning Goals for students. Each Goal names a category of knowledge or ability that students will gain in their writing class. Everything you do in your class, from discussion of assigned readings to major projects, is designed to help you meet one or more of these Goals and their associated Student Learning Outcomes.

Knowing the Learning Goals and Student Learning Outcomes (SLOs) for your class can help you to track your progress and meet your instructor's expectations for assignments and projects. For this reason, each part of the *Guide* includes an introductory chapter that will help familiarize you with one of the four Goals and the related Student Learning Outcomes. Additionally, the following four symbols appear throughout the book to help you quickly and easily identify the Goal(s) associated with a given activity, assignment, or lesson.

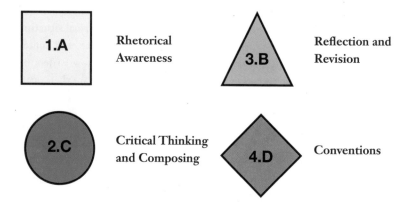

The number and letter in each SLO refers to the specific Learning Goal (1–4) and the specific related Student Learning Outcome (each goal has 5–6 SLOs; they are referred to with alphabet letters A–F). Read Chapter 2 for a more thorough introduction to using the Learning Goals and Student Learning Outcomes.

1.3 College Writing: Advice from Students

Although the course you are in is listed as an English course, it may be different from the English courses you took in high school. Students were asked about their high school and college experiences, and what advice they would offer to incoming students. The following are some of their responses:

"College Writing: Advice from Students"

By Faith Kurtyka

p. 7

Tips for Success from Student Writers

On Time Management:

> **"**Start writing early. Don't procrastinate. Even if it's a month away. You can wait a week, but make sure [you get started], even if it's a simple step such as writing an outline really quick.**"**

On Early **Drafts**:

> **"**Writing good first drafts helps a lot. For the first essay in our class, my rough draft was terrible. I didn't try on it at all. It was like 'Whatever, I just want to get this done.' And then when I had to write my final, I had to work so hard and it was so annoying. So for this second essay, I tried a lot harder on my outline, so writing the final wasn't as stressful.**"**

On Effort:

> **"**One paper can make or break your grade. So you want to do your best on every assignment, because you can't just make it up just like that.**"**

On Preparing to Write:

> **"**In high school, I would turn in papers and show up for tests, it's just the preparation in the meantime I never did. I would always just wing papers the night before and get high C's or B's on them. And so I settled on those grades, but here I can't settle on that. So I just do an outline just to get thoughts going, and then a few days later expand on it, three points for each major point. Just simple stuff—it really helps.**"**

The above quotes show how close attention to your writing process will likely be a major component of your foundations writing courses. Your instructor may assign invention activities that prompt you to generate ideas for your paper—an outline, a discussion or journal post, or even just time to write freely. Beginning the day the project is assigned, these activities can be instrumental in avoiding procrastination and allowing yourself the time to spread out your effort.

Read more about "Expectations for College Writing" within "Writing Processes" in *Writer's Help 2.0*.

LEARNING ACTIVITY:
Reflect on Writing in High School

To reflect on your own transition from high school to college writing and clarify some of your expectations for this class, discuss the questions below with your classmates and your instructor. If you are not coming straight out of high school, try to think of your more recent writing experiences instead.

- Describe some of the writing experiences you have had in high school or other settings (i.e., professional, online, etc.). What were the requirements? What was your writing process?

- What did you learn about writing in high school, professional, or other settings?

- What do you expect to learn about writing in college?

- How have your writing experiences in high school or other settings differed from the previous descriptions?

- What kind of student were you in high school (or another previous learning experience) and what kind of student do you want to be in college?

1.4 Grades and Rubrics in Foundations Writing

The previous section's focus on writing as an ongoing process is important for understanding the function of grading in your foundations writing classes. When assigning a grade, your instructor evaluates how well your writing achieves the goals of a particular assignment. This **feedback** can offer areas of focus for future writing assignments in your foundations writing courses and beyond. Grades are meant to help your writing improve over the entirety of a course, not to punish you for mistakes you make in a particular essay. However, in order to improve your writing, you must consider your grade and any instructor feedback carefully. Try to use any feedback to help direct your focus for future writing. For more on using instructor feedback, turn to Chapter 11.

1.4.1 Rubrics

A **rubric** is a tool that your instructor may use when grading your essays, offering feedback on a draft, or explaining the assignment guidelines and expectations. Many rubrics look like a chart with rows describing writing criteria and columns describing achievement levels, while others may look like checklists. The following sample rubric indicates the standards of the Writing Program broadly defined as content, organization, expression, and mechanics.

- *Content*: This category focuses on the ideas and information present in your writing. It usually includes a strong **thesis**, developed arguments, and a clear understanding of the assignment.

- *Organization/**Form***: This category focuses on how clearly organized your essay and **paragraphs** are and how effectively you have transitioned between different thoughts.

- *Expression/**Style***: This category focuses on the development of **tone** or **voice** appropriate to the assignment, as well as accurate and precise diction. It also takes into account a well-developed writing **persona**.

- *Mechanics/Conventions*: While this category includes grammatical conventions, it also focuses on proper MLA formatting, in-text citations, and the Works Cited page.

When instructors create rubrics, they typically fill in areas on the rubric with their own descriptions of each type of achievement. For example, they will use your assignment sheet to determine the required form or the necessary content for that specific essay. The completed section here focuses on the "Organization/Form" row and shows the shifting level of achievement in each progressive column. Keep in mind that the rubric your instructor uses may differ from this sample rubric, or he or she may choose tools other than rubrics to assign grades.

Sample Grading Rubric—Organization/Form Category

	Superior	Strong	Competent	Weak	Unacceptable
Organization/Form	Organization allows for a building and maintaining of momentum. Paragraphs are unified and consistently complement one another.	Ideas progress logically and clearly. Paragraphs are coherent and are mostly unified with very few breaks in transitions.	Essay is clearly organized. Paragraphs are focused, but are occasionally disconnected from others.	Essay lacks consistency in its organization. Paragraphs are unfocused, jumbled, and disconnected.	Order and emphasis of essay is nonexistent. Paragraphs are arbitrary, and are completely disconnected from one another.

After your instructor has graded your essay, you may see something similar to the circle on the sample rubric. This shows where your essay scored in that category. In this rubric, scores on the left side indicate fewer problems or errors in any given category while scores on the right side indicate more errors or problems. The middle column indicates competence. This column is used when a student shows adequate achievement in that category. Every move to the left of that column shows significant achievements above a competent performance.

Remember that writing is a process, as is your progress through foundations composition. The quality of your writing will improve as the course progresses if you use these rubrics as a tool to assist your learning. Instead of concentrating on one or two errors that you believe lowered your grade, look at the categories where you scored lowest overall and focus on improving in those areas on your next assignment. Finally, your instructor is likely to offer written comments on each of your essays whether or not they choose to use a rubric. You should read all comments with an eye to how they'll help you with your future writing. Feel free to ask questions about your grades and get clarification from your instructor on how you can improve your writing after reflecting on their comments. For more information on grading criteria, speak to your instructor directly.

1.4.2 Grade Appeals

The Writing Program is committed to providing you with fair, clear, and useful responses to your writing, and will process grade appeals in an efficient and objective fashion. A grade appeal is based on the quality of the writing produced by the student and the grades awarded to that writing by the instructor. If you disagree with a specific grade or if you have questions about the grading policy outlined in the course syllabus, speak with your instructor immediately. You may then speak with your instructor's faculty supervisor or the Course Director, but neither will become involved in considering changes in grades until you file a grade appeal after the end of the semester. If you believe your final grade in a writing course was unfairly or incorrectly assigned, you should first meet with your instructor and then with the Course Director. Go to the Writing Program office in Modern Languages for complete instructions.

1.5 Overview of the Foundations Writing Sequence ·

The UA Writing Program brings together students and instructors from a variety of cultures, languages, and academic disciplines. Instructors in the Writing Program come from various sub-disciplines within English studies, including creative writing, literature, applied linguistics, and **rhetoric** and composition; some instructors have degrees in disciplines outside of English. In addition, your peers represent the many possible majors around the university. Both instructors and students come from across the country and from around the world. The writing courses you take at this university will often provide opportunities to explore and challenge your understanding of difference through an exciting variety of materials, class activities, discussions, and assignments.

Instructors may encourage you to explore issues or **topics** that are challenging or even uncomfortable in order to push you to examine your ideas in writing. Sometimes you might struggle with the material because it conflicts with your belief system, but working with controversial issues can help you define and articulate your own ideas within the complicated context of a particular topic. You may even find that topics or issues that were initially uncomfortable lead you to produce your most interesting or thoughtful writing. For that to be a possibility, it is important that you communicate with your instructor when you find that a particular topic or issue brings up negative reactions. They are there to help you articulate and organize your responses to the material they assign.

Embracing the process of writing is a major emphasis for these courses. Class activities may include forms of **prewriting** such as brainstorming or outlining. Workshopping drafts of your essays with classmates will be an integral feature of each unit as you practice strategies for revising and editing your essays according to academic expectations. You will pay special attention to the situated nature of language use and come to understand that writing changes depending on the audience, context, and purpose.

1.5.1 Pathways through Foundations Writing

The most common pathway through the foundations writing requirement is typically two semesters. To date, there are numerous pathways to fulfill the foundations writing requirement. Students often take either 101A, 101, or 107 in their first semester, and follow with a second semester of either 102 or 108. However, students may also be placed in the honors variant of foundations writing, 109H, or 106, the "English Composition for ESL" course for international students. Students may also start in 107 and then take 102 or start in 101 and then take 108.

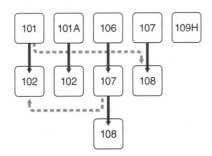

English 106, 107, and 108 are designed specifically for students writing in English as an additional language. Some features of these courses include:

- Addressing language-related concerns in class and through individualized feedback as needed.

- Beginning with the assumption that not all students will be familiar with certain U.S. educational practices, genres, popular cultural references, etc.

- Drawing on students' multilingual resources to support writing and language development.

1.5.2 The Courses

ENGL 101A

English 101A is a writing-intensive, four-credit course designed to help students practice the skills of **close reading** and critical analysis. Each week, you will be required to read assigned texts and respond to these texts through informal writing and class discussions. Three times during the semester, you will write well-developed essays that will each go through an extensive process of peer revision before the completion of the final draft. In addition to the two 75-minute classes, you will also be required to attend a 50-minute studio session once a week. Studio sessions provide further guidance on issues of craft, such as invention, drafting, and revision. With additional studio instruction, 101A provides extra support for students' reading and writing skills by offering small group class time with the instructor. Because of the small class size, students will have further opportunities to interact with the instructor and be engaged in small group discussions. Like art studio, adapted studio creates a learning play space for students to work creatively on projects while becoming mindful of effective writing habits.

ENGL 101/107

English 101/107 familiarizes students with the social and situated nature of writing—that is, with the ways in which writing is tied to purpose, audience/community, and topic/content. As such, there is a heavy emphasis on community, genre, and rhetorical situation. Through informal and formal writing, students will write in several genres, analyzing how purpose, audience, and context shape research, strategies for organization, and language usage, components that will be developed further in the second semester class. In addition, the course introduces practices of research **inquiry** in writing. Reflection on students' writing is also formally built into the entire course, culminating in a final portfolio.

ENGL 102/108

English 102/108 emphasizes rhetoric and research across contexts. Through reading and discussion of content, students engage in **rhetorical analysis**, research, persuasion, reflection, and revision. It is designed to help students recognize and learn to write for a variety of rhetorical situations, including different audiences, purposes, contexts, and genres. Students will conduct research inquiries, find and evaluate **sources**, and make critically aware decisions about how best to achieve their purposes. Further, it helps students become aware of their own writing processes and adjust them to whatever demands a particular writing situation places on them.

ENGL 106

In this course, international students for whom English is an additional/second language develop academic **literacy** skills for university writing. Through reading and discussion of academic content related to language use, students explore language and literacy practices, develop strategies for academic reading and writing, and reflect on their own development as academic writers. Students read and write texts intended for different audiences and purposes, and they'll practice modifying their own writing to be appropriate for different audiences or registers. Particular attention is given to expanding students' repertoire of academic language.

ENGL 109H

English 109H is an advanced, one-semester course that engages students in college-level writing practices and acclimates them to the four-year university as a new cultural context in which to place themselves as writers. Enrollment in English 109H is equivalent to the traditional Foundations Writing course sequence of English 101 + English 102.

In an accelerated learning environment, 109H students learn about the basics of academic research and writing, college-level argumentation, **rhetorical awareness** and practice facility with the conventions of writing in different genres. Because the course has a year's worth of writing instruction to cover in a single semester, the course moves very quickly. Students may be asked to read more challenging material, interact with denser philosophical or theoretical concepts, and experiment with different **technologies** as they practice inquiry, develop ideas, and engage in multiple revisions of their writing projects.

Whichever pathway you take through foundations writing at the University of Arizona will help you learn how to practice and improve your writing for a variety of circumstances through reading texts critically, conducting detailed and relevant research, reflecting on your writing process, and attending to conventions appropriate to the situation. By practicing and acquiring competence in these four areas, you will fulfill the Learning Goals for students in UA writing courses.

Outlining Theories of Writing and Learning

CHAPTER

2

2.1 Writing Development

At The University of Arizona, you will write a lot. You will write a lot in different settings. You may write in multiple academic disciplines, and you certainly will write in advanced courses in your major. In foundations writing, our aim is to prepare you for each of these settings, providing the foundation for future writing success. We know the following about writing development and student learning:

- Writing development progresses and regresses at various times (it is non-linear).

- Students develop effective writing skills when they receive ample **feedback** at various points in the writing process.

- Writing in different domains and across **contexts** supports development.

- Writing experiences outside of the classroom influence your **academic writing**.

In other words, writing is complex. It requires tremendous cognitive skill. It's no surprise, then, that writing is recursive in its development. You will show gains at times. You may struggle at times, especially when writing a **genre** that's new to you. To help writers with the recursive nature of learning to write, composition courses factor in the need for repetition. In this way, activities and homework will repeat relevant tasks that support writing across the semester.

A core part of writing development depends on promoting positive transfer of knowledge. Writers need resources and tools for writing in their future courses and careers to support transfer; composition courses highlight genre knowledge, rhetorical knowledge, writing process knowledge, and **discourse community** knowledge to provide students with an awareness of writing as it occurs across contexts for different communities, **purposes**, and **audiences**. In foundations writing, you will be asked to **reflect** on your writing in order to notice, discover, and explore writing concepts. You will reflect over time in order to draw upon prior knowledge, to describe critical incidents with writing, and to define your own needs, or self-knowledge, as a writer.

LEARNING ACTIVITY:
Reflect on a Writing Process

On a sheet of paper, draw your writing process for the last academic, "major," or "big" writing project you completed. Account for every step of the process, even procrastination. Then write a short reflection that explains your process and identifies what works well in the process and what works less well. Identify a goal for honing your writing process in your writing course.

Consider drawing a second map of a writing process based on another project. Compare and contrast the steps you took.

2.2 Writing Processes

Different writers often have distinct habits that dictate how they write. Dr. Lisa Ede, an English professor, identifies four types of writers in her book *Work in Progress: A Guide to Writing and Revising*. Keep in mind that you might fit into more than one category, or an entirely different one altogether.

- **Heavy Planners:** These writers "generally consider their ideas and plan their writing so carefully in their heads that their first drafts are often more like other writers' second or third drafts. As a consequence they often revise less intensively and frequently than other [writers]. Many [heavy planners] have disciplined themselves so that they can think about their writing in all sorts of places—on the subway, at work, in the garden pulling weeds, or in the car driving to and from school" (32).

- **Heavy Revisers:** These writers "need to find out what they want to say through the act of writing itself....Heavy revisers often state that writing their ideas out in a sustained spurt of activity reassures them that they have something to say and helps them avoid frustration. These writers may not seem to plan because they begin drafting so early. Actually, however, their planning occurs as they draft and especially as they revise. Heavy revisers typically spend a great deal of their writing time revising their initial drafts. To do so effectively, they must be able to read their work critically and be able…to discard substantial portions of the first draft" (32–33).

- **Sequential Composers:** These writers "devote roughly equal amounts of time to planning, drafting, and revising....[S]equential composers typically rely on written notes and plans to give shape and force to their ideas. And unlike heavy revisers, sequential composers need to have greater control over form and subject matter as they draft" (33). These writers often slowly work through **paragraph** after paragraph, rereading and revising as they draft, working from outlines, and planning ahead.

- **Procrastinators:** Although we all occasionally procrastinate, the group Ede labels as procrastinators are people who habitually delay writing anything until they write a final draft. They might wait until the night before the paper is due to begin; therefore, they only have time to create one draft and possibly proofread it before handing it in (36). Procrastinators may justify their process by claiming that they work well under pressure, but they have rarely explored alternative approaches.

It is not important to pinpoint exactly what kind of writer you are, but rather to recognize your general tendencies and consider the advantages and disadvantages of your approach. For example, if you know you are mostly a heavy planner, you can look more carefully at writing strategies described in that area to expand your approach to planning. In addition, you can deliberately work to develop new writing strategies by incorporating useful strategies from other writer categories. That way, if your usual method ever fails you, you will have another option to help you proceed.

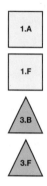

LEARNING ACTIVITY:
Reflect on Your Writing Processes

- What type(s) of writer do you consider yourself to be?
- Have you ever changed your process to incorporate approaches? (See list on page 17 for ideas.)
- In what ways has your approach to writing changed because of a particular assignment, activity, or concept you have learned?
- What does your writing process look like? Has it shifted throughout the course of the semester? Does it change for different writing situations?
- Did you try any new or different approaches to writing this semester? What worked? What didn't work? What might you try in future writing situations?

2.3 Theories of Teaching Writing

Adapted from pages 4–7 of Informed Choices, *by Tara Lockhart and Mark Roberge. Copyright © 2015 by Bedford/St. Martin's, an imprint of Macmillan Learning. Used by permission of the publisher.*

This section "Theories of Teaching Writing" is adapted from the section "Turning to the field: Mapping the terrain of teaching approaches" in *Informed Choices* by Tara Lockhart and Mark Roberge.

Over the past several decades, composition teachers and scholars have put forth a bewildering variety of theories, philosophies, approaches, pedagogies, and teaching practices. Scholars have also made numerous attempts to categorize and organize this thicket of scholarship. We believe that one of the most useful ways to think about these theories, philosophies, and pedagogies—especially for new student writers—is to ask what a particular philosophy or teaching approach emphasizes:

- Does it emphasize the features of the written **text** itself?

- Does it emphasize the role of the writer?

- Does it emphasize the context or culture in which the text is produced (i.e., the "real world")?

- Does it emphasize the roles of the reader (i.e., the potential audience for the text)?

In his article "Composition at the Turn of the Twenty-First Century," Richard Fulkerson argues that these four different emphases can be mapped onto specific historical periods in the field. Combining Fulkerson's ideas with our own taxonomy of teaching philosophies and practices, we can describe four general orientations—all of which are alive and well in our field today and all of which manifest themselves in one form or another in current composition pedagogies and current composition classrooms.

2.3.1 Text-focused Approaches

Texts (both those produced by students and those produced by professional and literary authors) have always been a focus of composition philosophies and pedagogies. Text-focused approaches became prominent in the early twentieth century as a large influx of students entered secondary and postsecondary schools. Faced with an overwhelming workload, secondary and postsecondary writing teachers resorted to teaching from stylebooks, which emphasized simplistic "rules" about good writing, and merely marking errors on student papers. The student writer, the potential audience of the student writing, and the "real world" in which the writing was produced and consumed took a backseat to textual features that could easily be marked, tallied, and graded.

In the late 1960s, many theorists and teachers began to move away from the strong emphasis on textual features. They disparagingly referred to the prior text-focused teaching approaches as "current-traditional" pedagogy, a term they used to describe English-teaching approaches that focused on formulaic writing, sentence diagramming, "skill and drill" instruction, grammatical correctness, and the errors marked in red pen.

Nonetheless, the text itself—whether a student text or a reading under discussion—still plays a prominent role in most current philosophies and pedagogies. In a society in which texts written in "Standard Written English" are seen as a key to social, political, and economic power, composition teachers feel called on both to enforce those standards and to assist students in gaining access to this language of power.

2.3.2 Writer-focused Approaches

The creative role of the author has long been emphasized in literary studies—think, for example, of literary Romanticism when the author was seen as a creative genius producing works of inspiration that expressed unique inner truths. However, in the late 1960s, composition researchers began to examine *student* writers and *student* writing processes, and pedagogies began to emphasize students' voices, their personal experiences and **narratives**, and their ways of making meaning through the writing process. The term *expressive* was used to signify this pedagogical movement, which composition historians have linked to the antiauthoritarian counterculture movements of the 1960s and the individualism of the 1970s. In the expressivist paradigm, texts are seen as vehicles for experimentations, exploration, and self-expression; meaning is located with the writer, and it is "discovered" during the writing process.

As theorists and teachers in the 1980s began to focus more on the real-world contexts of writing (such as writing within academia) and the real-world issues of power and **ideology** in writing, the term expressivism took on more negative **connotations** and was sometimes used disparagingly to denote self-indulgent, solipsistic, or overly "touchy-feely" pedagogies.

Nonetheless, composition teachers today still see students' confidence and self-efficacy as central to their development as writers, and thus the student-as-writer is still a prominent focus of most current composition philosophies and pedagogies. Many writing teachers assign some form of the personal narrative—ranging from **literacy narratives** to auto-ethnographies. The student writer's **voice** is also emphasized in much current pedagogy, particularly the voices of ethnolinguistic minority students, which have traditionally been marginalized or excluded from academic discourse. For example, many teachers allow or encourage hybrid discourse, colloquial voices, and code-switching (particularly in informal writing assignments, such as **blogging**). Such practices, which can be part of a larger critical pedagogy, aim to honor "students' right to their own language," an idea that was first articulated in the field of composition in the early 1970s.

2.3.3 Context/Culture-focused Approaches

In the 1980s and 1990s, the field of composition took what some refer to as "the social turn," moving away from a focus on the individual student writer toward a focus on the cultural and ideological **contexts** in which writing is produced and consumed. In this more sociocultural paradigm, meaning is not located solely within the text, nor is it located in the mind of the writer; rather, it resides in the intersection between writer, reader, and text, in particular social contexts.

Given that sociocultural approaches often drew from the intellectual work of the 1980s and 1990s, including cultural studies, feminism, critical theory, queer theory, and postcolonial theory, sociocultural theorists and teachers have sometimes disparaged writer-focused expressivist pedagogy for its lack of emphasis on social context. Instead, sociocultural pedagogies attempted to get students thinking about the larger systemic structures that shape their experiences of writing, education, language use, and power.

Today, the sociocultural orientation remains a dominant philosophy that informs composition pedagogy, and this can clearly be seen when surveying current textbooks, teachers' reading lists, and the writing assignments that students are asked to do. Whether students are writing about their own socially constructed identities, examining how discourse communities work to shape language use, investigating how specific generic conventions developed for a type of writing, or participating in collaborative, service-learning projects, sociocultural perspectives are often at play in shaping current writing pedagogies.

2.3.4 Reader-focused Approaches

Unlike the prior three orientations, reader-focused philosophies and pedagogies do not fall neatly into a single historical period or pedagogical movement. Instead, a focus on the readers or audience can be seen reappearing throughout the history of rhetoric and writing, from classical rhetoric (which focused on a physically present audience) to current-day Writing in the Disciplines pedagogies (which focus on an audience that shares professional knowledge and affiliation). In reader-focused pedagogies, then, the emphasis is clearly communicating a message that readers will readily understand or on persuading readers to think a particular way.

Each of the approaches we have explored thus far contains dimension of reader-focused pedagogy. Text-focused pedagogies include audience, but they have tended to construe audience (i.e., readers) as a community that shares a single set of stylistics and grammatical rules that the writer must adhere to; the composition teacher is thus the judge and enforcer of those rules. Writer-focused pedagogies also include audience, but they have tended to construe audience as a sounding board for the author; the composition teacher, as part of the audience, responds to student writing as an interested reader who can help the writer more clearly find and shape his or her message. Context-driven or sociocultural pedagogies not only have included audience but have in fact tended to turn the focus toward the audience itself—including the audience's ideologies and power relations surrounding the audiences, texts, and writers.

> Read more about "Academic, Professional, and Public Writing" in *Writer's Help 2.0*.

The four orientations are not distinct, mutually exclusive entities. In fact, teachers and scholars generally draw on ideas and practices from all four orientations. We must thus be cautious not to put ourselves, as writers, in a box in terms of our thinking about how writing works or is taught.

LEARNING ACTIVITY:
Define "Good Writing"

Based on what you read, as well as your experiences with writing, how do you define "good writing"? Try using some of the terms, concepts, and ideas from above to help articulate your thinking.

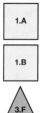

1.A

1.B

3.F

2.4 Theories of Learning

In their book *New Learning*, Mary Kalantzis and Bill Cope map out a comparative description of how interdependent features of learning are applied across contexts.

	Mass Institutional Education: The Modern Past	"Progressive" Educational Modernisation: More Recent Times	Innovations Anticipating the Near Future: New Learning
Dimension 1: The social significance of education	Always important in imparting basic skills and social discipline	More important as an economic force, as a path to participation and as a means of personal enablement	A central part of the emerging "knowledge society"
Dimension 2: The institutional locations of learning	Located mainly in formal institutions: schools, colleges and universities	Happening more and more outside the formal institutions	Something that happens everywhere: at work, at play, through the media; mixing formal, semi-formal and informal learning
Dimension 3: The tools of learning	Based on tools of teacher talk, textbooks and student workbooks	Using a broader range of instructional media	Communicated in part through new media (such as the internet and other new media) that don't need the students to be in the classroom and "on the same page"
Dimension 4: The outcomes of learning	Grounded in subject content, the things you know	Increasingly focused on learning how to learn	Grounded in capabilities, or the things you can do, including the capacity to find out what you don't know
Dimension 5: The balance of agency	A relationship of authority in which teacher and text transmit knowledge to learners	A relationship in which learners are more actively engaged	A relationship in which teachers build an environment of active knowledge making by learners
Dimension 6: The significance of learner differences	A place where one-size-fits-all curriculum seems easiest and best	A place where differences are increasingly recognized	A place where it is clear that effective teaching for learner differences make a difference in outcomes
Dimension 7: The relation of the new to the old	An institution that is quite consistent and predictable	An institution that is challenged by the increasing variety of approaches to education	A series of places where there are many forms of learning; new as well as revived versions of older learning approaches
Dimension 8: The professional role of the teacher	A workplace where teachers are loyal workers who take orders and teach the curricula they are given	A workplace where teachers are expected to take more responsibilities	A workplace of responsible self-managing professionals, who are also intellectuals and social scientists

Kalantzis, M., & Cope, B. (2012). *New learning: Elements of science education* (2nd ed.). Cambridge: Cambridge University Press.

LEARNING ACTIVITY:
Apply Theories to Specific Contexts

Think of a class you've had in the past year. Think of a class or learning experience 5+ years ago. For each experience, briefly freewrite about details you remember from the course; you might remember the space in which you learned, the teacher, the assignments, etc. Use those details to try and align that learning experience in one of the previous columns (the modern past, more recent times, or new learning). Describe why and how each experience fits best with a column; also discuss where and how it broke away from the column.

LEARNING ACTIVITY:
Synthesize Theories

Compare and contrast the "Theories of Teaching Writing" with the "Theories of Learning." Where might different theories of teaching writing fit into the chart? Why might certain elements outlined in the chart be important in supporting a specific theory of teaching writing?

As described in Dimension 7 under the New Learning column, many of the instructors in the writing program incorporate a variety of learning forms, some more current in theory, philosophy, and methodology with others "revived" from the past. This mix is based on their prior teaching and learning experiences, the objectives of their course and lessons, as well as their understanding of specific students' needs and expectations.

LEARNING ACTIVITY:
Extrapolate about Writing Curriculum

Carefully reread the "New Learning" column (consider rereading all columns so you better understand them in contrast to one another). Why might you, and the UA Writing Program, think the teaching and learning of writing is better facilitated within a "New Learning" curricular style?

2.5 Connections to Student Learning Outcomes

Theories of writing and learning inform major philosophies and processes that the University of Arizona's Writing Program promotes in their classes. The Program Goals and Student Learning Outcomes (Chapters 3, 6, 10, and 13) offer a road map for specific assignments and activities in your classes. The four program goals and twenty-two student learning outcomes (SLOs) are what you should be able to know, and do, once you've completed the Foundations requirement at the University of Arizona. Different courses in the Foundations Writing Program focus on specific SLOs. Your course syllabus should list specific SLOs. During the course you will continually be asked to reflect on your development in these SLOs. You will spend time identifying which assignments and activities support your learning in certain SLOs. At the end of the course you will be asked to complete a final reflection for the semester where you will implicitly or explicitly connect what you did and what you learned to course SLOs.

LEARNING ACTIVITY:
Connect to the SLOs

In the first week or two of your class, copy and paste your course-specific SLOs (they should be listed in your syllabus) into a new word processing document. For each SLO, read the introductory material found in Chapters 3, 6, 10, or 13. After you read each introduction, briefly reflect upon your previous knowledge and experience with the SLO. Write your reflections under each SLO.

Read more about "Reflecting to Learn" within "Writing Processes" in *Writer's Help* 2.0.

LEARNING ACTIVITY:
Reflect on Your Learning

After each major project/unit/module you complete in the course, return to the document you started above in the "Connect to the SLOs" activity. Reflect upon how materials you consumed, activities you completed, and texts you wrote contributed to your learning of each SLO. You might want to use bullet points to briefly list the text, activity, or example and then write 1–2 sentences about how it connects to the SLO.

LEARNING ACTIVITY:
Demonstrate Your Learning

At the end of the course, go back to your SLO document. Write a concluding reflection for each SLO. How has your understanding of that SLO changed over the course? What do you know or do well in relation to each SLO? What do you still need to work on in relation to some of the SLOs?

PART II:
RHETORICAL AWARENESS

Introducing Rhetorical Awareness

CHAPTER

3

3.1 Goal 1: Rhetorical Awareness

RA

Rhetorical Awareness. Learn strategies for analyzing texts' audiences, purposes, and contexts as a means of developing facility in reading and writing.

To best understand what a piece of writing means, or how to produce a successful writing project, audiences and authors need to understand a number of variables related to the text. For example, if a college student texted her roommate a note saying "gone to the cafe to grab some grub," we might have some questions about which cafe and what type of food. We might even wonder about the purpose of the message: is she inviting her roommate to join her for food or just leaving an update? The vagueness of this message suggests that the author and audience member probably know one another; the author expects that the reader is able to fill in the blanks.

What if this were the first or second week of classes, with new roommates? They might not feel comfortable sharing phone numbers yet. The message might be left as a physical note or sent as an email. The message might be both more formal and more detailed. It might look something like:

> TeAunna,
> I'm headed to the cafe across the street to eat some dinner. I'm bringing my laptop.
> I plan to stay a while and finish some homework. Feel free to join me if you wish; I
> know they have vegan options.
> Raquel

Both these messages have the same purpose: the writer wants the reader to know she is invited to come eat. However, the different contexts of the message account for differences in tone, style, and delivery. Having already sent a number of these messages during the semester would allow Raquel to send something so abrupt at the end of the year, knowing her roommate would be able to interpret the entire message without as many specific details.

Being rhetorically aware of a text's situation allows you to better design, deliver, and understand what is being communicated.

Read more about "Rhetorical Situations" within "Writing Processes" in *Writer's Help* 2.0.

To meet Goal 1: Rhetorical Awareness, students will be able to do the following at the end of the Foundations Writing sequence:

A. identify the **purposes** of, intended **audiences** for, and arguments in a **text**, as situated within particular cultural, economic, and political **contexts**.

B. analyze the ways a text's purposes, audiences, and contexts influence **rhetorical options**.

C. analyze how **genres** shape **reading** and **composing practices**.

D. read in ways that contribute to their **rhetorical knowledge** as writers.

E. respond to a variety of writing contexts calling for purposeful shifts in **structure**, **medium**, **design**, level of **formality**, **tone**, and/or **voice**.

3.2 Student Learning Outcomes: Descriptions and Key Terms

1.A: Identify the purposes of, intended audiences for, and arguments in a text, as situated within particular cultural, economic, and political contexts.

SLO 1.A emphasizes the need for writers to be able to carefully and critically read other texts. It's important to understand where a text comes from and why it exists so that you can understand why it works and how you might use it in your own writing or thinking. SLO 1.A also reminds us that all texts emerge out of a specific place and moment. To really understand a text, you must understand where and when it was created as well as where and when it is being read and used.

For example, *#BlackLivesMatter* as a political statement that helps define a particular movement is something that civil rights activists during the 1960s Civil Rights movement in the United States could have used. However, the use of the hashtag symbol as a way to digitally organize related content connected to digital social media applications, like *Twitter* and *Facebook*, is specific to the first few decades of the 21st century. Specific cultural, economic, and political contexts associated with specific moments in space and time impact our understanding of what a text means and how it functions within a given context.

During the medal ceremony at the 1968 Olympics in Mexico City, sprinters John Carlos and Tommie Smith hoisted their black-gloved fists up and demonstrated solidarity with the Black Power Movement of the late 1960s. The Black Power Salute, much like *#BlackLivesMatter*, spoke to many individuals who had struggled with racial discrimination and social injustice. And much like the hashtag, the salute became a symbol of tension at the height of the Civil Rights movement.

Photo by John Dominis/The LIFE Picture Collection/Getty Images

Purpose: the reasons and objectives for writing. An author's purpose might be persuading an audience to change their opinion, to feel a certain way, or to carry out a physical and measurable action. Purposes can also be more writer-focused, such as to plan something out or to express the writer's thoughts and emotions, as one would in a journal. A text will often carry out multiple purposes, and paying attention to them will help a writer consider which strategies can be helpful in achieving each purpose.

1.A

Audience: people who are engaging with a text, whether that be through reading, listening, or viewing. There are a variety of audiences who engage with any given text. A primary audience, for example, might be the person or people for whom a text is initially created. A **secondary audience** would include other people who come into contact with a text through other connections with and interests in the author, primary audience, or the topic itself.

Text: any artifact or object that can be experienced and engaged by an audience. A text might be written, aural, **visual**, or any combination among the three. In your writing class, you may be asked to produce texts in multiple media, sometimes without using any alphanumeric symbols.

Context: the circumstances surrounding the production and reception of a text. Context includes a text's setting and the knowledge that both author and audience bring into the text. Context also includes the text's cultural, political, and/or economic backgrounds, as these factors help dictate the author's and audience's ability to communicate through the text. For example, when giving a lecture, an instructor might consider the educational backgrounds of the students in a class, the time of day that the class is taking place, as well as the timeline in the semester. Each of these pieces of information will impact the students' ability to comprehend the information presented to them.

> Read more about "Reading Critically" within "Critical Thinking and Argument" in *Writer's Help 2.0*.

LEARNING ACTIVITY:
Prior Experience Matters

1.A

Describe a time when you did not understand what was going on with a particular text or communication situation. How did your lack of experience or lack of understanding of cultural, economic, or political elements impact your ability to understand the text's audience and purpose? What aspect of the context did you need to better understand to engage with the text in a more meaningful way?

1.B: Analyze the ways a text's purposes, audiences, and contexts influence rhetorical options.

1.B

Consider a professor preparing a PowerPoint lecture for a large class. If the purpose is for the students to understand the class material for an upcoming exam, what information is essential to include on the slides? Should the professor design dense slides that include an abundance of information to ensure that all of the required material is included on the slides? Should she aim for shorter slides and plan to supplement them with a prepared speech? Which font type would work best in a larger classroom? What color scheme?

An important point to consider is that there is no single answer for any of these questions, and each answer should always take into consideration who the author is, who the audience is, what the purpose might be, and what the context suggests. For example, dense slides might be a good choice if the content will be available for student use outside of the lecture when they study on their own; shorter slides might work if the professor is exceptional at speaking through main points and explaining them in ways that written text alone may not accomplish. If the contextual setting changes, then a formal presentation may not work best to facilitate discussion. For example, a total course enrollment of ten students in a senior seminar may prompt an instructor to have an outline for discussion with certain areas or concepts to emphasize rather than a presentation to lecture for the duration of a class.

As you analyze and compose texts, consider how different settings and options might impact an audience, and decide which options might prove to be more effective in aiding a text in achieving its purpose.

Rhetorical Options: the features that an author selects from when communicating with an audience. Rhetorical options include strategies and appeals, and they can range from choices in words and designs in a text to the actual medium in which that text is presented. In any writing situation, an author has multiple rhetorical options available to choose from, and each option may impact a primary or secondary audience in various ways.

1.C: Analyze how genres shape reading and composing practices.

Texts are written for many different purposes and audiences, in a variety of contexts, and in multiple **forms**. Texts that share the same or similar goals, audiences, contexts, and forms are classified together as a genre. Some everyday genres are wedding invitations, condolence cards, grocery lists, and event fliers that you might see posted on campus. Most academic texts can also be classified by genre, such as textbooks, lab reports, business case reports, and student fellowship applications. Texts within a genre tend to look similar because they have similar purposes, audiences, and contexts of use.

1.C

By analyzing genres, we can gain a better understanding of how to successfully read or write in them. More specifically, genre analysis includes understanding the various elements of a genre (its purposes, audiences, contexts of use, and common forms) and how they influence and shape each other. We read and compose wedding invitations, for example, very differently from how we read and compose lab reports—these different practices are related to the genres' goals, audiences, contexts, and forms.

For example, imagine that you work at a local grocery store and your supervisor wants to remind all employees that breaks should only be 15 minutes. The supervisor posts a reminder about break times on a board in the employee work room, but the reminder is in the genre of a memo. As an employee, how do you read this memo? Do you take time to read it carefully? Do you skim it or not read it at all? How would you read the reminder differently if it were written in the form of a post-it note?

As a university student, you will be asked to read many different genres. Imagine for a moment that your writing instructor assigns you to read "Mother Tongue," a personal **narrative** by Amy Tan. You might begin by looking through the text and considering the author's purpose or goal—to tell a personal story about language (sometimes called a "**literacy narrative**"). You might notice the specific rhetorical strategies Tan uses in order to tell this story, such as dialogue and other narrative elements. As you think about the purpose of this genre (a literacy narrative), you read in specific ways. For example, you might try to understand something new about language and literacy, or you might make connections to your own experiences with language and **literacy**. As a writer, you might also consider how Tan uses specific strategies to help her achieve her purpose and impact her readers. When you read a genre as a writer, you can begin to notice how other writers achieve their purposes so that you can incorporate these same strategies in your own writing.

Often in university classes, instructors will assign students to read one genre and write a response to it in another. For example, you might be asked to read "Mother Tongue" and respond to it by writing a short journal or discussion post about it. The lessons you've just learned about genres will still be useful. Before you begin writing your journal or discussion post, think about the purpose of the task and how the form, audience, and contexts might influence your writing and the rhetorical choices you make in it. Keep in mind that most texts try to achieve multiple purposes, for readers and writers. If you are ever unsure about what those purposes might be, ask your instructor.

Genres: categories that group texts based on their audience, purpose, content, and form. As a writer, understanding the genre of a text will help one in knowing the expectations and conventions surrounding that text and will help in distinguishing the rhetorical options that are available. As a reader, the ability to identify a text's genre will give hints to its purpose and will also provide an appropriate framework to aid in comprehension.

Reading Practices: the strategies and processes for consuming texts. You might think that there is only one way to read any text, but as you start reading any text, think about the particular genre, your purpose, and the context, and you can use a different reading strategy in order to help you reach that purpose. There are many ways to read any text, but asking yourself these kinds of questions is a place to start. Think of a *practice* as loosely defined steps—you might start with pre-reading questions, summarizing a section of a text, underlining terms, re-reading another section, skimming a section, writing connections in the margins, and/or underlining passages to use as quotes in a response paper. These different strategies can help you achieve your purposes as you read a text.

LEARNING ACTIVITY:
Interrogating a Text

Before you start reading a text, ask yourself a few questions:

- What would you call the genre? What expectations do you have about the text based on its genre?
- What is the author's purpose for composing the text?
- What do you know about the subject already?
- What is your purpose for reading?

As you read, think about the following:

- What strategies do you see the author using to fulfill their purpose?
- What are areas that confused you in the text?
- What ideas did you think were interesting?
- What ideas can you connect to your own life or to previous readings?
- How is the text similar to others texts of the same genre? Different?
- Is this a kind of genre that you will be asked to write in? If so, what characteristics about the genre can be employed in your own writing?

Composing Practices: the strategies and processes for producing texts. You might be used to writing a draft of a paper the night before it's due and turning it in the next day as a final submission. As you begin writing in college, you'll find that there are many steps in this process and, just like reading, the steps will depend on the elements of the rhetorical situation like the genre, purpose, audience, and context. As you begin composing, you might need to brainstorm some ideas, collect some information, then begin a draft of your essay, get **feedback**, and delete an entire section and start again, re-read an article to polish a line of reasoning, brainstorm ideas for a different section, and edit again before you turn in a final draft. There are multiple steps to think about as you are writing; it is important to think about and experiment with different strategies. As you begin your own writing, think about your purpose in writing a particular genre and how the form, purpose, content, and context will shape that writing. The genre, as well as the purpose, audience, and context, will greatly impact your composing process.

1.D: Read in ways that contribute to your rhetorical knowledge as writers.

Knowledge of the rhetorical situation can be very useful; for example, it can determine how you ask your roommate to take out the trash. For instance, you might consider your roommate's personality and your history with them. Do they often forget to take out the trash when it is their turn, or are they generally responsible in such matters? You are also likely to consider when and where to have the conversation. If your friend is going through a difficult time in their personal or academic life, you may choose to avoid the conversation. You may also find yourself reflecting on the purpose of the impending conversation: Is it more important that your roommate takes out the trash right away, or that they establish a more responsible routine in the future? Your answers to these questions make up the **rhetorical knowledge** that you will draw upon when making your case.

Writing research papers requires the same pre-reading of the rhetorical situation before entering it yourself. You'll want to understand how others have already discussed the topic, what has already been said and by whom. Preparing to write by both understanding elements of the rhetorical situation, especially audience and context, as well as understanding your topic prepares you with the available choices for your text.

Read more about "Reading Critically" within "Critical Thinking and Argument" in *Writer's Help 2.0*

Rhetorical Knowledge: an author's awareness of the choices available for communicating effectively with audiences. Authors make different choices depending on the audiences they desire to reach and the purposes they hope to achieve in particular circumstances. Awareness of these factors will enable you to discern why and how a particular text was produced. Your rhetorical knowledge as a reader can in turn help you to discern the **rhetorical situation**—the audience, context, and purpose—for your own writing, and to decide upon the strategies that you will employ to achieve your purposes.

1.E: Respond to a variety of writing contexts calling for purposeful shifts in structure, medium, design, level of formality, tone, and/or voice.

1.E

The context or circumstances in which you produce a text will influence the choices you make as a writer. Each choice must be weighed carefully, with an awareness of how it will help achieve the purpose and be received by readers. For example, John has decided to change his major; he will have to share this information with different audiences in different ways. His best friend, who does not attend UA, just gets a quick text message that excitedly "shouts" he's changed his major (image at right). However, as hinted at by the interchange with his best friend, this same message will probably not work for telling John's parents. Since John's parents were pretty insistent that they wanted him to

I'm changing my major!

what?

I'm changing my major

to what?

Mexican American Studies

Have you told your parents?

©Hayden-McNeil, LLC

major in business, his message—probably messages—with them will be longer, more formal, and require that he describe why he changed his major and defend his choice. John first crafts an email to send both parents that describes why he wants to change and includes a list of jobs he might apply for upon graduation.

He also includes a link to the *Time* magazine article "10 CEOs Who Prove Your Liberal Arts Degree Isn't Worthless." He then follows up with a phone call so that his parents might ask him more questions that he can then promptly answer.

The following are some of the considerations you may find yourself making based on the context for your writing:

Structure: the arrangement and organization of your writing and the relation of each part to the whole. Structure is always dependent on both content and contextual factors. Depending on your audience, you might present a certain type of **evidence** first; another audience might require emphasizing other evidence by presenting it first. For example, convincing a vegetarian friend to come to lunch at a certain restaurant might require discussing the vegetarian options first. A friend who has a tight budget might need the listing of the relatively low-cost meals presented first.

Medium: the form or material through which communication takes place or is finally delivered. For instance, an alphabetic print document communicates information differently than a painted mural. Audiences will therefore read and interpret a print document differently than a mural. Authors craft their work according to the expectations that govern the specific medium in which they are working. Some rhetorical choices are also constrained or afforded by medium; for example, you might include links to a review about a film in a text message or email inviting someone to go see it with you. If you leave a handwritten note, you cannot easily include the digital link to an online review.

Medium can be distinguished from genre, a category of communication that makes use of one or more different media. For instance, a medical patient's chart (genre) can be produced and consumed on paper or digitally in a laptop, tablet, and/or smartphone (medium). Some genres also combine media, as in the case of a news article, which combines the media of alphanumeric print and photography.

Design: the visual layout and presentation of information in a document. This includes the relationships among visual elements, such as images and graphics, and textual elements. The purpose of design is to enhance visual appeal and readability. For example, the structure of the job resume is compact, listing information pertinent to the candidate's qualifications in the space of one or two pages. This is because employers need to read through several resumes quickly. Many instructors ask that students submit papers in double-spaced **format** so that it is easier to read and make comments on the document.

Formality: observance of the rules or conventions that govern a particular genre or medium of communication. For example, the use of contractions ("We're," "Haven't," "It'll") is common in casual conversation but discouraged in the writing of some academic disciplines. In the earlier example, John could be more casual texting his best friend: not completing sentences and using **punctuation**. Both the genre and medium, as well as the expectations of his audience, did not demand formality. However, since he needs to demonstrate both seriousness and maturity to his parents, John writes a more formal letter in an email.

> **Medium, Mediums, Media...Oh My**
>
> The *Merriam-Webster Dictionary* says that *medium* is both an adjective, something that describes "something in the middle position," as well as a noun, "a means of effecting or conveying something." When referring to the plural of the noun, the dictionary explicitly distinguishes between using *mediums* and *media*. The plural term *mediums* is usually used to refer to individuals who say they can talk to spirits, or the dead. The term *media* usually refers to a type of communication or entertainment (as exemplified by the term mass media). When referring to the type of delivery method of your communicative act, use the singular term *medium* and the plural term *media*.

Tone: an author's attitude toward the reader, audience, or subject matter. Consider the difference that context makes in choosing the right tone for an email message. In a message to a friend or relative, you might use ALL CAPS to convey excitement about a job that you were offered. In an email to your future employer accepting the offer, your tone may be more reserved, expressing gratitude and enthusiasm to begin the job. Tone often refers to an emotional characteristic associated with the text; tone and formality are often intricately linked.

Voice: the style used to convey an individual author's, or **character's**, personality. Voice is usually composed of the amalgamation of the rhetorical choices in formality, tone, word choice, sentence style, etc. Over time, individuals develop certain writing patterns, just as they develop their speaking patterns; this is their individual voice.

LEARNING ACTIVITY:
Rhetorical Shift

1.E

Discuss a time when, like John, you needed to send the "same" message to two different audiences. How did the message change based on the wants and needs of your different audiences? Why did the differences better engage each audience? Be sure to make connections between specific details of the message with specific characteristics of your audience and purpose. What were the differences between structure, medium, design, formality, tone, and voice?

LEARNING ACTIVITY:
Formality, Voice, Tone, and Style

1.E

Search for a few websites that discuss and distinguish concepts like formality, voice, tone, and style (you might want to add the word *writing* to your search terms). Reflect back on a recent piece of writing. Try to describe it in terms of its formality, voice, tone, and style. Based on your understanding of your own writing, how are these aspects of writing different? How do they overlap?

CHAPTER

Entering Rhetorical
Situations

4.1 The Rhetorical Situation

When we use the term **rhetoric** in this book, we are referring to choices writers or speakers make in order to achieve a **purpose** and communicate in some way with a given **audience**. As rhetoricians, we strive to be aware of how language works in these situations so that we can be more effective communicators and more critical evaluators of the communications we receive every day. One of the ways this is accomplished is through acts of rhetorical **analysis**, which is a tool used to increase our **rhetorical awareness** in various composing and communicating situations.

We practice and perform **rhetorical analysis** every day, even if we are unaware of it. We are constantly thinking about different forms of communication and figuring out how they affect us. For example, when arguing with your roommates about whose turn it is to take out the trash, how do you make your case? Do you use personal attacks to make them feel guilty? Do you present **evidence** about how you have taken the trash out for the last three weeks, making it seem only logical that it is not your turn? Do you scare them by threatening to call the landlord? Or do you offer to help so as not to cause tension? Should you bring up this issue at breakfast or wait until right before bed? Do you call a house meeting, speak privately with a roommate, or leave a note? Do you communicate face-to-face or via text message? You will probably rely on your knowledge of your roommates' personalities, your type of relationship with them, and the surrounding circumstances such as time of day, location, etc., to make these types of decisions. Evaluating decisions or strategies used to achieve a particular purpose is at the heart of rhetorical analysis.

Read more about the "Rhetorical Situation" within "Writing Processes" in *Writer's Help 2.0*.

Rhetorical analysis asks you to examine and analyze how **arguments** are made in various **texts**. What **rhetorical strategies** do writers employ? Why? In order to evaluate the effectiveness of rhetorical strategies, you must first be aware of the text's **rhetorical situation**. Put simply, a rhetorical situation includes the **author/speaker**, the text's message and intended **purpose**, a specific audience, the **genre**, and the surrounding **context**. This chapter first focuses on recognizing and identifying the rhetorical situations that surround multiple moments of communication. From there, you will find projects and examples that walk you through different approaches to rhetorical analysis.

4.1.1 Author/Speaker

The author/speaker in a rhetorical situation is the person or people communicating a message to someone else. Depending on the **medium**, the author may take on different roles in the actual production of the text. For example, the author of a print text is usually the person who is writing the material; however, in films, the director would usually be considered the author for the purposes of analysis. In the roommate example at the beginning of the chapter, you are the author of whatever form of communication you choose.

In some rhetorical situations, it is easy to discover who is the author of the message. In many others, the author behind the message is less obvious. Consider a television advertisement for Welch's grape juice. While the visible speaker might be a little girl drinking a glass of grape juice, the author of the message in the advertisement is the juice company, specifically the marketing team of Welch's, who is trying to sell grape juice. Carefully consider who is responsible for the creation of the text and consider the following questions:

- Is the author immediately obvious? If not, who might be the author?

- What do you know about the author(s) of the text? Does prior knowledge about the author influence your reception of the text?

- How might another author compose the text differently?

- Do you get a sense of what the author values? How can you tell?

4.1.2 Audience

The primary audience is the person or people who the author/speaker intends to reach. Although it may be tempting to assert that an article or essay is written for a "general audience," most texts are targeted to a specific group of people. For example, when a United States President makes a primetime televised address that could be viewed by anybody with access to the speech, the primary audience is often comprised of a more specific audience of Americans and, even more specifically, voting Americans. Likewise, most material available on the internet could theoretically be read by almost anyone in the world, but **bloggers**, journalists for web publications, and other digital authors do not attempt to appeal to everyone in the world in their pieces; instead, they consider the people who are most likely to have an interest in their work and write with them in mind. Writers and speakers make choices based on what they know and what they assume about their intended audience.

Keep in mind, however, that the primary audience is only one of many audiences with access to a particular text. Although an author/speaker usually intends to reach a specific audience, there is often a secondary audience who may also encounter the text, whether or not the writer or speaker intended for this to happen. Consider again the problem with your hypothetical roommate. If you leave a note for your roommate to take out the trash, she is your primary audience. However, your other roommates may also read this note. Perhaps it will remind them that their turn is coming up, or maybe they will think you are being too pushy.

LEARNING ACTIVITY:
Identify Audience(s) Impact

1.A

1.B

1.D

When you analyze texts, begin by identifying the most likely primary audience, since this is the audience the author may have had in mind. Then you might explore any **secondary audiences** to analyze how the text affects them differently. After identifying the audience(s) of your text, consider these questions:

- Who is included in the primary audience and who is excluded? Is there an identifiable secondary audience? What details in the text help you to identify the audience(s)?
- What assumptions does the text make about the audience's values and expectations? What in the text helps you to identify these assumptions?
- What are the cultural and linguistic backgrounds of the primary and secondary audiences? How does the text account for these backgrounds and prior experiences?

4.1.3 Context

The context in a rhetorical situation asks you to consider the circumstances surrounding the creation and reception of a text. Every text reveals something about the context in which it was created. The context influences the author's rhetorical choices and the audience's reception of the text. Consider the garbage problem from the introduction of this chapter again. Perhaps this is the first time your roommate has forgotten to take out the trash, or you know they have a very understandable excuse. How you approach the situation within this context might be very different than how you deal with a roommate who consistently ignores his responsibilities. The way you communicate your request to your audience, including **format**, **tone**, word choice, emphasis, etc., is influenced by the context.

LEARNING ACTIVITY:
Analyze Context

1.A

1.B

1.D

Whether you are analyzing a written, **visual**, spatial, or oral text, consider the following questions about context:

- What is the date of publication or delivery?
- What medium is used to deliver the message? What "rules" or conventions are typical to the medium?
- What contemporary events may have shaped the author's views and the audience's responses?
- What social and historical movements are related to the **topic**?
- What are the physical and material surroundings of the event or text (i.e., the city where a speech is delivered or the magazine in which a text is published)?

- What other texts (i.e., texts of the same genre, by the same author, written in the same time period, etc.) relate to your text? In what ways might the text be responding to these other texts?
- If the audience is reading the text in a significantly different context to when the text was produced, how does the audience's context impact their understanding of the text?

In order to recognize the importance of context within a text, it may help to ask how a text would be different if it was written in a different era or was presented in a different medium. For example, a job resignation announced during a toast at a company party would probably be received much differently than the same resignation written in a formal letter and handed personally to the supervisor with a verbal explanation.

4.1.4 Message and Purpose

You leave a note on the counter that reads, "John—you forgot to take out the trash. Again. It smells." The message in this case is self-explanatory: this is what you did, and here is the consequence. However, the purpose of the note is somewhat different. The purpose is to get your roommate to take out the trash immediately. Hopefully, John will also feel so guilty that he will be more responsible in the future. Although the message was simply a statement of fact, your purpose is to inspire your roommate to action. In other situations, the message might be a set of instructions, a moral argument, or an idea. You might think of the message as what the text is "saying." The purpose is the action or response the author hopes to achieve with their message. In other words, what is the text attempting to do? It is also possible that a text might have several related messages and purposes.

Sometimes, like in the example with John, the message is fairly obvious and can usually be deciphered without too much analysis.

LEARNING ACTIVITY:
Analyze Purpose

The key to figuring out the purpose behind the message is to think about the author's specific goals. Does it appear that the author is trying to:

- express an idea or opinion?
- respond to a particular occasion or text?
- inform the reader about a topic that is often misunderstood?
- analyze, **synthesize**, or interpret?
- persuade an audience of, or to do, something?
- reflect on a topic?
- advocate for change?
- move the readers to feel certain emotions?

1.A

1.B

1.D

Of course, this list is far from complete. An author might have an entirely different purpose or try to achieve a combination of these purposes. Considering the purpose of a text is an important step in analyzing its effectiveness and/or understanding why the author used certain rhetorical strategies.

4.2 Rhetorical Situations at the University

An emphasis on rhetorical situations will help you as you move beyond your foundations writing course and into any writing situations that you might encounter within the university. When you're able to take note of your context and pay attention to your purpose for writing, as well as the expectations that your audience will have of you as the author, then your potential for successfully and effectively working through any writing situation will greatly increase.

4.2.1 Writing in an African-American Literature Course

Read more about "Writing for the Humanities" within "Academic, Professional, and Public Writing" in *Writer's Help 2.0.*

Let's consider a writing situation that might occur within an Intro to African-American Literature course, as it was once taught by Dr. Bryan Carter.

The specific assignment that we will consider asks for students to **reflect** on a text and consider what portions of the text and topic had an impact on them. Let's take a look at the wording from the assignment sheet:

Reflective Writing Exercise

This assignment asks you to "reflect" on a topic that you will select near the beginning of the semester. You are encouraged to choose one or more of the broad themes noted in the syllabus and apply your thoughts about that theme along with one or more of the texts we read into your essay. I would like for you to combine an analysis of one or more of your favorite readings along with your reflection of those readings which I expect to be more personal…tell me what you have received from this class, why the topic and associated readings you selected may remain with you for longer than the week after final exams, and relate that reflection to the topic…or even more personal, by incorporating any memories that may have been triggered by anything we read or discussed. I would like for you to make this both a personal reflection as well as an essay where you research your topic and relate it to something we read or discussed this semester. You will be evaluated on how well you integrate the above with the discussion of the work(s) you select. This exercise should be no longer than 3 pages in length, should contain quotes from the text(s), from which you are reflecting, in-text citations, and have a works cited page (not included in your page count). The paper is due on or before Midnight, May 2, and must be uploaded to the appropriate area on our Course Blog Site. Near the beginning of the semester we will begin one or more classes with time for you to ask questions or brain-storm with me and/or your classmates about your chosen topic. The exercise is worth a total of 100 points and worth 25% of your grade.

The assignment sheet gives hints that you should choose something that you have considered throughout the entirety of the semester. That being the case, your **reflective writing** should illustrate your thought process in a way that suggests repeated reflection on this topic over a period of time, in which case you might make it a priority to include some sort of development of your understanding of the topic as it has evolved throughout the semester.

Dr. Carter has also mentioned that the themes and topics that you are to choose from are available in the class syllabus. The syllabus mentions that one of the foundational themes of the course asks students to consider the relationship between race, representation and identity. This context clue will give you a hint that the better reflective essays are able to consider how these terms are working throughout some of the course readings, so it might be in your best interest as the writer to explicitly mention and reflect on how you understand these terms to be working in your own understanding of the material. Notes from class discussions and **annotations** you have made in your reading will aid in communicating how you see race, representation, and identity as terms that help you work through the content.

Assignment sheets also help you in understanding some key constraints that you should take note of. Due dates and minimum requirements, for example, all help you in planning out your writing situation. The due date for this specific assignment aligns with the end of the semester, so you should consider what constraints that timeline places on the assignment. It also asks that the reflective writing be no longer than three pages, which is to suggest a balance between expanding on key terms while understanding a need to be concise. Three pages is relatively little considering that there have been numerous publications and conversations about the role of race in identity and representation. To ensure that your reflection does not exceed the limitations of this one writing situation, consider focusing explicitly on how the theme is discussed in a specific reading or set of readings from your class, instead of making more generalized **claims** that would be impractical to talk through in a three-page paper.

LEARNING ACTIVITY:
Analyze Assignment Sheet

Use the following questions to analyze an assignment sheet from your freshman writing class, or another course that has a required writing assignment, and develop an approach to beginning work on this assignment.

1.A

1.B

1.C

4.B

Audience

- Does the assignment sheet designate an actual and/or hypothetical audience for this assignment? If not, can you infer an audience from the information provided in the assignment sheet?
- What can you learn about this audience's expectations from information provided in the assignment sheet? Consider:
  - How should the paper be organized for this audience?
  - What kind of tone is appropriate for this audience?
  - What type(s) of evidence does this audience find most persuasive?
  - What are the audience's expectations in terms of **mechanics** and formatting?
  - What **citation** style should you use for this audience?
  - What strategies will you use to meet this audience's expectations in your approach to this assignment?

Purpose

- Does the prompt designate a purpose or purposes for the assignment? For example, are you writing to reflect? To inform? To persuade? How will knowing the purpose affect your approach to this assignment?
- What learning goals or outcomes are associated with the assignment? What strategies can you apply to meet these goals/outcomes in your approach to the assignment?

Context

- Is there a reading or readings associated with this assignment? Does the prompt give instructions for responding to this reading in the assignment? For instance, are you reflecting on the reading from personal experience? Analyzing the reading according to a given set of criteria, such as rhetorical strategies? Comparing or contrasting one reading to another?
- What are the foundational themes or key terms of the course? Which of these themes or terms are relevant to this assignment? How might you incorporate or otherwise demonstrate your knowledge of these themes/terms in your assignment?

Read more about "Writing for Business" within "Academic, Professional, and Public Writing" in *Writer's Help 2.0.*

4.2.2 The Accounting Student's Rhetorical Situations

Leonel García-Iñiguez-Madero graduated from the University of Arizona with both a bachelor's and a master's degree in accounting, and he currently works for the University of Arizona's Financial Service Office in investment accounting. Leonel was interviewed concerning the application of rhetorical situations in both upper-level accounting courses and in professional situations.

Can you tell us about the types of writing that were required in your business classes?

During my time as an undergraduate accounting major and a master of accounting student, my studies required various different types of writing. The writing forms included, but were not limited to:

- Company analyses

- Memorandums

- Research essays on business topics

- Accounting theory research papers

- PowerPoint presentations

Analysis was a key word that guided most of the assignments. A company analysis, for example, looks at the intersecting factors for a client, such as the industry they are in, their history, their business models and daily practices, and their patterns as it pertains to their business's performance. From there, we would take note of any trends that are important to communicate to the client and make referrals or suggestions for them to consider. That last part of communication is important because our focus was to qualify the numbers in a way that makes sense for our clients.

Talk about the varieties of audiences you might write to in both your undergraduate and graduate coursework. What was the expectations of your instructors in terms of your written documents and assignments?

The audiences we had in our coursework were numerous. They ranged from simply persuading our professor(s) of a topic, to hypothetical clients, co-workers and managers, and to even actual business clients. The expectations of our written documents were highly focused on who we were writing for, and the expectation was that we were adhering to what was the business norm for each type of writing (e.g., if we were speaking to a manager—be more formal, if conveying bad news to a client—use the indirect approach of communication to explain the situation before disclosing the end result).

While a lot of our assignments had imagined audiences and operated on hypotheticals, I really valued the opportunities to work with real clients in real situations. I'm reminded of a contest that was a part of my junior year of undergraduate course work where we participated in a case competition sponsored by GEICO. The VP of marketing came to talk with us and mentioned their issues with retention for a younger customer base. So our task was to evaluate the situation, and as a group create a presentation that featured a PowerPoint or other presentation format, and handouts/other supplemental materials. The presentation also had to be timed effectively and well-rehearsed. I found that opportunity to do research for a popular company and make suggestions based off of research to be effective as it was as close to a high stakes simulation of real work experiences that we probably received.

What are some types of writing used in your profession? How did you learn the conventions for these different genres?

Some types of writing used in my profession are Memorandums, Reports, Emails, and PowerPoints. I learned about these conventions mostly through the study of business communication throughout my time as an undergraduate and graduate student at the University. For students at the Eller College of Management, business communication courses are required. It is in these classes that we learned not only what the form and **structure** was of these different genres, but how to effectively approach the audience in these writing formats. In addition, these courses provided my classmates and myself with what was considered "normal" business trade communication, to adjust to the climate of communication in the business industry.

What writing advice would you give to students seeking degrees and eventually professions in business?

The first of two pieces of writing advice I would have for students seeking degrees and professions in business is use the time that is already required of you in your first-year writing class to learn the importance of audience awareness. Most of my business experience has reflected the importance of understanding who you are writing to and for what purposes, and these first-year courses are the classes that help students better organize their thought process and their ability to utilize different types of writing applications effectively to any type of audience. With that comes my second piece of writing advice—during the time in business communication courses, take the **feedback** and review from not only your teachers, but also your peers, seriously. These are the times where learning how to perfect business communication comes to fruition. In any business school, there is that aspect of feedback and review process for writing assignments, so become involved in it as much as you can to learn about your writing style as it applies to business communication.

4.3 Rhetorical Interventions in Professions

Learning to analyze and respond to rhetorical situations now will also prepare you for the work you do beyond the university. According to a 2013 survey conducted by Hart Research Associates, 93% of employers say that communication skills are more important than a candidate's major in college. Whether it's responding to emails, interfacing in the workplace, or posting on social media, all industries value workers who can listen, speak, and write effectively. For this reason, the ability to assess and respond appropriately to a situation based on your purpose, audience, and context can help you to succeed in whatever career path you choose. This section provides a look into rhetorical situations that occur in the fields of graphic design and electrical engineering from the perspectives of working professionals in these industries.

4.3.1 The Graphic Designer's Rhetorical Situations

Courtesy of Christine Louise Larson.

Above is cover artwork created by freelance graphic designer Christine Louise for the 2014 Annual Report for the Center for Cultural Innovation, a non-profit organization based in Los Angeles. Christine was interviewed about her consideration of purpose, audience, and context when creating the artwork.

Can you tell us about the Center for Cultural Innovation and the genre of the Annual Report? What is the purpose of this document?

The Center for Cultural Innovation is a non-profit organization that works to support artists who are starting businesses or who already have small businesses to better establish themselves as entrepreneurs. Their Annual Report is a summary of what the organization did for that year [2014], such as initiatives and funding they worked on. It also includes testimony from the artists who have been supported by the organization. The report is given to the stakeholders for the organization so they can see what the organization has been doing. These are people who sit on the board, people who fund, guide, or represent the organization.

Who is the audience for the Annual Report? How did your knowledge of the audience affect your process of creating the cover artwork?

I was approached by the president of the organization to **design** the report. She told me that reports made in the past were fine; they were organized well and listed information that stakeholders needed. But they wanted something fresh, new, and innovative ("innovative" is in their title!). They're catering to a creative community and they wanted their report to reflect that. I suggested that we could focus on the cover and make it dynamic and interesting.

My goal was to illustrate what the center's mission is. On the bottom of the image is an artist or creative person who maybe doesn't have all the savvy to be a successful business person. But he finds a key that unlocks a machine with three major categories: knowledge, network and financial independence. He goes through the machine, and when he comes out he's still an artist but also has the savvy to be a successful business person.

In addition to the client, I inevitably ended up thinking about the stakeholders who would read the Report. It makes it easier to work when you actually think, "Who is going to be picking this document up?" Stakeholders are especially passionate about what the company is doing. If you think about what they're called—Center for Cultural Innovation—it's really cool. They're taking artists who are incredibly talented but might be lacking business experience, and giving them this tool to be savvy enough to make a living off of their talent. Thinking about it, I realized that's what's going to be so important to the stakeholders— that's why they're going to want to invest. So that made me think, "This piece really needs to represent what it is that the company is doing."

How did knowing the audience for the report affect your choices in terms of visual design, such as color, style, and tone?

Part of what you see is my aesthetic style as a designer. If I were to send you other things you'd probably look at them and think, she's got a clear aesthetic style that tends to use bright colors. I am drawn to things that make me feel happy, that make me feel good. I like when I look at something and there's lots to look at; so it keeps your eyes kind of busy and there are kind of details. A lot of the work I did once I found my aesthetic style were these kind of simple illustrations; that's what I really enjoy doing and what clients seem to like.

Because the artwork was created for a non-profit that supports artists, I felt like I had more leeway being whimsical than for a different organization. Plenty of annual reports are very serious, and they have photographs of people doing serious things. They could be laid out really well and the creator could have a great eye, and that could be what the client wanted. But I've seen so much of that serious tone—it gets a bit old, right? I wanted the final product to enhance the work that this organization does and make it come to life. The report is mostly text and the visual representation can bring it to life. They're doing lively things so to put a lively, colorful, active image on the cover helps to illustrate what it is that they're doing and kind of embellish the text.

At first I was a little nervous looking at it. Someone might look at that and have completely no idea what's going on. I made another version of the image that was still fun, but a little more safe. There wasn't as much room for interpretation. Ultimately they went with the more whimsical one. I felt that one would be okay, because obviously they're supporting artists and creative individuals, and they might be a little more supportive of that style.

How did contextual factors, such as the time and place in which you designed the artwork, influence the final product?

Just before designing the report I had watched the film *Babes in Toyland* (1961), which became the inspiration for the cover art. In the film there's a toymaker who works at this toyshop. At one point in the movie he makes a machine that makes toys. On the cover of the report, you see an artist who enters a fun, colorful, whimsical machine and it spurts out a more successful, more grounded individual. Now, in the movie the toymaker's machine ends up breaking [laughs]. So the analogy isn't perfect, but on a visual level it worked.

LEARNING ACTIVITY:
Outline a "Real-World" Rhetorical Situation

Think of a job, internship, or volunteer position that you have held in the past or hold currently. Use the following questions to construct an account of your rhetorical situation while working in this position. Share your answers in a group or with a partner.

| 1.A |

| 1.B |

| 1.C |

| 4.B |

Audience

- With whom did you communicate on a regular basis while working in this position? Consider co-workers, bosses, customers/clients, etc.
- What expectations did this audience hold for how you communicated and presented yourself? Consider:
    - tone
    - speaking style
    - body language
    - eye contact
    - dress
    - etiquette
    - writing **style**

- Think of a time you failed to communicate effectively with the above audience. What might you do, or have done, differently to improve communication with this audience?
- Think of a time you communicated effectively with the above audience. What did you do to communicate effectively in this instance? Why do you believe this interaction or exchange was a success?

Purpose

- What was the purpose or "mission" of the organization for which you worked/volunteered?

- What was your purpose as a worker/volunteer? What job or jobs were you tasked with in this position? How did this work contribute to the larger mission of the organization?
- Did knowing your purpose in the organization and/or the organization's mission help you to communicate more effectively to do your job? Why or why not?

Context

- What medium of communication did you use when communicating for this job? For example, were you communicating face-to-face? Over the phone? Via email?
- How did the medium of your communication affect, either positively or negatively, your ability to communicate effectively?
- Describe the culture of the company or organization for which you worked. Were there unspoken rules or expectations that dictated how people interacted in the workplace? Did these rules help or hinder you in achieving your purpose in the organization?

4.3.2 The Engineer's Rhetorical Situations

Rusita Desai-Brown is an electrical design engineer who specializes in products manufactured for aircrafts, such as commercial airplanes and private jets. She was interviewed about her consideration of purpose, audience, and context when writing a process specification, a genre of writing that is common in engineering.

Read more about "Writing for the Natural and Applied Sciences" within "Academic, Professional, and Public Writing" in *Writer's Help 2.0*.

Can you tell us about the genre of the process specification? What is the purpose of this document?

As an engineer, I need to have certain parts manufactured so I can use them to build my company's products. So I write up a specification, or "spec," that describes the parts I want and how to build them. For example, I wanted material coated with a particular kind of waterproof material, so I wrote out a spec that said (in summary): "I want this material and I want the waterproof coating in this location." And I sent it to a company that specializes in waterproof coating. And they wrote back, "We can do it based on your specifications for such and such price." So I placed the order.

Who is the primary audience for the process spec? How does your knowledge of the audience affect your process for writing a spec?

Specs are written, first, for the vendor who receives the spec and makes the part. I have to make sure the right kind of work is done, so I need to spell out every single thing in the document. For example, "You need to do this coating with class 3." The vendor holds my company to what I wrote in the spec. Once, I made a typo. One of the dimensions on my drawing was wrong. Then I had

200 boards that were off by a millimeter. They all got rejected when they came to our location. My company tried to return them to the vendor, but they [the vendor] referred back to the dimensions written in the spec. We kind of had to swallow it because the fault was in our paperwork.

Another time I ordered boards that needed to be spray-coated with a certain material. When we received them, the material was brushed—not sprayed—on. So we shipped them back to the vendor: $13,000 worth of boards! This time, it was the vendor who didn't follow the spec, so my company didn't have to pay for the boards. If I had missed that detail when writing the spec, my company would have had to pay for all of those boards.

Does anyone else read the process spec aside from the vendor?

Yes, vendors are not the only audience for specs. There is also the receiving department at my own company whose job it is to verify that the product from the vendor meets my specifications. In other words, someone within my company has to verify that what I expected to receive was received. Every time I receive something, they have to take dimensions of it, make sure the right parts are coated, etc. Unlike the vendor, this audience doesn't understand technical language, so I have to make sure all the details are included. I have to be very clear, specific, and detailed for that audience.

How do contextual factors, such as the time and place in which you write a process spec, influence the final product?

As an engineer, how you write a process spec depends on the company you're working for. Each company has its own expectations. I have seen examples of this in the process specifications my company receives for the products we manufacture and sell to our own customers. We get specs that are vague; they'll say, "Do whatever you want." Some are so detailed. They want everything perfect. They want **documentation** for everything. So, each company has its own criteria.

How you write the spec also depends on how a product is going to be used. If I know that the boards I am ordering are going in a plane's engine, I'll make sure my instructions are perfect. If the boards are just to play around with, fiddle with, try stuff with, then I don't care. It depends on your application.

Analyzing Rhetorical Situations

CHAPTER

5

(continued)

5.1 All Texts Are Rhetorical

Sometimes you may become confused about how your instructor uses the term *rhetoric*. Your instructor might ask you to analyze a **rhetorical situation** or ask you to conduct a **rhetorical analysis**. They may ask you to analyze how a **text** performs specific types of rhetorical reasoning or applies different **rhetorical strategies**. Don't be overwhelmed. Instead, first focus on what you are being asked to analyze.

5.1.1 Preparations to Produce Texts

Your instructor might ask you to rhetorically analyze a situation prior to you producing materials. You'll be asked to carefully articulate **purpose**, **audience**, **topic**, **context**, **genre**, **modality**, etc. In carefully understanding your situation, you will be able to make decisions about what you are doing to meet those variables. Writing a text for your roommate, you might leave off capitalization and **punctuation**. Writing an email to your instructor asking a question, you might want to include both. In short, understanding the rhetorical situation allows you to produce a more effective text. Chapter 4, Part 4.1 "The Rhetorical Situation," gives you a framework to analyze a rhetorical situation prior to producing a text.

5.1.2 Analyses of Existing Texts

Your instructor might ask you to conduct a rhetorical analysis of a text that already exists. In that instance, you'll carefully articulate the same elements of the rhetorical situation, and then discuss whether the text effectively meets, or not, those rhetorical requirements. You may even be asked to analyze your own writing as a form of reflection; you will be required to identify the rhetorical situation for which you wrote and then discuss how specific sections of your document support the situation.

The rest of this chapter supports the instances when your instructor asks you to rhetorically analyze a text. However, with a slight flip of perspective, most of this material is just as useful to help you produce your own texts.

5.2 Rhetorical Strategies

An **author** makes specific choices in order to influence the audience. Rhetorical strategies might include the following ranges:

- specific lines of reasoning and/or precise pieces of **evidence**,

- specific word choice and/or the organization of **paragraphs** in a written essay, or

- color choices and/or the arrangement of subjects in a painting.

Aristotle grouped common rhetorical choices into three types: strategies that an author uses to establish **credibility** or **character** (**ethos**), strategies that appeal to the emotions of the audience (**pathos**), and strategies that an author uses to appeal to the audience's sense of reason or logic (**logos**). The following lists of strategies are grouped in this way. Keep in mind that texts rely on multiple strategies to convey a purpose and that one strategy might affect or appeal to the audience in multiple ways.

> Read more about "Analyzing Arguments" within "Critical Thinking and Argument" in *Writer's Help 2.0.*

5.2.1 Appeals to Credibility and Character (Ethos)

An author establishes credibility in a variety of ways. Previous knowledge about the author, such as their qualifications or known affiliations, can immediately help establish their credibility. But you also want to consider what the author does specifically within the text to build their credibility. By expressing sound logic and demonstrating knowledge about a subject, authors can convincingly establish credibility and gain trust from their audience. Credibility can also be established visually and spatially; think of the ways that a speaker's choice of clothing, grooming, and body language makes us believe that he or she is worthy of our trust, or how the design of a website or poster can lend a sense of legitimacy to the writer.

Authors might also establish credibility by showing their quality of character. For example, an author writing a letter to parents about education reform might refer to personal experiences working as an elementary school principal and propose changes that directly impact students (such as access to technology and more counseling services on campus) in order to appear knowledgeable and personally invested in the well-being of students. An author should consider the qualities of character that the particular audience is likely to admire or respect and craft their ethos accordingly.

LEARNING ACTIVITY:
Analyze Ethos

Analyze a text to identify how the author developed their ethos. The following is a list of strategies that an author might employ to appear credible and of appropriate character:

1.B

2.B

4.C

- Personal stories
- References to credible **sources**
- Word choice
- **Tone**
- Visual arrangement
- Author's public image (i.e., reputation, physical appearance)
- Information about the author's expertise
- Acknowledgment of counterarguments and refutations to those arguments
- Appeals to values or beliefs shared by the audience

After identifying these strategies or other appeals to credibility and character in the text, ask yourself the following: How do these strategies affect the audience's perception of the author's credibility and character? How does the use of these strategies impact the effectiveness of the text's overall message? Are there any instances where the author's bias makes you doubt their credibility?

5.2.2 Appeals to Emotion (Pathos)

Authors might also employ a variety of strategies that appeal to an audience's emotions. In many cases there will be a definable emotion that the author draws on, such as humor or fear, but in certain situations there may appear to be very little emotional appeal. Even when it seems that a text lacks an emotional component, the author is making choices to that end. For example, consider why the writer of a lab report or a business memo might want to avoid provoking their reader.

LEARNING ACTIVITY:
Analyze Pathos

Try looking for the following strategies that can affect the audience's emotional response to a text:

- Personal stories or other emotionally compelling **narratives**
- Repetition of keywords
- Level of formality
- Humor
- Shocking statistics
- Images
- Color palette
- Music
- Sound effects
- Tone of **voice**

When identifying and analyzing these strategies, consider the following: What emotional response is the author attempting to create? Are these emotions effective or ineffective for this particular audience and rhetorical situation? How do these emotional appeals affect the credibility of the author or the argument of the text?

5.2.3 Appeals to Logic or Rational Decision Making (Logos)

There are many ways to judge how a speaker uses logic or reason to make a convincing argument. Keep in mind as you read this section that a logical appeal does not necessarily mean an author/speaker is using sound logic; even faulty logical appeals can sometimes be persuasive if they appeal to the audience's desires or needs in a particular way.

LEARNING ACTIVITY:
Analyze Logos

Use the following list of strategies to analyze how an author might make the message or purpose of a text appear logical to a specific audience:

- Examples and comparisons
- Historical records
- Statistics
- Interviews or expert opinions
- Effective organization of sentences, paragraphs, ideas, images, etc.
- Clear transitions between sections of text
- Arrangement of images/text for sequence
- Arrangement of images/text for emphasis/focus
- Size/color relationships between objects

When examining a text, you should also be aware of potential flaws in logic, also known as **logical fallacies**. While fallacies can be used strategically, make sure to analyze them carefully to figure out why an author/speaker has employed them.

5.2.4 Beyond Ethos, Pathos, and Logos

When rhetorically analyzing a text in terms of the three Classical appeals (ethos, logos, and pathos), it is important to think about the relationship(s) among these appeals. There is often much overlap between and among these three appeals. For instance, if an audience recognizes that a speaker is blatantly and carelessly manipulating their emotions, it would undermine the speaker's credibility. Similarly, an audience may not look favorably upon a speaker's character if she or he uses deceitful or illogical reasoning (fallacies).

If you review the strategies outlined throughout this section, you will notice that the same strategy can serve multiple purposes. As you conduct a rhetorical analysis, you will have to decide which strategies are the most important and why—and how—they are being employed toward an audience for a specific purpose. For example, an informal tone can help to build a certain kind of relationship between the author and the audience (ethos), which can, in turn, help the author to connect to the audience on an emotional level (pathos).

There is also more to a text than just ethos, logos, and pathos. These broad categories of appeal are present in all rhetorical acts and are a good starting point for your analysis, but remember that your focus should be on how specific strategies or choices work to serve the text's rhetorical situation (audience, purpose, genre, and context). Consider how the different strategies employed operate in relation to other elements of text.

5.3 Rhetorical Analysis Projects

"Example Rhetorical Analysis of a TED Talk"

By Maria Conti

pp. 58–62

5.3.1 Example Rhetorical Analysis of a TED Talk

TED (technology, entertainment, design) conferences are known for their engaging live speakers who focus on a variety of innovative ideas and perspectives. In this section, you will read about the process of rhetorically analyzing a TED Talk. Similar to rhetorically analyzing any other type of text, this process begins with identifying the TED Talk's rhetorical situation. From there you can evaluate the extent to which the chosen strategies are effective.

First, view the TED Talk "Our Century's Greatest Injustice" by Sheryl WuDunn.[1] You can find it on TED.com by typing the author or title into the search bar. After you've watched the talk, you might want to click on "View Interactive Transcript." This allows you to return to the written text for closer analysis.

1. Identify the Rhetorical Situation

Context

TED Talks often involve inspirational stories, passionate speakers, and activism for a specific cause or idea. Since texts are created in a specific time, space, and place, the genre of the TED Talk exists in a certain context of its own. WuDunn's talk is given at TEDGlobal, one of the versions of the TED conference (there are also local, independently organized versions of TED called TEDx). Specifically, this talk is one of many from the 2010 TEDGlobal conference in Oxford. People attending WuDunn's talk may have already listened to other presentations on the subject, which may impact their response to her presentation. Because the reception of a text's message is often influenced by contemporary events and social movements, Sheryl WuDunn needs to consider the global economic downturn of 2008 and 2009 and its effect on spending in order to make an effective appeal for donations and aid.

---

1 WuDunn, Sheryl. "Our Century's Greatest Injustice," *TED: Ideas worth spreading*, July 2010, http://www.ted.com/talks/sheryl_wudunn_our_century_s_greatest_injustice.

Medium

WuDunn is able to deliver a live presentation to appeal to audience members in keeping with the **medium** of the TED Talk. However, one of the limitations of a TED Talk (and other oral presentations) is that complex ideas can become distorted. WuDunn may have had to simplify her more complex arguments for a listening audience. In the same way, she may have had additional points that were constrained by time. It generally takes much longer to listen to a message than it does to read about it. Other media may have afforded her more room in these areas. TED Talks are usually accompanied by another medium: visual aids, such as slideshows and videos. WuDunn uses this medium to emphasize important points by providing accompanying images. Further on in this analysis, we will look at another way the visual medium allows WuDunn to appeal to her audience's emotions.

Author/Speaker/Composer

Prior knowledge about the speaker of a TED Talk can influence the audience's understanding of the message. Sheryl WuDunn is a well-known journalist. She and her husband, Nick Kristof, another renowned journalist, co-wrote the book *Half the Sky: Turning Oppression into Opportunity for Women Worldwide*. This book argues that empowering women can spur development. The audience for WuDunn's TED Talk may already be familiar with her work in this area, which may affect the way she addresses them.

Audience(s)

Primary Audience

The message of this TED Talk was created to appeal to a specific audience. The primary audience, based on an understanding of the context, is probably comprised of wealthy individuals who can afford the steep conference registration fee of $8,500 ("TED Conference"). However, a portion of the registration fee is tax-deductible ("TED Conference"), so people attending might consider this fee as a part of their annual charitable giving. Since this talk is about sex trafficking, health care, and women's education globally, the people attending may be interested in social justice and gender equality.

Secondary Audience

For TED Talks, it is important to consider the secondary audience—people who did not attend this talk but who can access it online. TED shares all of its talks on its website for the public to view. Even though everyone can technically access these talks, the secondary audience is not "everyone." It is likely that people interested in global change, resource-poor countries, and activism will click on this talk if they are browsing TED's website. Alternatively, think about the people who might click on this video if it were on their Facebook newsfeed or posted to YouTube and other social media sites.

Purpose

Often, authors do not explicitly state their purposes in their texts, especially as they might have multiple purposes. However, we can analyze their language and rhetorical strategies to make inferences and **claims**. An audience member might infer the following about WuDunn's purpose: WuDunn argues that the issues facing women globally are deserving of our attention. She hopes to educate her audience about poverty, maternal mortality, and barriers to girls' education. WuDunn also strives to encourage people to donate to organizations fighting these issues.

2. Look for Rhetorical Strategies

Now that you have identified the elements of the text's rhetorical situation, you can look at the specific strategies WuDunn uses to communicate her purpose in this context to the audience(s). Keep in mind that many of these concepts overlap. As you explore some strategies, you might refine your understanding of one or more elements of the rhetorical situation.

Appeals to Credibility or Character (Ethos)

WuDunn seems like a credible speaker due to her qualifications. These qualifications allow the audience to trust her message more implicitly than they would if she did not have relevant professional experience in these issues. In addition to professional experience, WuDunn also has life experience—she's traveled to many of these places and spoken to many of the people she cites, such as the village chief in Zimbabwe. Including details such as these adds authenticity to her talk. WuDunn wears professional clothing, and she appears prepared to deliver an engaging speech in a conversational tone without notes or other memory aids. These features of a live presentation allow WuDunn to present herself as trustworthy and responsible. Additionally, the images she incorporates are timed to relevant points in the talk. The images and slides are professional as well.

Character appeals involve the speaker or text connecting with the values and beliefs of the audience. WuDunn demonstrates that she is aware of the personal values that her audience holds when she argues that "individuals can make a difference" because, together, they can create a movement. By saying this, she hopes to convince her audience that their support matters. WuDunn likely knows that her audience is already invested in social justice causes. They may need the extra encouragement that their support, monetary or otherwise, actually matters.

Near the end of her talk, WuDunn also connects in a second way to her audience using character appeals. She asks, "What's in it for you?…Why should you care?" WuDunn explains that research shows that people can become happier if they contribute to a larger movement once they have addressed their own basic needs. By making this argument to her primary and secondary audiences,

WuDunn demonstrates that she understands that they may be busy or have other commitments that demand their attention, time, and resources. By claiming that supporting this cause will benefit her audience personally, WuDunn effectively addresses potential concerns about the personal value of this investment.

Appeals to Emotion (Pathos)

Although WuDunn provides statistics and other facts, she might lose her audience if she includes too many. Remember the context for this lecture. It is one talk at a conference that includes many other talks that audience members would have attended. Alternatively, people in the secondary audience who access this talk online may become distracted by something more entertaining on the web if she relies on statistics too heavily.

Instead, WuDunn uses emotional appeals to keep her audience engaged. She tells the stories of four main women: Dai Manju, Mahabuba, Saima, and Beatrice Birra. Each of these stories is carefully placed to emphasize points she has made about poverty, maternal mortality, and girls' education. Each time she introduces one of these women, she displays a photo on her slides. This visual appeal to pathos allows audience members to put a face to the story. It's more likely that the audience will have an emotional connection to WuDunn's topic if she provides both stories and photographs. WuDunn spends a lot of time on the harrowing details of each story, especially Mahabuba's, to convey the significance of her argument. She needs to demonstrate to her audience that the causes they support affect real people. WuDunn also uses the inflection of her voice and her gestures to communicate the seriousness of this issue.

Appeals to Logic (Logos)

WuDunn's argument itself is logically organized, and there are clear linguistic signposts for the audience to follow. She articulates her first major point clearly: "And that brings me to my first major tenet of Half the Sky." To show a transition to her next point, WuDunn's linguistic cue is similar: "The second tenet of Half the Sky." When she needs to transition to the story of a new woman, she always uses the phrase, "Let me tell you about." She also numbers her main points and communicates this verbally. By providing these signposts for her audience, WuDunn makes it easy for her audience to follow her points.

Another way that WuDunn demonstrates effective logos is by providing a counterargument to her point. WuDunn knows that her audience, especially the primary audience of wealthy individuals, may be reluctant to donate if they have encountered other arguments about the futility of global aid. In expressing this counterargument, she mentions Bill Easterly's book *Dead Aid*, as well as personal experiences as a witness of abandoned water-well and chicken-coop projects. WuDunn then provides a refutation to the counterargument: "You don't throw the baby out with the bathwater; you actually improve. You learn from your mistakes." She advocates for revising projects instead of abandoning them completely. By acknowledging the fact that unsuccessful projects can serve as lessons for improvement, she addresses concerns that her audience may already have toward aid. This allows her to predict and respond to issues the audience may have with her main argument before she moves to the conclusion.

5.3.2 Rhetorical Analysis Process

Remember, when you analyze a text's rhetorical effectiveness, you are looking at how an author gets the message across. It's important to make your most informed guess as to the rhetorical situation. Then, the strategies that you identify should correspond well to the elements of the rhetorical situation. If they do not, the text is not as rhetorically effective as it could be. Some texts may be partially effective; they can be effective in some areas and ineffective in others. Learning to analyze texts rhetorically can help you compose more effective texts of your own. Work to become comfortable with the rhetorical concepts of context, author/speaker/composer, audience, purpose, and the rhetorical strategies of ethos, pathos, and logos so that you can consider them in your own work.

Theodore was assigned to write a rhetorical analysis for his foundations writing class. For this assignment, he decided to write about the strategies used by the "Kony 2012" video. If you are unfamiliar with this video, you can watch it here: http://invisiblechildren.com/kony/. The producers of the short film claimed that their purpose was to promote the awareness and eventual arrest of African cult and militia leader Joseph Kony. After conducting his analysis, Theodore determined that the video, which became the fastest-growing viral video at the time and yielded over 3.7 million signatures in support of Kony's arrest, had mixed results due to the rhetorical strategies used in the film.

The following is Theodore's introductory paragraph and **thesis** statement. In it, he contextualizes the situation and connects some of the rhetorical strategies in the "Kony 2012" video with its intended audience, purpose, and overall effectiveness:

> *Even though the video was clearly popular and its message reached many people worldwide, critics have argued that the "Kony 2012" video was inherently flawed and presented a simplistic, stereotyped, and ethnocentric view of the African conflict, instead of encouraging viewers to learn more. Critics have also argued that the film promoted a form of political activism for the truly lazy where viewers were given the naive idea that all they had to do was click on an icon, sign a petition, or post a sign to bring a warlord to justice. However, I argue that the film was a success in raising awareness about an important conflict. The same factors that made the "Kony 2012" video a huge success amongst its target audience of American youth also created*

the video's failures and controversies. The film's simplistic conclusions and focus on its American narrator allowed the filmmakers to connect with their young American audience. While the film's request that viewers share the video seems like a simple or naive solution for fighting against Joseph Kony's brutality against children, the video did create worldwide awareness of Kony and his brutal army and did build a community of youthful activists who might otherwise be unaware of the conflict.

LEARNING ACTIVITY:
Examine Theodore's Introduction

- What elements of the rhetorical situation does Theodore identify in his introduction? Having seen the video, do you agree with Theodore's interpretation of the rhetorical situation?
- Underline Theodore's thesis statement. How is his position on the video different from that of previous critics? How does his interpretation of the rhetorical situation lead him to this position?
- What rhetorical strategies do you think Theodore will discuss in this essay? Why?
- Notice how Theodore does not use the terms ethos, logos, or pathos, and instead focuses on the specific strategies used by the producers. Based on this introduction, what do you think is the main rhetorical appeal being used by the producers?

In his body paragraphs, Theodore demonstrates how the simplicity of the film, the use of an American narrator, and the request for viewers to share the video help the video creators connect with American youth and create a community of young activists. These different aspects of the video constitute the **evidence** that Theodore uses to support his thesis—that while the film hasn't yet resulted in the arrest of Kony, it did raise awareness on the part of the American people. Whenever you rhetorically analyze a text, the evidence that you identify and your ability to fully explain how it functions rhetorically will determine the persuasiveness of your analysis. Take a look at Theodore's use of evidence in the following body paragraph:

> *Prior media coverage of the conflict between the Lord's Resistance Army and the Ugandan government may have been more complete and realistic in describing the complexities of the war, but this coverage did not impact an audience outside of a small, politically informed group. The "Kony 2012" video presents a simplistic view of the conflict in Uganda that ignores many of the war's political*

and diplomatic complexities, and perhaps reinforces stereotypical views of Africa. But a simple message is sometimes more clear and effective than a complex one. The video used one child, Jacob, to represent the story of all the children victimized, or living in fear of the LRA. While Jacob's experience might not be representative of all the LRA's victims, it is easier for us to relate to the story of one individual. Jacob's story appeals to our emotions. When he says he doesn't want to go on living if things don't change, the viewer can clearly see the need for action. Then Russell, the narrator, tells viewers how they can take action. While the actions are simple, they are actions that most people could easily do. The video does focus on an idealistic, but ultimately unsuccessful goal—the arrest of Kony by the end of 2012. Although the goal was unmet, the video is successful in making viewers aware of the LRA problem and prompting many to take some action.

LEARNING ACTIVITY:
Examine Theodore's Evidence

- Underline Theodore's main point. How does it relate to the thesis?
- Highlight the evidence used to support the main point. What makes this evidence convincing? Do you see a need for further evidence?
- How does Theodore analyze this evidence and connect it back to the main point? Is he explaining how and why this strategy serves the text's purpose, makes the text effective for a particular audience in a particular way, and/or is relevant given the context?
- Having watched Kony 2012, do you agree with Theodore's analysis of the video? Why or why not?

As with any thesis statement, your rhetorical analysis thesis statement should act as a road map for your paper. If the purpose of your rhetorical analysis is to explain how an author/speaker works within a particular rhetorical situation to achieve a specific purpose, your thesis statement should help address this question. Some of the information about audience, context, the author/speaker, etc., might be embedded in your introduction, but your essay should still have an identifiable thesis statement that indicates which rhetorical strategies you will focus on in your analysis.

LEARNING ACTIVITY: Create a Rhetorical Analysis Thesis Statement

1. Start by listing all of the pertinent information about the rhetorical situation and rhetorical strategies found in your text.

2. Now circle the parts of the rhetorical situation and the specific rhetorical strategies that you know you want to focus on in your essay because you find them the most compelling, convincing, etc.

3. Try combining all of these circled parts into a thesis statement. Your thesis might now include a combination of elements of the rhetorical situation and specific rhetorical strategies. A rhetorical analysis thesis is often highly complex because you are identifying many elements in the text and trying to put them all together in a statement.

4. Look at how the following thesis combines information about the author, rhetorical strategies, the audience, the message, the purpose, the context, and some of the effects on the audience. This statement could be worded in several other ways, and you may not find it necessary to mention as much information in your own thesis. For example:

> In his 2013 inaugural address, President Obama uses repetitive phrases such as "we, the people" and an inclusive tone to convince his American audience of both his supporters and non-supporters that they must unite together to defend freedom. Although he is generally effective in evoking hope through his references to historical successes and goals for the future, his lack of specificity in regards to how his future plans will be carried out makes his message less convincing for those who did not vote for him and are perhaps skeptical of his capabilities as president.

5. After creating your thesis, make sure that it explains how the author is attempting to achieve a specific purpose. If your thesis sounds like a **summary**, you need to consider how you can turn that summary into a compelling analysis.

5.4 Discovering Rhetoric in the World

5.4.1 Rhetorically Analyzing Advertisements

As a global, multi-billion dollar industry, advertising is a constant part of our lives. We see advertisements while traveling to school or work, flipping through a magazine, watching television, and even just browsing the internet. Advertisements often use both words and images to achieve a desired effect.

"Rhetorically Analyzing Advertisements"

By Al Harahap

pp. 65–68

Unlike most other genres of communication, advertisements appear in many different media, with each medium relying on different ways of appealing to readers, listeners, or viewers. A magazine or newspaper advertisement may use words, images, or both, while a television or internet advertisement is likely to incorporate moving images and audio in the form of speech, sound effects, or music.

Advertisements are complicated texts designed by professionals to be extremely persuasive, and analyzing them can be intimidating. The following print advertisement could be found on a college campus very much like this one, and, although it may seem fairly straightforward, there is plenty here for a rhetorical analysis. When you approach an advertisement in order to perform a rhetorical analysis, you might find it helpful to move through the following steps:

Step One

Examine the advertisement and look for any images and words that stand out, but do not make any conclusions yet. Also pay attention to the elements of **visual rhetoric** mentioned in the "Reading Visual Rhetoric" section in this chapter.

Step Two

Make sure to identify and understand the advertisement's rhetorical situation. Remember that on the surface, an advertisement's message might be to sell you a product, but it might have a greater cultural influence on the audience than just convincing them to buy something. To begin building an understanding of the advertisement's context, start by answering the following questions about the rhetorical situation:

Who is the author/speaker?

The medical center's logo makes clear that the event is related to a science-oriented educational institution. Although this does not give the identity of the specific person who generated this document, it does make the organization the author is representing clear.

What is the image conveying?

The viewer is struck by a long and obviously complex equation worked out on a chalkboard. However, contrary to the viewer's expectations, the person solving the equation is not a university professor, but a young boy. Why would the advertisement play with the viewer's expectations in this way? In that moment, the advertisement has created an element of surprise, which has the effect of drawing the viewer further in.

What are the message and purpose of the text?

Looking at the largest textual element, "Learning…it's all in your mind," does not help much because it is a slogan that sounds catchy but does not necessarily give much information. However, the next largest text, "Upper Westside University Medical Center Invites You to Our Summer Open House," reveals that this ad is trying to get people to come to an open house. This flyer does not announce the date or time of the event, so it is safe to assume that the audience has some prior knowledge about the event. Perhaps this lack of specificity can help us determine the intended audience.

Who is the audience?

Given the information we have about the event, we can hypothesize that Upper Westside University Medical Center is a teaching hospital similar to the University Medical Center on the University of Arizona campus. In this context, the focus of the image and heading font, with their emphasis on education, make sense in combination with an event that appears to be promoting community health. The audience might possibly include K–12 students who are not yet in college and their parents because the message of the image advocates investing in children's education from a young age.

Step Three

Identify the rhetorical strategies employed in the advertisement and determine how they work together to help the advertiser achieve a desired effect on the intended audience. How does the author make appeals to character or credibility and/or appeal to the audience's emotions or sense of logic? You could choose to analyze specific strategies such as the font, the placement of information, the use of the bulleted list, or even the race and gender of the subject in the photo.

The genre of advertisements might also impact how an audience receives a text's message and reacts to its purpose. How does this advertisement use the visual conventions of a modern print advertisement to make its argument? Think about its use of a logo, the combination of images and words, and the inclusion of a URL. You might also consider the types of emotional appeals commonly used in this genre. For example, in the genre of advertisements, desire is frequently an important appeal. With many advertisements that are selling physical, tangible products, the creators are appealing to their audience's material desire for something by making the product the primary focus of the advertisement. However, all advertisements are also appealing to some kind of intangible, cultural desire, such as the desire to easily connect with people, made possible by the latest smartphone or social networking site. What kinds of cultural values might the medical center in this advertisement be appealing to?

5.4.2 Examining Culture through Everyday Objects

"Examining Culture through Everyday Objects"

By Alan Chu

pp. 68–69

Culture can be a particularly powerful lens for rhetorically analyzing a text. Because it asks you to think critically about the way a given cultural context influences the way we look at the world, practicing cultural analysis has the potential to change the way you see the world. Yet, before you attempt to understand these connections, it is important to consider a crucial question: what, exactly, constitutes an appropriate text for cultural analysis?

The field of Cultural Studies has helped expand the definition of what we consider a text. For cultural critics, the empty Coke bottle in the trash can or the University of Arizona flag above Arizona Stadium can be read as texts laden with complex cultural meaning. Considering everyday objects as meaningful texts significantly widens the scope of objects that invite analysis. For instance, consider the Coke bottle:

First, take a close look at its physical properties. What are the dimensions? Is it in a 12 oz., 16 oz., 20 oz., or 2-liter container? At first glance, the size of the container may not offer much in the way of useful cultural analysis. However, like any text, the Coke bottle is designed for a specific audience. If the bottle is located on campus, what does its size mean in relation to its audience? In other words, how would university students react if the vending machines around campus only offered 2-liter (about 66 oz.) Cokes instead of 20 oz. bottles? Would it help or hinder its designed function as a product for consumption? Additionally, consider what is important to its target audience of college students. 20 oz. bottles are certainly more portable than a 2-liter container, and yet they offer a greater volume of soda for consumption than a 12 oz. can. Each bottle, as opposed to a can with a tab, comes equipped with a twist-off cap, allowing for convenient storage and reuse. Finally, the 20 oz. bottle's size, dimensions, and physical makeup are an indication that the bottle is a disposable item. Its ergonomic shape and volume suggests that its contents are a single serving—despite its designation by the FDA as containing the equivalent of 2.5 servings per bottle.

Based on this brief description, one can assume that the players participating in this cultural production are the University of Arizona, Coca-Cola Corporation, American culture with its capitalist **ideology**, and you, the university student, its target consumer. Now, apply this critical lens to the other components that you notice on the Coke bottle: its colors, logo, and physical makeup—is it made of plastic or glass? After a bit of practice and reflection, it should become clear that each one of these properties offers an abundance of insight for cultural analysis.

The Coke bottle is but one example. Take a second look at the many objects that you are intimately familiar with and try to complicate your understanding of these artifacts. In other words, take what's familiar and make it strange. Whether at home, at a friend's apartment, outdoors, or working at a restaurant, there are innumerable artifacts that we encounter every day but give very little thought as to their connections to culture. Ask yourself: what is the cultural significance of a PlayStation controller? Why do some women's restrooms have couches? And what is the point of the sunglasses on that moose's head at the restaurant where you work? By conceptualizing your artifact through a cultural lens, this may very well change not only your relationship with the object, but deepen your understanding of how culture influences everything around us, from trash on the ground to flags fluttering in the sky.

LEARNING ACTIVITY:
Analyze an Everyday Object

To begin a rhetorical analysis of an everyday object, first attempt to disassociate your prior knowledge and experience from the object, which we will refer to as an artifact. Examine how the artifact is both a product of culture and one that produces culture. By analyzing everyday objects as "unfamiliar" cultural artifacts, you can begin to answer several key questions:

1.A

1.B

1.C

1. What is the user's relationship to the artifact? Conversely, what does that relationship reveal about the user?

2. What is the economic value of the artifact? What is its value to the people for whom it was originally produced?

3. In what historical period was the artifact created? How does it reflect the customs and assumptions of that period? If the artifact has evolved over time, what does that evolution suggest about changes in the associated culture?

4. Who has access to the artifact? What factors (e.g., cost, availability, size) impact access?

5. What is the artifact's relationship to other similar objects found in the same cultural context?

6. Does the artifact reflect a particular ideology? If so, how does the artifact's ideology reproduce the culture from which it came?

7. What other factors are important to understanding the specific artifact being examined?

"Reading Visual Rhetoric"

By Amy Parziale

p. 70

Read more about "Analyzing Appeals within a Visual Argument" under "Analyzing Arguments" within "Critical Thinking and Argument" in *Writer's Help 2.0*.

5.4.3 Reading Visual Rhetoric

Visual rhetoric is a form of communication in which visual elements create meanings and arguments. Advertising is one form of visual rhetoric in the contemporary world, but works of art, photographs, websites, brochures, and even bumper stickers contain and create visual rhetoric. Just like textual rhetoric, the author's purpose in using visual rhetoric is to best persuade her audience of her position—whether it is which shampoo to purchase or who to vote for in an election. Thus, there are some overlaps between analyzing visual rhetoric and analyzing textual rhetoric. As with textual rhetoric, when you analyze visual rhetoric you should consider the rhetorical situation: the author, audience, message, intended purpose, and surrounding context.

When you analyze visual rhetoric, you should also be aware of some elements worth analyzing that are not usually present in written texts. These elements include:

- The type of visual (text, images, clip art, photographs, etc.)

- Color palette (individual element's color, background, **contrast**, etc.)

- Font choices (size, color, typeface, etc.)

- Organization and arrangement of the elements in the work (foreground, background, top, bottom, etc.)

LEARNING ACTIVITY:
Analyze Visual Rhetoric

To examine a work's visual rhetoric, start by writing down everything you see.

- **Visual Composition:** What elements make up the piece? How are they arranged? How are they related? What shapes, colors, textures, lighting, shadows, and types of lines are used? What is lightest? What is darkest? Do the elements complement or contrast with each other? Is a specific element repeated? Is there variety in the elements?

- **Technique:** How do you think the piece was created (photography, painting, film, computer-generated techniques, etc.)?

- **Focus:** What is in focus and what is out of focus? What size are the objects in comparison to each other? Are the objects to **scale**? How does your eye move around the piece? What elements draw your eye, and how is that accomplished?

- **Space:** What sense of space is created? Do objects overlap? What is in the foreground, middle ground, and background? What is in each third of the piece—top, middle, bottom, left, middle, and right?
- **Point of View:** From what vantage point is the piece created? How is the piece **framed**? What is included? What do you think lies beyond the edges?
- **Organization and Arrangement:** How are the people in a photograph posed? Do their movements or positions seem natural or artificially imposed? How are visual elements arranged? What is your eye drawn to first? What does the organization of elements seem to be emphasizing?

Once you have observed the many choices present in the visual text, try to infer how these choices shape, modify, or enhance the message and purpose. Understanding visual rhetoric allows us to engage with the multitude of images we are bombarded with each day on a more critical level. The next time you are driving by a billboard, strolling through a museum, or flipping through a magazine, pause and consider how the image engages its audience through visual rhetoric.

PART III:
CRITICAL THINKING AND COMPOSING

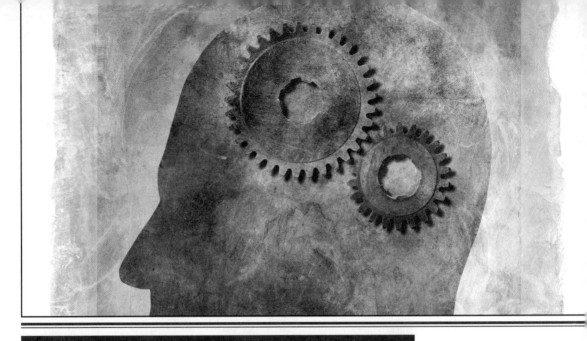

Introducing Critical Thinking and Composing

6.1 Goal 2: Critical Thinking and Composing

Critical Thinking and Composing: Use reading and writing for purposes of critical thinking, research, problem solving, action, and participation in conversations within and across different communities.

Regardless of your chosen career, you will do a lot of reading and writing in college and for most of your professional life. When you read an academic text, read it critically. This does not necessarily mean that you need to disagree with the author. It means that as you read, you are putting the author's ideas into your own words, connecting those ideas to your own experience and to other texts, and thinking about what the author is trying to do or accomplish through the text. By engaging with the text in this way, you are having a conversation (of sorts) with the author, and when you begin to compose your own writing, you are continuing that conversation, whether it is about a research topic, a specific problem or question within a field of study, or a local issue that needs to be addressed.

Composing texts requires the same level of critical engagement. Organizing ideas is a form of thinking, so you can use writing as a way to clarify your own thinking and help you work through complex ideas. Your first draft may be vague and disconnected, and through drafting, you come to a clarified and coherent idea. The process of writing can you help you as you explore and work through ideas.

To meet Goal 2: Critical Thinking and Composing, at the end of Foundations Writing, students will be able to:

A. employ a variety of **research methods,** including **primary** and/or **secondary** research, for purposes of inquiry.

B. evaluate the **quality, appropriateness**, and **credibility** of sources.

C. incorporate evidence, such as through **summaries, paraphrases, quotations**, and **visuals**.

D. **synthesize** research findings in development of an argument.

E. support ideas or positions with compelling discussion of **evidence** from multiple sources.

F. compose persuasive researched arguments for various audiences and purposes, and in multiple **modalities**.

6.2 Student Learning Outcomes: Descriptions and Key Terms

2.A: Employ a variety of research methods, including primary and/or secondary research, for purposes of inquiry.

Once a writer has a research topic in mind, she will pose research questions in order to clarify for herself what she knows and what she needs to find out in order to be well informed on the topic. These questions can be answered by engaging in a variety of kinds of research.

When writers engage in primary research they collect data from the primary object of study. When collecting primary data from people, researchers usually use interviews, surveys, and/or questionnaires in order to make original discoveries about their topic. This is sometimes called *fieldwork*; the writer becomes a researcher who goes out into the "field" to make discoveries. A historian or literary scholar, however, conducts primary research by conducting focused analyses on historical or literary texts.

When writers engage in secondary research, they read the work of other primary researchers (such as pre-existing articles, interviews, and/or studies) and attempt to synthesize that information to increase their understanding of the subject. This can also be thought of as *deskwork*. The writer can conduct their secondary research from their desk, their dorm room, their living room, their office, or their school library. All they need is access to the internet and/or their school library's resources.

Secondary sources can come from a wide variety of media types.

- They can be **digital** or **print** sources, such as popular magazines, newspapers, news sites, professional blogs, academic journals, books, etc.

- They can be **video** sources, such as television programs, films and documentaries, filmed interviews, clips from television and film on *Youtube* or other video-based websites, etc.

- They can be **audio** sources, such as radio programs, podcasts, audio-recorded interviews, music, etc.

- They can be **social media** sources, such as posts on *Facebook* or *Twitter*, *Reddit* threads, discussion boards, photo-based sites like *Instagram*, or non-professional blog posts on *Tumblr*, *Wordpress* or other blogging platforms, etc.

Consider the following example: Marisol is working on an anthropology paper about horror movie fandom. She generates some research questions:

- Why do some people enjoy the experience of being scared/shocked?

- Are there certain kinds of people who enjoy being scared more than others? Why?

- What does neuroscience have to say about the physiological response of the brain/body to horror movies?

- Is liking horror movies a cultural tradition? Or a personal preference?

Marisol starts by conducting some secondary research. She uses the library catalog to determine a number of resources that might give her insight into why people like horror movies; she finds:

- the 1993 book *Men, Women, and Chainsaws: Gender and the Modern Horror Film* by Carol J. Clover.

- the 2014 documentary *Why Horror?* directed by Nicolas Kleiman and Rob Lindsay.

- a 2013 article from *The Atlantic* titled "Why Do Some Brains Enjoy Fear?" by Allegra Ringo.

- a 2015 article from *Psychology Today* titled "Why Do We Like Watching Scary Films?" by Mark D. Griffiths.

- a 2014 *YouTube* video titled "Why do people like horror?," uploaded by the Oxford University Press.

- a 2015 *Reddit* post on the "Dreadit" sub-reddit titled "Why do you love horror movies?"

- a segment from a 2013 *All Things Considered* broadcast on NPR titled "Why Latinos Heart Horror Films" by Vanessa Rancaño.

To contextualize her study to students at the University of Arizona, Marisol decides to conduct some primary research. Based on some of the information she has learned from her secondary research, she develops a short online questionnaire meant to capture students' attitudes towards horror films. She distributes it via email to everyone on campus, giving students two weeks to respond. After collecting the primary data, she synthesizes her results from both the primary and secondary data before reporting initial answers to her research questions.

Research Methods: the means by which a writer acquires information and data about a subject of interest. Researchers may be asked to articulate specific methods they used to collect, manage, and analyze data.

Primary Research: any type of research where writers directly interrogate the object of study and collect new data for themselves. If researching flowers, the researcher will observe or experiment with flowers. If researching students' attitudes about required general education courses, the researcher will ask students what they think directly. Much primary research is completed outside of the classroom, library, or office; it requires that researchers go out into the field.

Secondary Research: any type of research where the writer discovers information about the specific topic generated by other writers/researchers.

Inquiry: the process of investigating a question or series of questions about a topic of interest.

LEARNING ACTIVITY:
Distinguish between Primary and
Secondary Research

The Daily Wildcat has asked that you conduct a review of a new restaurant that opened near campus. What type of data might you collect as a form of primary research? What secondary sources might you look at?

Read more about "Preparing for Research" and "Conducting Research" within "Research" in *Writer's Help 2.0*.

2.B: Evaluate the quality, appropriateness, and credibility of sources.

When conducting secondary research, writers pursuing a line of inquiry will need to gather sources that provide them with information or insight into their topic. With the proliferation of information across the internet and the many genres of sources available online (print text, video, audio, social media, etc.), it is imperative that writers are able to judge which sources are most and least useful to them.

What makes a source *useful* for one writing situation might not hold true for another. So SLO 2.B truly builds upon the rhetorical awareness in Goal 1. Writers engaged in inquiry-based research will need to consider the following types of questions as they locate sources:

- Who wrote/created a source?

- What is the source's purpose?

- When was the source created?

- Where is the source found?

- Why was the source created?

- How is the source constructed?

A critical requirement for college students is to understand scholarly, peer-reviewed sources. Most academic publications require that the article or book be reviewed by other scholars in the field. Those reviewers usually require that the author revise the text before it is accepted for final publication. Therefore, a scholarly, peer-reviewed source has usually been written by someone with appropriate credentials and experience and has been reviewed by others with relevant credentials and experience.

SLO 2.B is also about media literacy and awareness. For example, writers should understand:

- What the major papers of record are in the country/your state/your city or region.

- What the major popular magazines or websites are for a given subject.

- What is being created and aired on premium cable TV, basic cable, and public access TV.

- How NPR works.

- How radio works.

- The world of podcasts.

- The world of social media.

Consider the following example: Ami is working on a research paper about domestic violence. Via a quick Google search, she finds the article "New York City Council Speaker Melissa Mark-Viverito Will Not Stay Silent on Domestic Violence" on the website *Jezebel*. The author of the article is listed as Julianne Escobedo Shepherd.

Ami decides to do some research into this source by:

- Reading the *Wikipedia* page about *Jezebel* (It's a media site founded by Gawker Media and Anna Holmes in 2007 and is currently owned by Univision; its tagline is "Celebrity, Sex, Fashion for Women. Without Airbrushing").

- Finding Julianne Escobedo Shepherd's *Twitter* feed (@jawnita).

- Finding Julianne Escobedo Shepherd's Adjunct Faculty page on the NYU website.

- Finding Julianne Escobedo Shepherd's *Tumblr* account.

- Finding, via Google, that Julianne Escobedo Shepherd has also written for *Rolling Stone, Rookie, The FADER*, and *Pitchfork*.

- Discovering that Shepherd's piece hyperlinks to the following sources: the website for the New York City Economic Development Commission, the *New York Post*, the *New York Times*, *The Slot*, a press release on the New York City Council website, the website for the National Coalition Against Domestic Violence, the *New York Daily News*, the website for the New York Giants, and *ESPN.com*.

Ami uses this information to assess the authority and **credibility** of both *Jezebel* as a publication as well as Julianne Escobedo Shepherd as an author.

LEARNING ACTIVITY:
Assessing Authority

Based on what you read above about Julianne Escobedo Shepherd and the article "New York City Council Speaker Melissa Mark-Viverito Will Not Stay Silent on Domestic Violence," would you categorize this text as authoritative and credible? Why or why not? What specific audiences would find this text more or less credible?

Quality: the accuracy and reliability of the information contained in the source. One way to assess a source's quality is to determine whether it was self-published (without the input of an editor or editorial team) or published via a media company (with the assistance and input of an editor or editorial team).

Appropriateness: the relevance of the source for our writing situation. For example, if you are looking for the opinions of female voters on the 2016 presidential candidates, then a thinkpiece written by a male pundit would not be appropriate to the situation. However, a faculty member (male or female) in a women's studies department probably is appropriate. Appropriateness is usually vetted by how well the piece addresses the specific research question as well as the needs of the rhetorical situation, including purpose, audience, context, and genre.

Credibility: how trustworthy or reliable a source is for an author's purpose. You might consider the identity of the source's author, who published it, where and when it was published, the target audience for the source, and the timeliness and relevance of the information. Different purposes might determine different levels of credibility. For example, if you are writing an ethnography of alt-right white nationalists, then a series of anti-Semitic comments on a Jewish journalist's published article might be credible sources for the project (especially if you can use the commenter's name to discover his *Twitter* feed, personal blog or other information that corroborates his identity).

LEARNING ACTIVITY:
To Wiki or Not to Wiki

Why is the quality of *Wikipedia* entries usually dismissed by college instructors? Come up with 2–3 rhetorical situations (purposes, audiences, topics, and genres) where using *Wikipedia* as a source might be credible and appropriate. Describe why.

Read more about "Evaluating Sources" within "Research" in *Writer's Help 2.0*.

2.C: Incorporate evidence, such as through summaries, paraphrases, quotations, and visuals.

When making claims about a subject, authors construct reasons and use evidence to support those reasons. For example, a restaurant review might claim that the restaurant is worth the visit because it has good:

1. food,
2. wait staff, and
3. environment.

These three reasons would then need different types of **evidence** for support. Much of the evidence you will use in texts for your writing courses will be from other texts, or primary data collected from the object of study (like a book, poem, or movie) or individuals. In either case, when you decide to present evidence from the source, you will need to decide whether to **summarize**, **paraphrase**, or directly **quote** the source.

Evidence: specific pieces of information or data used to support a reason that then supports a larger claim. Evidence can be from either primary or secondary data.

Summaries: brief overviews of a specific text. Summaries usually include the who, what, why, when, where, and how of a given text.

Paraphrases: presentation of another's thoughts or ideas in your own language. Paraphrases usually include the same level of detail as the original text; however, they are presented as a type of translation by the author. Paraphrases help the audience better understand the original text and why it is important to the author's argument.

Quotations: presentation of another's thoughts or ideas in their specific language. Quotations present the original text as is, without any adaptation.

Visuals: a graphic, image, or other type of text that is perceived through the audience's optical sense. Visual texts may be used as specific pieces of evidence in an argument. For example, presenting quantitative data in tables or charts makes them usually more easily understood to an audience (a type of synthesizing and paraphrasing of quantitative data). Images might also be used to demonstrate different types of data, such as examples of flower petals in a botany paper.

LEARNING ACTIVITY:
Articulate Types of Evidence

Pretend you are writing the restaurant review discussed above. What might be the different types of evidence you could include in the review? Design and complete something like the following table.

*   **Summaries:** Who might you summarize? Why might you need to summarize something instead of providing all the details?

- **Paraphrases:** Who might you paraphrase? Why might you need to translate someone else's language for your audience?
- **Quotations:** Who might you quote? Why might it be more important to use their language instead of your own?
- **Visuals:** What images might you include? How do the images support a specific reason or provide specific evidence (not just provide something to look at)?

Reasons	Types of Evidence			
	Summaries	Paraphrases	Quotations	Visuals
The food is good.				
The wait staff is friendly and helpful.				
The restaurant has a great atmosphere.				

2.D: Synthesize research findings in development of an argument.

An important part of the research process is learning what others have said about the question or issue that you are researching. As you locate and read sources that are relevant to your subject, you will notice patterns of similarity and difference in the views expressed and the ways that authors express those views. For example, a voter researching the candidates running in a presidential primary may notice that they hold similar positions on many issues but have different styles of speaking about those issues in speeches and debates. This person has begun to **synthesize** her sources of information, or put them in conversation with each other. By doing so, she may be moving closer to a decision on who to vote for.

2.D

Read more about "Integrating Sources" within "Research" in *Writer's Help 2.0.*

A writer who has synthesized what has been said on a particular topic can begin to identity informational or conceptual gaps in the current conversation. These are places in the conversation where the author feels something could or should be said but hasn't yet. A person reading about vandalism on college campuses may observe many disagreements about how to stop vandalism and insufficient attention given to the reasons why people vandalize school property. Recognizing this gap in the conversation, the author may be able to develop an argument that contributes new and original insight to the conversation.

Synthesize: to combine or put sources of information into conversation as a way to develop understanding or a new meaning. A writer who synthesizes primary data and secondary sources compares and contrasts information looking for trends, themes, similarities, and differences. Synthesized information should move from having separate pieces to a more fused whole (or something new).

LEARNING ACTIVITY:
Compare, Contrast, and Synthesize

Photo by jesse1dog on Flickr. https://www.flickr.com/photos/jesseflickrdog/30942439731. CC BY 2.0 license. https://creativecommons.org/licenses/by/2.0/

How is comparing and contrasting information different from synthesizing information? Find an image that represents or visualizes comparing and contrasting. Find another that represents or visualizes synthesizing.

Read more about "Synthesizing Sources" under "Integrating Sources" within "Research" in *Writer's Help 2.0.*

2.E: Support ideas or positions with compelling discussion of evidence from multiple sources.

Most people are not going to believe an argument that you make just because you say it's true. That's why arguments require evidence. Often an audience will desire evidence from a variety of sources. For example, suppose you meet a friend at the Student Union for lunch. Soon you are joined by other friends, one of whom begins telling a story about seeing a UFO the previous weekend when he was hiking in the mountains. Some of your friends seem impressed by the story and think the descriptive details are especially convincing. But the friend you originally met for lunch is skeptical. She thinks the details are typical of stories about UFO sightings and asks if the storyteller contacted the park officials where he was hiking or the nearest police station to see if anyone else reported a sighting. She also asks if the news on TV or the internet mentioned anything about a UFO sighting or something the UFO could have been, such as a weather balloon. In other words, she wants more evidence than just the storyteller's personal experience to support his story.

In Western cultures, empirical evidence is given the most credibility. Western cultures value what can be observed and verified. Even so, personal experiences often carry a great deal of weight in an argument, especially if those experiences are carefully presented with specific details that feel "authentic" and narratives that elicit emotions from the audience. Further, common knowledge or values/ beliefs can serve as evidence for an audience that accepts that knowledge or those values as true. Ultimately, the effectiveness of the evidence in supporting an argument depends on the audience the argument is targeting.

As you are writing an argument, know the audience you want to appeal to and the kinds of evidence that this audience will find most persuasive. Also, consider using several different kinds of evidence to make your argument as convincing as possible. Rarely does an audience find one kind of evidence persuasive by itself. Finally, integrate evidence into your argument and analyze it to show how and why it works to support your points.

> Read more about "Constructing Arguments" within "Critical Thinking and Argument" in *Writer's Help* 2.0.

LEARNING ACTIVITY:
Identifying Evidence

Think about various arguments you have read or heard. What arguments did you find most convincing? Which didn't persuade you at all? List both convincing and unconvincing arguments you have recently come across. Then list the types of evidence you found persuasive in the convincing arguments. Consider why the arguments you found unpersuasive didn't work for you. What kind of evidence (or lack thereof) did they use? List these kinds of evidence too. Think about why you are persuaded by some kinds of evidence and not by others. Is it the quality of the evidence itself or how it is used?

2.F: Compose persuasive researched arguments for various audiences and purposes, and in multiple modalities.

During your college years and your professional life, you will have occasion to write different kinds of arguments:

- from the formal academic argument you write for one of your major courses to a proposal for a project at work,

- from the application letter for your dream job to a letter to the editor of your local newspaper, and

- from an impassioned speech to your mom asking for permission to spend Spring Break in Mazatlán with your friends to an email to your teacher requesting an extension on your essay.

Arguments come in many different forms, genres, and media and are directed at many different audiences for different purposes.

Read more about "Writing a Research Project" within "Research" in *Writer's Help 2.0.*

You will need to create arguments that are appropriate for various kinds of venues requiring alternative genres and media. The kinds of academic arguments you may be used to writing are only one genre. In your profession, you may need to create visual arguments in PowerPoint or Prezi as well as arguments on paper, and each profession has its own format and expectations for arguments. In your public life, you may give arguments in the form of speeches, pamphlets, editorials, or even blogs. And in your personal life you will write letters, emails, and texts, as well as participate in spoken arguments. Knowing how to "read" your rhetorical situation—your audience, purpose, context, and genre—will help you create successful arguments for all of these different occasions.

CHAPTER 7

Researching to Write

(continued)

7.1 Research: An Overview

This chapter provides an introduction to the important role research plays in foundations writing at the University of Arizona. It will give you a foundation for doing research in your future classes by going through the process of developing a research topic and question, evaluating and keeping track of sources, and eventually writing an annotated bibliography.

> Read more about doing research and using sources in "Research" in *Writer's Help 2.0.*

You can also learn a great deal about conducting research by going to the Main Library. UA Library's website has online lessons and other support materials. Consult with librarians at the Information Commons Reference Desk or via the "Chat" function on the UA library website. You might also schedule an appointment to meet with a specific member of the library staff in person. The library staff is specially trained in finding and evaluating information and will serve as a valuable asset to you throughout your college career. The University of Arizona libraries also makes course-specific resources; look for some under the "Research by course" menu option.

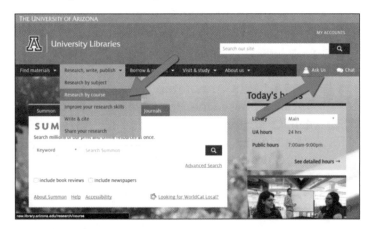

As you begin your own research project, remember that all well-researched ideas build on existing conversations. Learning how to choose appropriate sources, engage them in analysis, and incorporate them properly into a paper will help you enter these conversations in foundations writing and beyond.

7.2 Developing a Research Topic

Sometimes discovering what you want to write about and finding an appropriate focus are the hardest parts of writing a research paper. Some students are accustomed to working with assigned topics and may find it difficult to choose one that they find sufficiently interesting to research. Others are interested in so many ideas that they find it difficult to select just one topic. Some instructors will assign a specific topic, while others may require that your topic fit within a predetermined theme. However you come to your topic, keep in mind that you will spend a great deal of time thinking, reading, talking, and writing about your research; be sure that the topic is one you are committed to exploring. Your instructor can help you decide if your topic is appropriate for the assignment, but you should begin by thinking of several possible research topics from which to choose.

Most foundations writing classes will include assignments that ask you to find a topic that has multiple viewpoints; this is typically called a debatable topic. Debatable topics must fulfill two criteria. First, they have to stimulate some sort of argument or disagreement, meaning they go beyond reporting undisputed facts. Second, others will have written enough about a debatable topic for you to be able to locate multiple perspectives to inform your understanding of the issues involved.

LEARNING ACTIVITY:
Identify a Research Topic

Identify a topic or issue introduced in one of your classes. A good place to begin exploring topics is to reflect on the discussions and readings in your classes. If you are taking a history class, for example, you might research a contested historical event brought up in a lecture and decide which of the several interpretations seems most compelling. Many foundations writing courses are organized around particular themes that will provide various ways to approach your research topic.

1.A

- **Research an issue in your chosen major:** Each academic discipline contains its own hot topics or controversial issues. If you are interested in a particular field of study or career, you may find it helpful to discover what topics are currently debated in that discipline. For example, a pharmacy student may want to consider the merits of current laws that require medications containing pseudoephedrine to be dispensed only from behind the counter because of the use of that substance in manufacturing methamphetamines. An aspiring teacher may choose to explore the validity of current testing methodologies in evaluating student learning and teacher performances or the effectiveness of teachers' unions in promoting a better quality of life for teachers and better outcomes for students.

- **Investigate an extracurricular interest:** Your instructor may ask you to identify some non-academic interests as a way of discovering issues to write about. For example, students who are passionate about fishing might investigate the environmental issues surrounding the stocking of trout at Rose Canyon Lake on Mount Lemmon, while students who enjoy reading might investigate changing literacy practices in relation to technological developments.

No matter what approach you take when choosing a topic, it is important to maintain an appropriate authorial voice for the project. Balancing careful research with your own claims and perspectives can be tricky. Keep in mind that the research you present should achieve several goals. It should show that you are informed about the topic; you are aware of the complexities of the debate you are entering; and you have considered the various definitions, contexts, counter-arguments, and assumptions underlying your argument. Focusing on these goals will demonstrate attention to the ongoing conversation and strengthen your argument for your readers.

Read more about "Narrowing a topic for a research project" under "Preparing for a Research Project" within "Research" in *Writer's Help 2.0*.

7.3 Narrowing Your Research Topic

Sometimes a research idea that seems like a good topic for a class project turns out to be so broad that sifting through all the available research will be overwhelming. It is crucial to find a topic large enough that others have published information about it but also narrow enough for you to identify the most important sources and arguments within a limited time frame. If you are working with an unfamiliar topic, you will probably need to do some research before selecting a narrower focus. You may want to read several encyclopedic entries and introductory articles about the broader topic in order to give yourself a basic foundation of knowledge from which you can investigate more nuanced issues.

LEARNING ACTIVITY:
Narrow Your Research Topic

1.A

After you have found a topic that interests you, try making it even more specific by breaking it down further or investigating specific arguments within the broader context of your topic. Preliminary research can help you identify sub-topics. The UA research librarians recommend checking out what has been written about your topic in *CQ Researcher* or another UA library database to begin narrowing your topic.

Broad topic: Alternative energy sources

Possible sub-topics found through preliminary research: biofuels, electric cars, solar power, environmental activism efforts in Tucson

Through your research, you might find that even a sub-topic can be narrowed further.

New topic: Solar power

> Possible sub-topics: solar-powered high-speed trains, solar ovens, solar panels on electric cars

1. **Pair your topic with a related issue:** Sometimes pairing one topic with a second one helps to provide a more specific and defined lens for your research. As you do preliminary research on your topic, keep an eye out for an angle that you might bring to your research idea.

   - **Research topic**: Solar ovens

   - **Possible pairings**: Solar ovens in disaster zones, solar ovens in developing countries, solar ovens and elementary education

2. **Ground your research in something you know:** Approaching a research topic that you already know something about may help you develop a personal stake in your findings. Similarly, it helps to narrow any abstract ideas into more concrete subjects. Mechanical engineering majors might narrow "alternative energy sources" to solar-powered cars, for example, whereas an environmental science major might be more interested in studying environmental activism in Tucson.

   Ask yourself: "What do I have to say about this topic?"

3. **Write a pointed research question:** A clear, focused research question helps you narrow your topic and stay focused throughout the research process. Remember that if you are not interested in learning the answer to your question, your audience will probably not be very interested in the answer either. Focus your research on a question you are interested in answering and that others might find interesting as well. If the answer to your research question is clear before reading and synthesizing the research, then the topic is either not debatable or not specialized enough to warrant such research.

   Try listing a bunch of possible questions using a journalist's question words: *who, what, when, where, why,* and *how.*

   - **Research topic:** Solar ovens

     - **Research Question 1:** How have solar ovens been used recently in disaster zones, and what were the positive and negative effects of this use?

     - **Research Question 2:** What environmental factors influence the effectiveness of solar ovens, and does this make them better suited for use in certain geographic regions?

     - **Research Question 3:** How are solar ovens built, and what impact does the selection of a particular building material have on the cooking effectiveness of the finished oven?

- Strong research questions share a few qualities:

  - They are clearly significant; they carry an answer to the "so what?" question. For example, Research Question 2 above sets the writer up for an argument about why solar ovens should only be used in certain parts of the world.

  - They can be answered in the space you have available. It would be nearly impossible to find a definitive answer to the world's reliance on oil in the space of a five-page paper, for example. However, it might be manageable to examine the political reasons for and economic impacts of raising fuel standards for vehicles made during the 2011 model year.

  - They have no obvious or definitive right answer—at least, not one that is common knowledge. For instance, asking, "What is climate change?" is not an original research question, as it can be answered with minimal research and does not engage in a debate or discussion. Questions that ask for definitions and standard explanations are useful to explain the basis of your inquiry, but are not appropriate for the focus of a research project.

  - Having a strong research question will be key to finding sources and evaluating their effectiveness.

7.4 Evaluating Sources

Read more about "Evaluating Sources" within "Research" in *Writer's Help 2.0*.

When conducting research in an academic setting, your job as a student and critical thinker is to sift through the many claims and competing opinions and decide which are the most credible and reliable. Begin evaluating your sources by focusing on how the information is portrayed to its primary audience. Be aware that information is often portrayed differently in scholarly and popular sources. Both types of sources can help you gain a more thorough understanding of the way different publics view and understand your topic. Always check your assignment to see if your instructor requires certain kinds of sources.

- A **scholarly source** is a text written by and for researchers and scholars with specialized knowledge about a particular subject. Sometimes scholarly sources are also referred to as "academic sources," meaning they are written by and for academics, peer reviewed, and published in academic journals or books.

- A **popular source** is written for a broader audience and seeks to engage in a public debate or conversation. Popular sources include magazines and newspapers as well as videos, websites, blogs, and other media. They can be written by professional writers, journalists, or anyone with publishing capabilities.

See the following table to compare the major distinctions between scholarly and popular sources.

7.4.1 Scholarly vs. Popular Sources: A Quick Reference Guide

Characteristic	Scholarly Source	Popular Source
What does it look like?	• Usually includes many citations referencing other scholarly sources using an established citation system (MLA, APA, etc.). • Front covers are often plain with few pictures. • Usually takes the form of extended written texts that sometimes include charts, graphs, or related images.	• Includes few end citations. Sources cited using signal phrases, reference to credentials, or other means. • Front covers and inside pages are often full of photographs and short snippets of text. • Tends to be shorter and less formal, and may include images, graphics, or video.
What is its purpose?	• Seeks to contribute to an ongoing academic debate or a discussion in a specific field.	• Seeks to engage in a public debate or conversation.
How and where is it published?	• Published through a process called "peer review," which means that before being accepted for publication, the article is read by experts in the field who assess its reliability, relevance, and the quality of its research and writing. • Generally found in academic books and academic journals.	• If it is edited, editors are usually journalists or professional editors who may or may not be specialists in the topic the work covers. • Generally found in newspapers, magazines, books, and online sources.
What kinds of sources does it cite?	• Usually references published research to back up claims. • Almost always includes in-text citations and a bibliography of cited texts. Sources may be referenced in quotations, paraphrases, summaries, footnotes, endnotes, and bibliographies. • Quotes illustrate the existing scholarly conversation on the topic, provide textual evidence, and guide readers to the other credible sources.	• May reference sources ranging from experts to everyday people who have a stake in the conversation. • Does not always provide information on how to access sources beyond naming them. In other words, does not always include in-text citations. • Quotes usually serve as evidence for the claim the work is seeking to make.

Characteristic	Scholarly Source	Popular Source
Who is the author?	• Authors are faculty, researchers, or scholars writing for others in their field. • Many scholarly sources are written by professors at colleges and universities like the UA.	• Authors may be anyone from researchers to teen bloggers writing for a more public audience.
Who is the intended audience?	• Intended to be read by an audience with interest in the field. • Assumes readers already have some specialized knowledge.	• Written for the publication's intended audience. For instance, *Wired* magazine has a very different audience than *National Geographic*. • May not assume their readers have specialized knowledge.
How did I find it?	• Accessible through academic databases like *JSTOR* or *Academic Search Complete*. • Often found in academic libraries such as the UA Main Library.	• Generally accessible using popular search engines such as *Google* or *Yahoo!*, or library databases such as *LexisNexis Academic*. • Often sold at newsstands or at bookstores.
What are some examples?	• *Arizona Quarterly, Journal of Insect Science, Community Literacy Journal*	• *Time, The Wall Street Journal, Popular Science, Slate, Salon, Radiolab, NPR*

7.4.2 Evaluating Internet Sources

As more material becomes available on the internet, it is increasingly important to know how to evaluate the credibility of online sources. In fact, one of the first discussions about research in your foundations writing courses will probably center on the differences between using a search engine such as *Google* and using a library database such as *Academic Search Complete* or *LexisNexis Academic Universe*. All students at the University of Arizona have access through the library to multiple academic search engines and electronic journals. Generally speaking, most texts you find using library databases are either scholarly sources or popular journalism, both of which are generally considered credible resources. On the other hand, sources available through widely used search engines like *Google* range in terms of credibility from well-researched information published by respectable organizations to incorrect assertions published by misinformed independent authors.

Many Web pages are not subject to the review process of a peer-reviewed scholarly source or even that of a respected popular source such as *The New York Times* or *Time* magazine. Anyone with the technical skills and access to the internet can publish a Web page on any topic, even if they do not have expertise in the subject. For instance, an angry consumer can publish a review denouncing a certain product even if the consumer's dissatisfaction arose out of misuse rather than a defect of the product itself. If you were to rely only on that consumer's opinion, the research would be flawed and, at best, misleading. However, because they are not subject to review, Web pages can also provide a space for voices that are not normally heard in official publications. Unmonitored websites might also provide a more accurate, uncensored picture of what members of the public think or feel regarding a specific topic. As with any careful reading, it is important to employ the skills of rhetorical analysis when evaluating internet sources. Reading critically for audience and purpose can shed light on the credibility of the source.

Online encyclopedias are commonly cited internet resources, and they range from *Encyclopedia Britannica*, available through the university library, to *Wikipedia*, a free online resource edited by users. Your instructor may or may not allow you to use encyclopedias; if you consult these sources, you should be aware of the distinctions between them. Although *Wikipedia* may well be authoritative in certain contexts, its reliability is not monitored in the same way as an encyclopedia such as the *Encyclopedia Britannica*.

If your instructor does allow you to use popular sources in your research papers, it is important to evaluate their credibility. Even when a Web page looks and sounds official, you should be careful to examine its claims. Evaluating websites carefully is an essential part of your research process, since the reliability of your own argument in an academic context will depend in large part upon the credibility of your **citations** and sources. Whenever you are in doubt about the suitability of a certain source, consult your instructor or the UA librarians.

LEARNING ACTIVITY:
Evaluate Internet Sources

When you find a website you think you would like to use in your research, ask the following questions to assess its credibility:

- **URL:** What is the URL? Does it end with .com, .edu, .org, .gov, .biz, .name, .info, or .net? What does each of these domain names imply? Which would indicate that the source is credible?

- **Author:** Can you identify an author for the information? Can you verify the author's qualifications?

- **Last Updated:** Does the Web page provide information about when it was last updated? Is there any way of determining whether the material is out of date? What sorts of links are on the page? Where do these links lead you? Are the links still working?

- **Purpose:** What is the text trying to accomplish? Is its purpose to inform, entertain, or persuade the reader? Does it appear to be promoting a commercial product, an idea, a philosophy, or some other way of seeing something?

- **Graphics:** Are there graphics? If so, what do they illustrate and why?

- **Position on Subject:** Does the source seem biased, one-sided, incomplete, or erroneous? Who profits if viewers of the website believe its information to be true? Can you verify the information with other online or print sources?

- **Links:** Does the source suggest avenues for further inquiry such as possible readings, research, or links? Does it cite reputable sources or note the extent to which claims in the text are connected to recognized authorities in the field?

7.5 Primary Research

All research projects require that you conduct **secondary research** (when the writer discovers information about the specific topic generated by other writers/researchers); however, your project might also require that you conduct **primary research** (when writers directly interrogate the object of study and collect new data for themselves). If you are studying a specific object, like a literary novel, your primary research might be carefully reading and collecting evidence from the text itself. You might also collect data from observing people and places as well as engaging with people through interviews, questionnaires, and surveys.

7.5.1 Textual Analysis

We often read texts just once or scan them for relevant information. For example, you might skim the "Arts & Leisure" section of the newspaper to find film times, or you might read the *Wikipedia* entry about the *Mona Lisa* quickly for the information you are most interested in. You might also scan a chapter in a biology textbook to look for important terms that will be on your next exam. Surface reading alone and reading for an answer to a predetermined question can lead to an insufficient understanding of the text. It may neglect the importance of language and detail in creating meaning which, in turn, can lead to an incomplete analysis. However, this practice of surface-level reading can be helpful when you are concerned with finding a specific piece of information. If your purpose, though, is to understand a text and the author's messages, you must read the text more carefully. **Close reading** happens before you can make an argument about the text or determine the text's purpose. It is essential to all forms of textual analysis.

Close reading helps you to look at a text carefully and uncover how an author uses language, imagery, details, and form to convey or complicate ideas and feelings. Often a close reading will give you a more thorough understanding of the main messages of a text while also revealing some of the text's more intricate and implicit ideas. One common way to think about the strategies you use when you read is to divide the process into three phases: The first occurs before reading, the second during active reading, and the third when reviewing your notes and the text. The strategies that follow in this chapter can be applied to many reading experiences. For example, you can close read a poem, story, scholarly article, blog post, or even a music video, and you can be an active reader when conducting research or reviewing a course syllabus. Since close reading involves the practice of observing and questioning details, consider how this practice applies to non-written texts including visual art, human subjects, and spaces. Whatever your purpose might be, practicing to become a more efficient and critical reader will help you in any situation where a thorough understanding of a text is important; such situations include the reading you will do for your UA composition classes and other university courses, applying to job listings, and understanding professional correspondences. You will even apply close-reading skills to social situations as you try to analyze people's body language and facial expressions.

7.5.1.1 Why Annotate?

Annotation is the process of writing notes and comments about a text. When you write in the margins, highlight or underline important passages, and take notes on the pages, you make the most of your ability to understand and write about the text. You can also annotate texts on a separate paper if you are borrowing books from the library or analyzing something like a music video. Just remember to keep track of the details of the text—like the page numbers and lines from the text you are annotating or the timestamp from the music video—so you can return to it later.

Annotation makes thinking deeply about the text you are reading much easier. Maybe you realize that you circled a certain word more than once—why? Maybe there was something that confused you at the beginning but that makes more sense after reading the whole text. Maybe you noticed certain kinds of images popping up more than once or elements of the writer's language that create a certain feeling or response. Or perhaps you start to notice something from a different perspective.

Read more about "Reading Critically" within "Critical Thinking and Argument" in *Writer's Help 2.0.*

If you are actively reading and processing the text as you go, writing down ideas as they come to you and marking sections to refer back to and ponder, you are starting to take apart the text to see how it works, which is the basic process of analysis. Whether you are reading a written text or conducting a "reading" of a person, place, or thing, writing down your observations and questions will help you remember your impressions, organize your thoughts, and discover some of the patterns and special exceptions that help make meaning in a text.

7.5.1.2 Phase One: Pre-Reading

Before you start reading, take time to scan the text and consider the general questions that follow. It's important to first establish the genre because different genres carry their own expectations for how one might "read" them. For example, alliteration or line spacing might be more significant in poetry than in an academic article. Familiarizing yourself with elements such as the title, genre, medium, organization, and any introductory materials will help you begin to anticipate what you will encounter as you engage with the text.

LEARNING ACTIVITY:
Pre-Read

1.D

While pre-reading a text, consider the following questions:

- What is the genre? What is the usual purpose of that genre? What expectations might you (and other readers) bring to this particular genre?

- Are there any chapters or sections with designated headings? Is there another indication of structure? What might this structure suggest?

- What information does the title offer?

- Are there any visuals, such as graphs or pictures? How do they influence what you expect from the text?

- Do you expect the language to be literal or figurative? Should we expect to find many symbols, metaphors, and similes?

- Can you expect a story arc, an argument, or a collection of images?

- If the text contains sound, what kinds of sounds do you expect to hear?

- Are there many printed words or just a few? How does that impact how much attention you should pay to each word?

- Do you know anything about the author or artist?

7.5.1.3 Phase Two: Active Reading (Observations, Questions, and First Interpretations)

Now that you have scanned the text, you are ready to take a closer look at its content. Your first reading is like the first day of class. You become familiar with features of the course such as the teacher, the structure, the theme, and the basic requirements. However, you will have to attend again, multiple times, before you have mastered the goals of the course and answered all of your questions.

When you practice close reading, you might think of yourself as an active participant engaging with the material rather than as a passive observer. Reading actively will make it easier for you to remember what you have read and will enable you to respond effectively when writing about the text. As an active reader, you have two goals during your first reading:

Goal 1: Read and take notes. Record your initial reactions and impressions while also trying to understand the text. Your focus should be on what is happening in the text on a literal or basic level. Don't skip on observing the obvious. If you are reading a short story, for instance, talk back to that story by annotating and writing in your journal or notebook, recording your thoughts about the narrative, the characters, and the plot. If you are reading an academic article, your responses might be focused more on the writer's ideas, use of evidence, or connections to other arguments. If you are looking at a visual, write down exactly what you see and describe the details.

LEARNING ACTIVITY:
Make Observations

When making observations about a text, your responses should reflect what you are noticing about the text and what you find interesting. You may want to begin by identifying the who, what, where, and when of a text. The following is a limited sample of the questions readers might answer in their observations throughout their first reading:

- Is there a narrator, voice, or speaker? How would you describe it?

- Who/what are the subjects or characters (if any)? How would you describe them?

- What verb tenses are used? Are they active or passive? Who is doing the actions?

- What happens in the text? Does anything in the text seem figurative or symbolic?

- Is there anything that confuses you? Does anything surprise you? Why?

- What images, ideas, or words are repeated? Do some of them seem more important than others?

- Does the text indicate any suggestion of place or location?

- Where does the text present its main ideas? What else do you notice about the organization of the text?

- Does the mood seem to change in different places? Try tracing how the text makes you feel at various points. Does the speaker or narrator seem to contradict your own feelings? Do you think the author shares the same feelings as the narrator/speaker?

Goal 2: Ask questions. You want to start locating places in the texts that you don't understand or have questions about. Recording the questions that arise as you read is another way to actively engage with a text. Take notes in the margins of the text or in a writing journal. This way, you can return to your questions and read the text again with these questions in mind to help you see the text differently. You might also use these questions as discussion-starters to begin a dialogue with others who have read the text. Below are a few examples of Goal 2 annotations, but your own questions will vary according to your medium.

- What does this word mean?

- What is important about this detail?

- What is the motive for this action?

As you read, you will start to make some inferences about your observations and questions. During your first reading, try not to think of inferences or claims about the text as "finding the right answer" to the text, but rather as one possible interpretation. A second reading might produce other observations, questions, interpretations, or reactions.

7.5.1.4 Phase Three: Directed Reading (Inferences, Answers, Nuanced Meaning, and Evidence)

During active reading, you were taking notes on the who, what, when, and where of the text. With directed reading, you are looking at the how and why. To begin this phase of annotation, revisit your initial observations and questions. Use these observations and questions to guide your second reading of the text. Try to understand how different elements of the text function and why certain aspects of the text seem confusing, important, or intriguing. In this phase, you will address your questions and look for patterns that might relate to possible themes, ideas, complications, and interpretations.

While your Phase 2 reading mostly produces observations and questions, the Phase 3 reading allows you to start analyzing the ideas of the text and how they are produced. This is when you are best equipped to begin to identify the author's purpose and message. It is also the time to identify potential symbolic or figurative meanings and alternative interpretations.

LEARNING ACTIVITY:
Analysis and Synthesis in Textual Analysis

2.D

After pre-reading and making observations of your text, start making your own meaning through analysis and synthesis of what you've noted.

- Try to start answering some of the questions from your first reading.

- Review everything that seemed strange or didn't seem to fit. Are these passages more meaningful now that you have a better understanding of the text?

- Return to your initial observations and annotations. Do any of them seem particularly striking now that you've read the text again? Why did you make note of certain details? Do you notice any patterns in your annotations?

- Look for contradictions and changes in the ideas or form. What are the purposes of these conflicts in meaning, tone, characterization, interpretation, connotation, etc.?

- Locate connections between repeated words, images, and ideas.

- Write down any ideas that arise when you read certain phrases or think of particular images. Is there evidence for a symbolic or figurative reading in addition to the literal reading?

Once you have finished your second reading, you should try to organize your notes and look for some general conclusions and initial claims. Organizing your ideas now will help you to be better prepared to write and talk about the text since you will have narrowed your observations down to some main ideas.

7.5.2 The "I" of Eye: Theories of Looking

"The 'I' of Eye: Theories of Looking"

By Casely E. Coan and Devon R. Kehler

pp. 101–104

Our eyes have a lot to do with the ways we experience pleasure, and they also impact the way we understand the power roles in our relationships with others. Eyes complexly interact with the rest of our body in the struggle to make sense of the world around us. This section explores how meaning is made not only by one's eyes and viewing experience in the moment, but also by the histories and socially situated identities that viewers and authors bring to a film or photograph. This section provides some key terms for how eyes look and gaze at images captured by cameras. Additionally, you are asked to examine how pleasure and power operate in visual texts by paying attention to the ways looking and gazing produce feelings, thoughts, and bodily sensations.

Laura Mulvey,[1] a frequently cited writer on cinema, calls our attention to the "pleasure of looking." She suggests that the pleasure the eye receives from looking and being looked at is not innocent. The concept of "gaze" as explained by Jonathan Schroeder can help us explain how looking is more than just an act of seeing. Schroeder claims, "to gaze implies more than to look at—it signifies a psychological relationship of power, in which the gazer is superior to the object of the gaze" (208). In other words, gazing has a purpose: it puts the one looking in a position of power over whatever is being seen.

When analyzing a visual text, especially those with human subjects, certain language is needed to discuss differing sorts of relationships between the looker and the looked at.

Spectator's Gaze: Within this particular context, we can understand the "spectator" as equivalent to the "audience." The spectator's gaze is your gaze when you are viewing a film or photograph. As such, this gaze is influenced by those

---

1 Mulvey, Laura. "Visual Pleasure and Narrative Cinema." *Film Theory and Criticism: Introductory Reading*, edited by Leo Braud and Marshall Cohen, New York: Oxford UP, 1999, pp. 833–44.

contexts you bring to the text: your identity, background, experiences, and social and cultural positions. Voyeuristic spectatorship is one mode of gazing in which the watcher experiences power and pleasure.

- What do you feel as a viewer? Do you feel pleasure and/or power? How? Why?

- How do your own experiences or background impact your understanding of the image?

Eye of the Camera: The camera—and the person or people operating it—create certain "conditions for viewing," meaning a viewer does not get to see the whole picture, but only what was captured by a lens. Sometimes, the camera's eye places our eyes in a passive position; sometimes, the eye of the camera places us in a position of dominance.

- How does the camera position you as viewer? From what angle are you viewing the action?

- What was captured in the frame? What isn't shown? Why?

- Does the camera place viewers in a position of passivity or dominance? What about the image, the angle, the framing, the lighting, the cropping, etc., makes you feel this way?

Intra-diegetic Gaze: In film and photography involving human subjects, the characters within the text also use their gaze to create dynamics of power and pleasure. A filmmaker or photographer may employ this gaze in different ways, asking the audience to identify with either the one looking (that is, the one exercising the intra-diegetic gaze) or the one being looked at. This gaze promotes sympathy between audience and character and creates experiences of power or pleasure in looking or being looked at.

- Where are the characters in the image looking? What are they looking at? Why?

- How does their gaze indicate their position of power? Are they enacting power over another figure or object in the picture?

- Does their gaze indicate if/how they are taking pleasure in something?

- Who do you identify with in the film or photograph? Why?

Extra-diegetic Gaze: This occurs when people depicted in a visual text appear to be looking directly out of the frame at viewers. Power is primarily located with the person(s) depicted. Consider one of the most common experiences viewers have when gazing at the *Mona Lisa*: the intense sensation of being looked at or watched.

- Are any figures in the image looking directly at the camera?

- How are the figures trying to engage you as a viewer?

• Do any figures indicate a sense of pleasure in being gazed at?

Now that we have introduced some terminology that enables us to better engage how looking, power, and pleasure interact, let's apply these terms to the photo below. We'll ask questions while inviting you to engage in the analysis process with the following photograph from Lauren Greenfield's *Girl Culture*.

Lauren Greenfield/INSTITUTE

Eye of the Camera: This photograph is part of a larger project seeking to display everyday practices of girlhood. The camera sets these girls outside a suburban home, in a suburban neighborhood. How does this setting affect your interpretation of the photograph? What might you assume about the subjects based on this setting and their attire? What is or isn't captured in this frame? What does the arrangement of the girls in front of the camera suggest about their relationship with the photographer? With you as a viewer? Considering the purpose of this photo project, what does this particular frame ask you to see about the "everyday practices of girlhood"?

Intra-diegetic Gaze: Consider Berit on the far right. She does not engage the camera. Instead her gaze is directed towards the girls posed beside her. What does this say about the pleasure Berit experiences in being photographed? What's her relationship to the camera in comparison to the rest of the girls? How does Berit acquire power for herself and/or grant power to the other girls by the way she gazes away from the camera and towards her friends?

Extra-diegetic Gaze: Alli, Annie, and Hannah are all looking at the photographer and, therefore, the audience. But they aren't gazing in the same way. How can we see them enacting the extra-diegetic gaze differently from one another? What do their varying postures say about the relationship between them and the camera? How does their willingness to engage the camera communicate their pleasure in being gazed at? As a viewer, how do you feel yourself responding differently to being looked at by them?

Spectator's Gaze: As a viewer, how does the composition of the photograph position you in the girls' world? Do you feel pleasure in looking at them? Power? How do these dynamics shift as you consider the girls looking back at you versus the girl avoiding eye contact with the camera? How do your own experiences or identity impact your understanding of the girls and situation depicted by Greenfield?

For a more nuanced analysis, return to the photograph multiple times, with greater attention to what captures your gaze on repeat viewings.

"Interviews:
Bringing Your
Research Topic to
Life"

By Rachael Wendler

pp. 104–105

7.5.3 Interviews: Bringing Your Research Topic to Life

Having the opportunity to speak with a research source can be exciting, but effective interviewing takes thought and preparation. These steps will walk you through the process.

Step 1: Choosing an Interviewee

Consider people with different kinds of knowledge:

- Academic knowledge (a professor who studies autism)

- Professional knowledge (a staff member at a local autism advocacy organization)

- Experiential knowledge (a parent of an autistic child)

Try googling "Tucson" or "University of Arizona" and your topic to get a sense of local resources. You might also explore faculty profiles in relevant departments or think about your personal networks. You might also think about interviewing someone who disagrees with you to better understand alternate views.

Step 2: Requesting an Interview

Remember that an interview is a favor, so ask nicely! In your interview request:

- introduce yourself (if needed), the purpose of your project, and the interview topic

- explain why this person would be a good interviewee

- specify how much time the interview would take, when you need it completed, and the format (in person, phone, email) and location (someplace convenient for the interviewee)

Make contact as soon as possible, so you have time to find someone else if your first choice is unavailable.

Step 3: Preparing

Begin by researching your interviewee—asking for information that is available online shows a lack of consideration for your interviewee's time. Has your interviewee published something? Read it. Does she work for an organization? Check out its website. Consider what holes you have in your data and what this interviewee could offer from his or her expertise. Brainstorm questions (~8–12 for a 20-minute interview), making sure to avoid questions that could be offensive or overly intrusive. Try for open-ended questions (why/how/in what way) rather than closed questions that can be answered with a simple yes or no.

Once you have a list, put questions in an order that makes sense, such as chronologically or by topic. If there are any sensitive questions, put those at the end, after the interviewee has had time to warm up and you've had an opportunity to feel out whether the question is appropriate. Finally, prioritize your questions, bolding the ones that are most important, so if time runs short, you can jump straight to the key points.

Step 4: The Interview

Bring your typed questions, a hard-backed notebook to write on, a pen, and two ways to record in case one doesn't work (hint: there are many free recording apps for smartphones). Be sure to ask permission before you start recording. Dress professionally if you'll be interviewing in a professional context. Establish rapport through small talk first, and then ask permission to record before turning on your device and asking questions. Don't feel tied to your questions—follow your interviewee's lead if he or she brings up something interesting, and improvise follow-up questions. Pay attention to your body language (eye contact!) and your interviewee's (is a certain topic making him uncomfortable?). Don't take more time than you requested unless your interviewee invites you to talk longer, and make sure to say thanks!

Step 5: Following Up

Send a thank-you card or email, and offer to share your final paper.

7.6 Keeping Track of and Engaging with Sources

As you research your topic, make a conscious effort to keep track of the sources you find. Keeping track of sources will help you stay organized and will save you time in the long run. In addition, you can begin the actual writing process as you collect your sources by taking notes and interacting with each source. This section will address both aspects of tracking sources. Instructors often require an annotated bibliography for the research assignments in the foundations composition sequence. Alternatively, they may ask you to place each of your sources on a spectrum of possible opinions. In addition to taking thorough and accurate notes regarding your sources' arguments, evidence, and ideas, you will also want to takes notes on where you found the source so that you may return to it with ease.

7.6.1 Recording Crucial Information

Your research project will probably require you to identify your sources with in-text citations and a Works Cited page. It can be time-consuming and frustrating to retrace your steps later to find a publisher's name, a page number, or the database for an online article. Here are a few tips to assist your process:

- **Keep track of your research in a research log.** To do this, record the databases and indexes you search and the keywords that you use in each database. Keep this log with the notes you take on the books and articles you are reading. This will help you keep track of where you have looked and what sources were good for your topic. Also write down sources you review that are not helpful so that you do not waste time by accidentally reviewing a source twice. See pages 107–108 for an example.

- **Copy materials you cannot check out of the library for an extended period (such as journals).** Print or download articles or texts that you find online. Do not assume that you will be able to find such sources again later; they may be in use or in the process of being reshelved when you look for them again. In the case of online materials, do not assume that you can find the article again easily. It will save you time to print or download the article at the time you find it. The UA library has many print stations that you can access through the computers nearby. You might also consider saving article PDFs to your own computer or memory drive.

- **Try using *RefWorks*.** Another option for compiling resources is an application available through the UA libraries called *RefWorks*, which formats and organizes your citations and bibliographies as you work. A librarian can help you learn to use this resource.

- **Immediately write down any information that you will need** every time you copy or print materials out of a book, journal, or online database. This information will include the page numbers you read as well as all of the bibliographic information for the source. Make a habit of writing this information on the first page of anything you copy or print, and record it in your research log. You can find an in-depth explanation of how to cite various types of sources under "Documentation" in *Writer's Help 2.0*.

- **Compile an annotated bibliography**, in which you include all the bibliographic information (in the format required for your paper) and a brief description of each text. This will help you keep track of who said what. You can easily flip through it to remind yourself of each author's main points. You might also want to make note of the rhetorical situation of each source, including which rhetorical strategies they rely on to persuade their readers. See the discussion of annotated bibliographies in the next section of this chapter.

- **Write the citation as soon as you use a quote, summary, or paraphrase of any source, and immediately add that source to your Works Cited page.** This way you can be certain you cited all your sources, and when you revise, you won't have to look through all your materials to find the correct citation information.

- Refer to the appropriate citation style in "Documenting Sources" in *Writer's Help 2.0*. Also check out the UA libraries' "Write & Cite" Web page (http://new.library.arizona.edu/research/write-cite). Note that depending on your class, instructor, or academic discipline, you may need to use a different citation system than what is covered in these resources, like IEEE or AMA. Always make sure to check the formatting expectations before you begin integrating your sources.

7.6.1.1 Sample Research Log

Keeping a research log can help you stay organized throughout the research process. It can also help you keep track of where and how you found your sources and serve as the starting point for an annotated bibliography. In the sample below, UA student Justin Frere demonstrates how to turn a research question into search terms for an academic database. Notice how he records the database, the search string, and the articles that this search produced. This way, Justin can remember which sources he has already found and which search terms he has already used. To improve the effectiveness of this research log, Justin would want to include notes on the content of each of his sources. Though this sample shows the selected results of only one attempted search, Justin will probably want to try different search strings in order to identify the best sources for his research project.

You can learn more about searching online databases—including identifying keywords and creating searches with Boolean operators (AND, OR)—by viewing the "How to Search Effectively" tutorial on the University Libraries website.

First, highlight or underline the key terms in your research question and create a list of searchable keywords. Also consider if there are other important terms that are not in your question. In this case, Justin added "university" to his list because of the setting of his research.

Since different terms will yield different results, it is important to consider alternative words you can use to represent the key terms in your question.

Research Question: How does student–teacher communication in a large lecture setting impact student experience?

Keywords	Synonyms and Other Related Words
student	pupil, audience
teacher	mentor, faculty, professor, instructor
communication	interaction, contact, learning
lecture	lecture hall, auditorium, class, large, big
university	college
student experience	attitude, learning, mindset

Record the database and search string, so you can remember what terms you have already used. Justin used the ERIC database because his topic relates to education.

Note how Justin strategically used his keywords in combination with Boolean operators (AND, OR) to narrow his results.

Write a brief annotation for each source you open. You might also include the author's credential and a short summary. You will modify this list as you locate more sources and determine which will be most appropriate for your project. You can add information to this list to create an annotated bibliography.

Search #1

Database: ERIC

Search String: (student OR pupil) AND (teacher OR faculty) AND (lecture OR seminar OR auditorium) AND (communication OR interaction OR contact) AND (large OR big)—189 results

Title: "Student Response Systems and Facilitating the Large Lecture Basic Communication Course: Assessing Engagement and Learning"

- Author(s): Denker, Katherine J.
- Publication: *Communication Teacher*, v27 n1 p50–69 2013.
- Title: "Digital or Didactic: Using Learning Technology to Confront the Challenge of Large Cohort Teaching"
    - Author(s): Saunders, Fiona C.; Gale, Andrew W.
    - Publication: *British Journal of Educational Technology*, v43 n6 p847–858 Nov 2012.
- Title: "'Supersizing' the College Classroom: How One Instructor Teaches 2,670 Students"
    - Author(s): Parry, Marc
    - Publication: *Chronicle of Higher Education*, Apr 2012.
- Title: "'That's It for Today': Academic Lecture Closings and the Impact of Class Size"
    - Author(s): Cheng, Stephanie W.
    - Publication: *English for Specific Purposes*, v31 n4 p234–248 Oct 2012.
- Title: "Student Engagement in Very Large Classes: The Teachers' Perspective"
    - Author(s): Exeter, Daniel J.; Ameratunga, Shanthi; Ratima, Matiu; Morton, Susan; Dickson, Martin; Hsu, Dennis; Jackson, Rod
    - Publication: *Studies in Higher Education*, v35 n7 p761–775 Nov 2010.

7.6.2 Engaging with Your Sources

Engaged reading requires more than just reading through a text and underlining passages. One of the best ways to engage with your sources is to take notes as you read, a practice known as annotation. Think about annotation as having a conversation with the author or authors of the source and asking them the questions you might address in your paper. Asking questions and making comments in the margins while you read can help you remember why you took note of that section. Annotation can also help you see patterns developing across sources, which may help you identify how you would like to enter the conversation.

Thorough notes will help you to group sources together based on patterns such as their position on an issue or use of rhetorical strategies. You may also realize that your sources only represent one side of an issue and that you need to find more sources to fill in any gaps.

7.6.2.1 Sample Research Notes

Below you'll find sample research notes. This two-column strategy helps you to record the ideas you have about specific parts of a text and can save you from having to go back and hunt down specific quotations later in the writing process. The following example uses direct quotations from a source; however, you may wish to include a combination of direct quotations, paraphrases, and summaries. Remember to always include the page number for summaries and paraphrases; it is also useful, for your own reference, to include the page numbers of the sections you summarize. These notes, taken by a UA student, were provided by UA librarian Vicki Mills. This student's research project explores how minority children in elementary school are able, or unable, to relate to the characters in the books they read.

Tolson, Nancy. "Making Books Available: The Role of Early Libraries, Librarians, and Booksellers in the Promotion of African American Children's Literature." *African American Review*, vol. 32, no. 1, 1998, pp. 9–16. *JSTOR*, http://www.jstor.org.ezproxy2.library.arizona.edu/stable/3042263.

In the left column, write the page number and a quote or paraphrase that you find interesting, relevant, or even incorrect or confusing. Writing the quotation will help you consider it more fully than if you just looked at it on the page and recorded the page number.

Source Material	Notes, Questions, etc.
"African American children's books are in existence today because of the determination and dedication of African Americans who decided more than sixty years ago to remove negative depictions of servile, impoverished African Americans from library shelves. These people were able to establish criteria, petition publishers, and creatively write stories for African American children that reflected positive images at a time when few of these books could get published" (Tolson 15).	I agree with Tolson's thesis. The focus is pretty historical throughout the article though. My question is, what is happening with the depiction of minorities in children's books now? Surely they are still problematic at times. **Look for more contemporary articles on this. Also, what did these negative depictions do to children's desire to read and to their own identity? I need to look for other articles that relate the lack of books with positive minority role models to the reading ability of minority children.

In the right column, record your response to the passage on the left.

Your notes should include questions or challenges you have for the text, as well as your possible responses to these questions.

Note other research you need to do, including new searches and looking up experts named in the source text.

Write yourself notes that will help you to construct your argument when you start drafting.

Don't worry about writing in full sentences; taking notes is like talking back to your sources. Being casual can make the process more comfortable and generative, and you can always dress up your language in your actual draft.

This kind of research note might very well become a central part of your paper. Keeping research notes helps to save these important insights you have as you engage with your sources.

"Bontemps, being both an educator and the father of six children, knew the importance of writing books that would reflect positive African American images; this meant, among other things, freeing his African American characters from the heavy dialect that most other authors had imposed upon them" (10).

This is one way I might go with this paper—the importance of parents reading to children and the problem of minority parents finding enough appropriate books to read. Like how Tolson says that the depictions in Bontemps' books meant "freeing… characters from the heavy dialect." The same thing happens in the depiction of other minority characters—American Indian, Hispanic, or Asian American—they are basically trapped and limited by the language and the behavior the author assigns them (particularly if that author is not from the minority group).

Now that you have seen how you might take notes from a source, try it yourself. Find an article online that relates to your topic—either popular or scholarly—and create your own research notes to share in class. Make sure to keep this article handy, as you can use it again to work on an annotation for your annotated bibliography assignment in the next section.

Read more about "Keeping a Working Bibliography" under "Evaluating Sources" within "Research" in *Writer's Help 2.0*.

7.7 The Annotated Bibliography

Writing an annotated bibliography for your research projects will help you gather and analyze information before you sit down to draft your project. When working with many sources, it can be very helpful to have brief summaries of each article as a quick reference.

An annotated bibliography lists carefully formatted citations for topic-related sources. Each citation is then followed by a brief summary of the source and an evaluation of how and why you plan on using it in your research process. Annotated bibliographies are highly valued by scholars because they allow researchers to quickly review the best sources on a given topic. Even if you do not end up publishing your annotated bibliography for other researchers, it can be a useful way for you to keep track of the best sources for your research topic.

Let's take a look at one annotation from UA student Stephenie Mirka. As you read, note how in this entry Stephenie considers not only what the source is about, but also how it could contribute to her research.

Annotated Bibliography

Hardesty, Dawn Wotapka. "Long Island Landlord Group: Sex Offender Law Goes Too Far." *Long Island Business News*, 17 Nov. 2006. General OneFile, go.galegroup.com/ps/i.do?p=ITOF&sw=w&u=uarizona_mai n&v=2.1&id=GALE%7CA154587611&it=r&asid=8a6f9fe342cf79abd1 c3609d16ea4b9e.

Hardesty claims that a bill in Long Island, regarding landlords renting to sex offenders, is ridiculous. The author utilizes many quotes from people, who agree and disagree with her claim. By including both points of view in her argument, she strengthens her essay. She also explains the disadvantages of this law, and how it victimizes sexual offenders. Her purpose is to show that some sex offender laws are too extreme. This article will provide a point of view different than mine for my persuasive essay. It will give me an example of a sexual offender law that is creating problems for landlords. Hardesty provides information from the creator of the bill, which will be useful to back up my claims. I chose this source because it gave a good example of why some laws do not work against sexual offenders.

Let's see how Stephenie's annotated bibliography entry meets or does not meet the criteria in the section entitled "Write the Annotation" below. First, Stephenie begins by stating the overall claim of Hardesty's argument: a new bill making it illegal to rent apartments to sex offenders is ridiculous. Then, she moves to a brief summary of Hardesty's methods (citing other interviews and balancing multiple points of view). Finally, she states Hardesty's main point, which is that sex offender laws are too extreme. Stephenie lets her readers know that she will be using this article to show how this proposed bill is problematic for landlords. It is also clear that this is a good resource for helping Stephenie learn about the bill, its creation, and its intended execution.

LEARNING ACTIVITY:
Write the Annotation

Consider the following template for an annotated bibliography entry. Following these guidelines can help ensure you have included all the information you need in your own work so that your audience clearly understands the major arguments in each source and how you plan to use them.

1. **Describe the purpose of the article.**

   - *Context*: Contextualize the purpose in one sentence. Why was the article written?

   - *Audience*: Identify the primary audience for the article.

   - *Purpose*: State the overall thesis of the article in one sentence.

2. **Summarize the methods.**

   - Mention how any studies were conducted and what resources the author depends on to make their case.

   - Omit specific details (save these for your notes and the final essay).

3. **Describe the major observations/findings/results.**

   - Provide the key ideas and takeaways.

   - Omit any specific details (save these for your notes and the final essay).

4. **Forecast the future use.**

   - Include the ways in which you plan to use the article in your essay.

Here are a few more entries in Stephenie's annotated bibliography. Now that you understand the basic parts of an annotation, read to see how she relates each source to her overall argument.

Longo, Robert E. "Megan's Law Does Little to Increase Safety in US." *Community Care*, 3 Aug. 2006, www.communitycare.co.uk/2006/08/03/megans-law-does-little-to-increase-safety-in-us/.

Longo claims that the development of Megan's Law has not been proven to decrease the number of sexual abuse cases within the United States. The author proves this by including background information, statistics, and examples. He discusses the many implications of Megan's Law, such as cost and victimization of sexual offenders. This victimization has caused many to become offenders again because they are not able to live normal lives after their release from prison. Longo's purpose is to show his readers that the only way to put an end to sexual abuse is to stop it before it occurs. Megan's Law does not aid in this since no evidence exists to prove that it has prevented recurrences of sexual abuse. This article will aid in my research question of deciding whether sexual offenders should be integrated back into society. It shows examples and statistics that could be used in my paper.

Miller, Kathleen. "Wyoming Fears It's Luring Sex Offenders." *Chron.com*, 25 Feb. 2007, www.chron.com/news/nation-world/article/Wyoming-fears-it-s-luring-sex-offenders-1835130.php.

Miller discusses the number of sex offenders that are moving to Wyoming as a result of the harsh laws in other states. Miller uses quotes from a representative of the U.S. House of Representatives, sex offenders, a police officer, and many others. These add substance to her article, when used with background information and other facts regarding laws in Wyoming. Miller's purpose is to inform people of the lack of laws for sexual predators. She wants this to change so that more sexual predators will have to be registered, and harsher laws will be created. In my paper, this article can provide me with an opposing point of view. This will help me to draw my own conclusions about the opposing viewpoint.

Seipp, Catherine. "The Sex-Offender Lobby." The Wall Street Journal, 6 Oct. 2005, www.wsj.com/articles/SB112855797963161192.

Seipp states in her editorial that laws regarding sex offenders and landlords in California do not coincide well. She proves her point by explaining Megan's Law. Also, Seipp's article contains quotes from opponents and advocates of Megan's Law. By including the views of a landlord who is unable to move a sex offender out of his mobile-home park, but still needs to inform angry residents of the offender's presence, she makes her case far more understandable to the reader. The author's purpose is to let people know that lawmakers should not oppose Megan's Law. This applies to my research question by showing the opposing point of view. I can use this in my persuasive essay to show readers what others think regarding the issue of sex offenders. Seipp includes various quotes, which could be added into my paper to expand on the opposing viewpoint.

LEARNING ACTIVITY:
Complete the Research Checklist

The following checklist can help you keep track of all the stages in the research process and assess your progress. Keep this list handy and check off items as you complete them.

Check the assignment sheet to find the due date for the initial and final drafts of your essay as well as any other assignment to be turned in along the way, such as an annotated bibliography. Be sure to write down all of your work; much of your notes might help produce your first draft.

1. Write down relevant due dates:

    • Rough Draft(s):

    • Final Draft:

    • Other Requirements:

2. Brainstorm topics.

3. Browse a site like *CQ Researcher* or the "Research by Course" section on the library's website to gather ideas about topics.

4. Narrow down your list of possible topics to one or two ideas.

5. Get more details and sources on your topic or topics using keyword searches in the Library Catalog and databases like *Academic Search Complete*. Remember, you can also find other good sources from the references cited in the books and articles you find.

6. Record promising sources: email lists of links to full-text articles, call numbers, and other information to yourself and/or print out reference pages and full-text articles. Keep notes about print sources in a well-organized notebook or folder or make photocopies you can write on. You may also want to use a service like *RefWorks* or *Zotero* to keep track of your sources.

7. Explore the library's book collection.

8. Formulate focused research questions.

9. Continue to search for sources based on your focused research question.

10. Meet with a librarian, either at a reference desk or by appointment.

11. Read through your sources. Take notes, summarize, and evaluate your best sources.

12. Consider writing an annotated bibliography to help keep track of your sources and their primary arguments in relation to your paper.

13. Schedule an interview with an expert on the issue you are interested in. Prepare questions ahead of time. Send a thank-you note afterwards.

14. Start analyzing and synthesizing your notes (see Chapter 8 of this text).

15. Double-check that you have all of the sources you need. Check that you've written down all information needed for your own Works Cited or Reference list.

| Analyzing and Synthesizing Information | CHAPTER **8** |

8.1 Analysis and Synthesis: An Overview

All of the assignments you will complete in your foundations writing courses require **analysis**. The word analysis means "a breaking up, a loosening, a releasing" ("Analysis"[1]). When you analyze something, you "break it up" to examine its parts and see how the individual elements of your object of analysis work together as a whole to achieve its purpose. In fact, in much of the work you do at the university, you will be asked to analyze something and provide evidence to support your interpretation. In your foundations writing class, that "something" might be a written text, an image, an audience, or a literacy event in your life. In an art history class, you might be asked to analyze a particular social or historical context, an artist's technique, or a particular medium; in a biology class, you might analyze cellular function, an ecosystem, or the life cycle of a particular organism. Regardless of what you are analyzing, you are essentially performing the same cognitive task: closely examining a subject in an attempt to understand or interpret it.

In your foundations writing courses, analysis requires an ability to explain how and why a text works to make meaning. Whether you are analyzing a short story or a literacy event in your life, you participate in creating meaning by exploring and building an argument around your particular interpretation. In an analysis, you will be challenged to think beyond the surface-level message of the texts you read. In order to offer a complex and interesting analysis of any text, you

---

1 "Analysis." *Etymonline.com*. 2013. 15 Oct. 2013.

must read it closely, interact with it, locate sites of inquiry, and use your own experiences to guide your responses.

You **synthesize** when you combine together the analysis of multiple texts. You may be comparing and contrasting literary or visual texts or you might be weaving together multiple sources from a research project. You might even synthesize what you have learned from collecting primary data from interviews or observations with information you learned from secondary sources like scholarly articles from peer-reviewed journals.

Before moving into a discussion of specific types of analysis and synthesis, take a moment to consider the following key terms:

- **Analysis:** The act of breaking a text into parts and examining how those parts affect the audience's understanding of the text or the overall function of the text. Analysis moves beyond summary and description. Summary and description explain what is happening while analysis explains how and why something is happening. Remember that analytical statements reveal a careful consideration of the text beyond its main point and open a space for dialogue about the text and what it "means" to an audience.

- **Synthesis:** The act of comparing and contrasting multiple sources and/or pieces of data to identify trends or absences. Synthesis requires that you both understand the various texts on a basic level (summary and description) as well as understand how they work (analysis). Synthesis requires that you critically compare multiple texts to understand a larger picture or context.

- **Text:** Any artifact or object that you analyze. A text might refer to a book, a newspaper article, a scholarly article, a short story, a poem, a speech, a movie, a picture, a video game, a person, an event, a space, a place, and so on.

When composing a written analysis, it is important to focus on a specific argument. No single essay can say everything about a particular text or experience. If you try to take on too much in your essay, you will find that the thesis lacks specificity and the paragraphs make imprecise claims.

> Read more about "Analyzing Arguments" within "Critical Thinking and Argument" in *Writer's Help 2.0.*

8.2 Strategies for Analyzing Texts

In your foundations writing course, you may be asked to perform different types of analysis including textual, visual, spatial, and experiential analysis. Textual analysis refers to examining a written text like a poem or short story while visual analysis deals with films, music videos, photos, and works of art. Spatial analysis examines places you have visited or a space you use, while experiential analysis involves self-reflection focused on a personal experience, such as your relationship with language. You might even analyze your own experiences as with the literacy narrative. In the following pages, you will find individual sections with suggestions and strategies for performing analysis on various types of texts.

8.2.1 Journalist Questions

Asking key questions is a common technique that a reporter might use when investigating a story. These questions include the five Ws that enable a journalist to get the crucial details for a story: who, what, when, where, and why. A reporter may then ask a sixth question to deepen his or her sense of what happened: how did the event occur? Using these questions will help you consider a topic or analyze a text from various angles. For example, consider how the following basic questions might apply to texts such as the Harry Potter novels:

1. **Who** is the author? Who are the main characters? Who are the primary and secondary audiences? Who might have influenced J.K. Rowling's writing of this series?

2. **What** are the important plot points? What happens to the main character? What happened to the author before, during, and after writing the series?

3. **When** did Rowling write the first novel? When does it take place? Are there historical connections with events and themes during the time the novel was written and during the time the novel is set?

4. **Where** do the novels take place and what do we learn by comparing and contrasting the different settings? Are these settings real or fictional (or some combination of the two)? Why did the author choose these locations?

5. **Why** does Harry take such risks against his powerful enemies? Why do some people identify with his character while others find him annoying?

6. **How** does Rowling generate specific emotional reactions, such as fear and sympathy, from her readers? How does the series reflect cultural aspects of the time and place in which the novels were written? How do the novels invite us to reflect on social issues such as inequalities of race, class, and gender?

As you can see, these questions move from basic description to the kinds of analytic questions that may help you generate a thesis statement about the text. You could use the same technique with topics as diverse as stem cell research or restrictions on streetlights in Tucson. You can also use the questions to interrogate non-fiction texts like scholarly and news articles.

8.2.2 The Observations/Inferences Chart

"The Observations/
Inferences Chart"

By Carie Schneider

pp. 118–120

The observations/inferences chart is a simple method for organizing your thoughts and annotations. It can also help you construct a thesis for a textual analysis assignment. When taking notes, first focus on the techniques, features, or images that you immediately notice. These should be actual observations that are physically present in the text, which no reasonable person would disagree with—things like "he uses repetition," "lots of metaphors," "there are two characters in the frame." These are observations; you are just noting content from the text (this is Phase Two: Active Reading from Chapter 7). Then go back through your observations and try to figure out what each of these features could mean, signify, symbolize, or represent (this is Phase Three: Directed Reading from Chapter 7). These can be whatever comes to mind. They do not have to be provable; they are just whatever you infer from the features you noticed. List these under the "Inferences" column.

Following is an example observations/inferences chart for a visual analysis of two panels from a comic composed by Ryan Winet. The first five observations in the chart relate to the first panel.

Panel One:

Panel Four:

Artwork courtesy of Ryan Winet

Observations	Inferences
Swinging door, barrel, wood construction	Swinging door reminds me of saloons in Western movies. Seems like this might be a "Western"
There are two characters facing each other with hands at their sides	If this is a Western, there will probably be a duel
Character on the left has disheveled hair, a crooked nose, and bandolier	These characteristics seem to imply the "bad guy"
Character on the right has lighter hair and wears a cowboy hat and cravat (neckband)	The standard cowboy outfit leads to a "good guy" association. The cravat reminds me of the Boy Scouts. Is this an American association with courage or "good"?
Text in a box highlighted by a colored background	The background of the text box means the text is not part of the scene. Is there some kind of narrator? The font is an interesting choice, too—it looks playful like Comic Sans which doesn't seem to fit a Western. Why might this be?
Crooked-nose character appears juxtaposed with the word "BANG!"; same shape coming from his gun and the cowboy's hand	It's a gunfight. The artist shows motion by using words and images
Both characters have their mouths open	There are no words printed, but it looks like they might both be screaming. One out of anger and the other from pain or fear?

After reading the entire cartoon and completing an observations/inferences chart, you need to organize your thoughts even further to move toward a thesis statement by grouping the techniques or features ("observations") into categories and trying to decide what the overall message or meaning of the text is.

Looking back at the sample chart, it seems that some of the main categories of features could be "composition" or "character depictions," "juxtaposition," and maybe "symbolism." These categories could be body paragraph topics, and the order of these can be changed during the writing and revision process.

LEARNING ACTIVITY:
Practice Observations and Inferences

Take a look at a text assigned by your instructor and fill in the observations/ inferences chart below. Then, as in the example in this section, identify some main features or patterns and begin to make claims.

Observations	Inferences

Next, you will have to figure out what the text means; you will need to interpret the overall message for the reader. Based on the notes in the sample chart, we can start to come up with some ideas. For example, one might use the inferences about the characters to argue that the Western genre relies heavily on stereotypes. Or maybe the juxtaposition of playful font and violence is suggesting something about depictions of violence in popular media.

As long as you can back up your thesis with strong evidence from the text, you have a lot of freedom in terms of what you would like to argue about this particular cartoon.

8.2.3 Section Summaries

Summaries can help you map the development of a text so you can see where it is going and how it gets there. For example, if you are writing an analysis of an academic journal article and your entire paper depends on your understanding of it, you may want to create thorough summaries of each section or paragraph that highlight the author's main points and the ways in which those points are supported. This summary would also be important when reading a short story or novel because understanding narrative structure is a crucial step to writing about literature.

> Read more about "Summarizing a Text" under "Reading Critically" within "Critical Thinking and Argument" in *Writer's Help 2.0.*

A section summary can be as simple as a short description of each paragraph. The main advantage of section summaries is that they are quick to construct, especially if you have already annotated the text. When creating a section summary, you should accurately describe the main ideas in a portion of the text. Focus on larger themes rather than specific textual strategies and try to paraphrase the author in your own words.

LEARNING ACTIVITY:
Practice Section Summaries

Practice below by creating section summaries of the first three paragraphs of one of your assigned readings.

Section Summary Practice	
Paragraph 1:	
Paragraph 2:	
Paragraph 3:	

8.2.4 Rhetorical Précis

Writing a concise, focused summary of a text is also a form of analysis. In French, the word "précis" (pronounced "pray-see") means "summary." The purpose of the rhetorical précis is to offer a short account of an article that does more than summarize the content. The rhetorical précis, which is generally four sentences long, accounts for the author's main assertion as well as an explanation of how the author develops or supports the thesis. The précis also includes the author's purpose for writing, a description of the intended audience, and the relationship the author establishes with that audience (Woodworth 156–164[2]). Examining issues of audience and purpose are essential to writing descriptions that analyze rather than summarize the content of a source.

Sentences of the Précis:

1. **Name of author, [optional: a phrase describing author]; genre and title of work, date in parentheses; a rhetorically accurate verb (such as "asserts," "argues," "suggests," "implies," "claims," etc.); and a "that" clause containing a major assertion (thesis statement) of the work.**

2 Woodworth, Margaret K. "The Rhetorical Précis." *Rhetoric Review* 7.1 (1998): 156–64.

2. An explanation of how the author develops and/or supports the thesis, usually in chronological order.

3. A statement of the author's apparent purpose, followed by an "in order" phrase indicating the change the author wants to effect in the audience.

4. **A description of the intended audience and the relationship the author established with the audience.**

Sample:

> In a *New York Times* opinion article entitled "Finally, Good News About School Lunches" (2011), food writer Mark Bittman argues that while the new federal guidelines for school lunches are not perfect, they are effective and are a positive step forward. Bittman supports his thesis by outlining the pros and cons of the new bill, comparing the new guidelines to previous ones, and placing the new guidelines in the context of a larger cultural and political conversation about health and the food industry. His purpose is to persuade potential supporters who may be disappointed by compromise that the new bill is indeed a victory. **Bittman establishes an informal tone ("let's remember") and places his argument in political terms in order to connect with similarly-minded readers.**

8.2.5 Literary Analysis of Written Texts

In order to produce an analysis of a written text, you should first review your notes from your close reading of the text. You might want to look through Chapter 7 again to remind yourself of some of the questions and strategies that can help you produce your own interpretation of a text's meaning. Consider focusing on the patterns and repeated ideas you discovered while reading, including patterns in the arguments a text is making (themes or ideas) and how it makes these arguments (literary devices and form). On the following pages, you will find suggestions for two types of literary analysis essays: one based on thematic content and one based on the author's use of literary devices. However, there are many other types of literary analysis essays, and you should make sure that you are following your teacher's assignment instructions and guidelines.

> Read more about "Writing for the Humanities" within "Academic, Professional, and Public Writing" in *Writer's Help 2.0.*

8.2.5.1 Thematic Literary Analysis

The goal of this type of analysis is to explain how a text engages, promotes, or challenges specific ideas or themes. The theme is a message that one interprets from the text rather than the main topic(s) of the text. A text may even place two or more ideas or themes in opposition to each other, calling for an interpretation that makes sense of a contradictory relationship.

In a thematic literary analysis, writers usually identify and support their interpretation of a text based on the author's use of details, setting, characterizations, images, descriptions, etc. To make sure you are not merely summarizing the text, consider looking at complex, ambiguous, or secondary issues within the text. Take note of your close-reading annotations again and focus on phrases, images, or descriptive language that seem particularly thought-provoking, important, or unusual. Consider any sections with unclear purposes. If you wonder why an author used a particular detail or described a particular event, there is a good chance that she is complicating the main issues of the text in ways you have yet to consider. Remember, a text doesn't happen by accident and authors often contradict, elaborate on, or redirect what appears to be their main purpose or message.

How many different ideas or themes are present within your text? How can you connect these ideas or group them together? Are any of the connections surprising or unusual? Does the author challenge or subvert the positive or negative values traditionally associated with these ideas or themes?

LEARNING ACTIVITY:
Examine Thematic Literary Analysis

When performing a literary analysis, you can also consider two different themes in conversation with each other. For example, Salman Rushdie's short story "At the Auction of the Ruby Slippers" includes themes such as consumerism, violence, institutional religion, nostalgia, unrequited love, and celebrity culture, among others. Consider how UA student Chloe Cho analyzes the relationship between religion and materialism in the text in order to produce a specific interpretation of Rushdie's story:

> The short story "At the Auction of the Ruby Slippers" by Salman Rushdie depicts the materialistic era and the consequential emptiness of worshiping the unachievable object. While some people consider the Ruby Slippers as just a special and glamorous object, the majority of the population idolizes the Ruby Slippers. The story mainly focuses on the narrator's point of view. He considered the Ruby Slippers as a magical object that will help him regain his romantic relationship. However, as he realizes that his desires are unattainable, he experiences bitter feelings of emptiness. Since materialism functions as religion in the story, people tend to depend on the fictional object, the Ruby Slippers, rather than acknowledging and improving their dissatisfying conditions.

Following up on student writing:

- In your own words, what is Chloe saying about the text?

- How does Chloe's thesis move her beyond summary into an analysis of Rushdie's story?

- How does Chloe introduce the two complex themes and her interpretation without being too vague or giving away too many details?

- How might Chloe structure her essay around the relationship of material-ism and religious devotion?

It is important to notice that Chloe's thesis does not simply state that the short story reflects two ideas, religion and materialism, but rather that these two themes combine to produce a message within the text. Remember, like the definition of analysis in section 8.1, it is always important to demonstrate how your interpretations of the author's ideas (or the "parts" of the text) connect back to a larger idea or message (or the "whole" of the text).

8.2.5.2 Literary Device-Based Analysis

In order to perform an analysis based on the literary devices or techniques used by the author, consider the following steps:

Use your close reading to identify a theme, message, or purpose present in the text (often based on patterns or repetitions of language and form).

1. Correctly identify specific literary devices related to this theme/message/purpose. (See the sample list of literary devices that follows on page 126.)

2. Group examples from the text together by literary device or technique. For example, you might place all similes together. You might also consider grouping examples together based on larger categories that produce similar effects like sound or image. Symbol, simile, and metaphor can be grouped together as they all create mental images, while assonance and alliteration might be grouped together because they produce specific sound effects.

3. Based on your teacher's assignment, select an appropriate number of devices to analyze for your essay. You may be asked to discuss the author's use of a single device at length, or you might be asked to demonstrate how the author uses multiple devices for a single purpose. When you select devices and examples, be sure to select those that have a strong impact on the theme or message you wish to discuss in your essay.

4. For each example, you should explain how the technique affects the audience's reading of the text. For instance, you might explain that the use of alliteration in a poem increases the tempo of the poem, making the audience read a specific line faster and with more urgency. You should make sure this explanation is supported with evidence from your text, using quoted words or phrases.

5. You should also explain how the specific devices, or examples of a device, impact the overall meaning of the text and the audience's understanding. In addition to the literal effect of the device on how a text is read (step 4), you should also explain how the example creates or affects the overall meaning or purpose of a text.

LEARNING ACTIVITY:
Examine Literary Device Analysis

1.A

2.A

2.B

Consider this example of a literary device-based analysis, written by UA student Haley Gray about Michael Lassell's poem "How to Watch Your Brother Die."

> Lassell utilizes enjambment when describing a phone conversation between the speaker and his wife, discussing the brother's grim fate. He includes, "Hear her say / 'Please. I don't want to know all the details'" (Lassell 481). Lassell chooses to roll over "Please. I don't want to know all the details" to put the sole emphasis on her words. He does this to pinpoint for the reader the wife's uncomfortable attitude towards the brother's homosexuality. Lassell highlights the wife's disinterest in the brother's illness solely due to his sexual preferences. He implements these line breaks to amplify a specific part of the line, to evoke emotions from the reader.

Following up on student writing:

1. How does Haley incorporate evidence from the text to support her interpretation?

2. Where does Haley describe how the literal effect of enjambment impacts the process of reading?

3. Where does Haley describe how the literary device impacts her interpretation of the text?

When you are writing your own textual analysis, keep in mind that you will need to move between evidence and an explanation of the evidence to prove your points. See 8.2.2 "The Observations/Inferences Chart," in this chapter for some examples of how to effectively move between evidence and explanations in your own writing.

The following strategies are defined in *The Bedford Glossary of Critical and Literary Terms*. Your instructor may introduce other terms that relate to the texts in your class.

8.2.5.3 Sample List of Textual Strategies

- **Alliteration:** the repetition of sounds in a sequence of words. Alliteration generally refers to repeated consonant sounds. For example, "Peter Piper picked a peck of pickled peppers."

- **Allusion:** an indirect reference, often to a person, event, statement, theme, or work. Allusions enrich meaning through the connotations they carry or the associations that they evoke in a reader's mind. Examples of allusions include references to historical events or plays by Shakespeare made by the author.

- **Assonance:** the repetition of identical or similar vowel sounds, as in "fate" and "cave."

- **Atmosphere:** the general feeling created for the reader or audience by a text at a given point. While this is sometimes referred to as tone, the two words have different meanings. Tone is an author's attitude toward the reader, audience, or subject matter, whereas atmosphere is the feeling or mood the text evokes for the reader.

- **Cliché:** an expression used so often that it has become commonplace and has lost its original impact. For example, using "a picture is worth a thousand words" to indicate that a single image expresses many feelings or ideas is a cliché.

- **Figurative language:** language that employs one or more figures of speech, such as metaphor or simile. A simile compares two distinct things by using comparative terms including "like" or "as," while a metaphor associates two distinct things directly using literal language. "That child is like a cyclone" is a simile, while "that child is a mouse" is a metaphor.

- **Foreshadowing:** the technique of introducing material that prepares the reader for future events or revelations. Examples of foreshadowing include mentioning a gun that will later be used to shoot someone in the narrative or implying that a character is threatening through suggestive language before his or her actions become villainous.

- **Hyperbole:** employing deliberate, emphatic exaggeration, sometimes intended for ironic effect. Saying something is "the very best in the world" could be a hyperbolic statement. The opposite of this is understatement.

- **Point of view:** the vantage point from which a narrative is told. First-person and third-person are the most commonly used, while second-person is only occasionally encountered. First-person narratives are told by a narrator who refers to himself or herself as "I" and is often a part of the action. Third-person narrators can either be omniscient (all-knowing and reliable) or limited (restricted to the perspective of a single character at a time). Second-person narrators speak directly to the reader as "you."

- **Symbolism:** the sustained use of symbols to represent or suggest associations or ideas that are not part of a thing's literal meaning. For example, you could say that an author "uses symbols of nature" to evoke a sense of freedom for the reader.

8.2.6 Visual Analysis

Like written texts, visual texts can lead toward a variety of potential interpretations and messages. Messages in visual texts are communicated primarily through images, illustrations, and design. As a reader, you will notice different aspects of visual texts than you would in written ones. For example, in written texts, a comparison using the words "like" or "as" signals a simile. In visual texts, where words may or may not be present, such a comparison would be made through visual cues within the text—perhaps by juxtaposing two images in an unexpected way. You would have to read the visual elements of the text closely, just as you would a written text, in order to make such an interpretation. As you investigate visuals, look for aspects of the text that spark your interest. Ask yourself why those particular aspects had an effect on you. You will want to consider how certain visual strategies or techniques (design choices, areas of emphasis, symbolic representation, and so forth) work to construct meaning.

8.2.6.1 Sample List of Visual Strategies

The following key terms and questions for visual analysis, from the guidelines for analyzing a photo presented by the UA Center for Creative Photography, will help you develop the language to analyze a visual text, whether it is a painting, a photograph, or a digital image. An understanding of these basic strategies can lead you to an analysis of the artist's overall message(s).

> Read more about "Analyzing Visual Texts" under "Reading Critically" within "Critical Thinking and Argument" in *Writer's Help 2.0*.

- **Angle:** From what vantage point was the photograph taken? Imagine the photograph taken from a higher or lower angle or view. How does the vantage point affect the meaning or viewer's interpretation of the photograph?

- **Framing:** Describe the edges of the view. What is included? What is not included, and why?

- **Dominance:** Close your eyes. When you open them and look at the photograph, what is the first thing you notice? Why is your attention drawn there?

- **Balance:** Is the visual weight on one side of the photograph about the same as the other—is there more to grab your attention on one side than the other?

- **Contrast:** Are there strong visual contrasts—lights and darks, shadows, textures, solids, voids, and so forth? Why might the artist have chosen to emphasize contrast between two parts of the image?

- **Focus:** What parts of the image are clearly in focus? Are some out of focus? Why?

- **Scale:** Discuss the size of the objects within the work. Does the scale seem natural? How does it change the way you look at the image when one of its parts seems unnaturally large or small?

Depending on your assignment, you may be asked to discuss the use of a single visual element at length, or you might be asked to describe the effects of multiple strategies for a single purpose. When you select examples and devices, be sure to select those that have a strong impact on a theme or message you wish to discuss in your essay. For each example, you should explain the effect of the strategy or visual element on the audience's experience of the text. For instance, you might explain that the specific framing in a photo causes the audience to focus on the space between two figures. You also want to explain how a specific strategy or visual element impacts the overall meaning of the text. You might suggest that this framing makes an argument about the vast distance between these two figures or about their inability to connect.

LEARNING ACTIVITY:
Analyze a Photograph

Photo by D.R. Ransdell

Using the strategies listed in this section, practice analyzing this photograph of people lined up to enter a monument. You might want to start with an observation/inferences chart before answering these questions.

1. What aspects of the picture do you find most interesting and why?

2. What do you believe the photographer wants the viewers to think about after viewing this image?

3. What specific strategies used by the photographer lead you to this interpretation?

4. What larger claim do you believe you could make about this photograph, given the information you have and the interpretation you have developed?

"Film Analysis"

By Amy Parziale

pp. 130–132

8.2.7 Film Analysis

We tend to interpret films without acknowledging that we are thinking critically about the images we see. When asked about a film, you might answer, "I really liked that film," or "I hated it." You may not immediately be able to articulate why you had such a reaction, but, if pressed, most people will actually provide a more in-depth critique or analysis: "The dialogue was stilted and unrealistic," or "The main character wasn't fully developed, so I didn't care about her." These close readings are the beginning of film interpretation. By examining a film critically, you will be able to analyze the messages it expresses as opposed to simply summarizing the plot. As with other types of analysis, you will need to come up with a unique argument about the film and prove your claims by explaining the use of specific strategies.

8.2.7.1 Sample List of Film Strategies

Following are a list of cinematic terms and techniques commonly used when analyzing films:

- **Mise-en-scène:** literally "put on stage" in French. In films, mise-en-scène is created by four components: lighting, setting/props, makeup/costume, and figure behavior.

    - **Lighting:** the type of light used in a particular shot or sequence of shots. The most common lighting technique is three-point lighting, which consists of a backlight, key light, and fill light. By using these three points of light, the human face can be lit in such a way that there are no shadows on the face, thus allowing the viewer to see even minute changes in the actor's face. Backlighting is a technique used to illuminate the set from behind. Key lighting is the brightest light in three-point lighting and generally illuminates the face from the front. Because this bright light creates shadows, three-point lighting also uses a fill light, which fills in the shadows created by the key light. The fill light is generally positioned to one side of the character and near the camera to eliminate shadows. High-key lighting refers to a scene with a very bright key light, causing the scene to have almost no shadows. Low-key lighting refers to a noticeable difference between the brightness of the key and fill lights, creating deep shadows.

    - **Setting:** the location of the film. The setting can be on location, on a set, or created digitally.

    - **Props:** any object in the setting that has a function within the film. "Prop" is actually short for "property" and is a term borrowed from the theater. Props can act as catalysts for action, as a motif, or as foreshadowing. A famous example of a prop used as a foreshadowing motif is the use of oranges in *The Godfather* trilogy to symbolize death and betrayal.

- **Costume and makeup:** how the characters are dressed and styled.

- **Figure behavior:** the movement and behavior of an actor or other element (animal, object, etc.). Figure behavior includes expression, movement, and posture, as well as acting style and degree of realism.

- **Shot:** what is captured during an uninterrupted period of time by one camera. An establishing shot is an initial shot that establishes the setting and orients the viewer to the world of the film. Shot/reverse shot is an editing technique often used to show a relationship between characters or actions. This technique is most often used during conversations to capture both the speaker and the reaction of the person being spoken to.

- **Cut:** the process by which two shots are joined during editing; in the finished film, cuts appear as the instantaneous transition from one shot to another. The cut is the most common technique used to transition between shots. Other transition techniques include wipes, iris open/close, dissolves, fade-in/fade-out, and fade to black or white.

- **Continuity editing:** the system by which most films' shots are combined. A take is the amount of time a particular camera rolls without stopping. In continuity editing, filmmakers tend not to use particularly short or long takes. Filmmakers may decide, however, to build suspense by quickly cutting between the same shot/reverse shot over and over again, or they may decide to use a long take in which viewers will become uncomfortable because they are not used to watching from one position for a long period of time.

- **Diegesis:** the world of the film. On-screen space is the space seen within the frame. Off-screen space is the space not seen within the frame. When a character or object is off-screen, the viewer will continue to believe in its presence unless the film gives them reason to believe otherwise.

- **Framing:** the use of the camera's spatial limits to determine what appears on screen and what does not. Mobile framing is framing in which the camera moves. Some common types of mobile framing include handheld shots, crane shots, dolly or tracking shots, panning (in which the camera moves on a vertical axis), and tilting (in which the camera moves on a horizontal axis).

- **Shot scale:** the distance of framing in a shot or how much is captured by the camera. There are seven generally accepted shot scales.

  - **Extreme long shot:** captures more than the human body (may show landscape, building, or crowd)

  - **Long shot:** captures the entire human body

  - **Medium long shot:** captures the human body from the knee up

  - **Medium shot:** captures a person from the waist up

- **Medium close-up:** captures a person from the chest up

- **Close-up:** any object shown up close so it appears quite large and fills the majority of the screen

- **Extreme close-up:** shows part of a larger object, part of the human body, or a very small object

- **Shot angle:** the angle of the camera lens relative to what it is capturing. A high angle shot looks down at its subject from a higher angle and can evoke powerlessness. A low angle shot looks up at the subject from below and can evoke power and importance.

- **Sound:** There are two major types of sound in film: diegetic and non-diegetic.

  - **Diegetic sound** is produced by something within the world of the film.

  - **Non-diegetic sound** is produced by something outside the time and space of the film, such as voice-over narration or soundtrack.

- **Film genres:** There are many different genres and subgenres of film that have particular narrative and thematic conventions. Some examples of genres are western, horror, musical, comedy, action, mystery, and romance. Because viewers understand the conventions of each genre, filmmakers can play with audience expectations.

As with other kinds of texts, these techniques (which are manipulated by the screenwriter, producer, editor, director, and others) are used to help viewers "read" and respond to film in various ways. For instance, think about the way that *Star Wars, Episode IV: A New Hope* opens and immediately sets up the paradigm of "good versus evil." After the text crawl that sets the scene along with the non-diegetic soundtrack, the camera tilts down through space to show viewers a planet with two moons. A spaceship enters from the upper-right portion of the screen to the center, and then another spaceship enters from the same direction. This second ship is massive compared to the one it is chasing. The ships exchange fire. This long take establishes the central conflict without ever actually telling the viewer anything at all: this is a story of the Rebels against the Empire.

As you can see in the preceding example, focusing on the non-diegetic soundtrack, the direction of the objects entering the frame, and the long take all contribute to our understanding of the film's main idea. Remember, it is necessary to not only explain the literal effect created by the specific film techniques, but also how that effect impacts meaning and the audience's understanding.

8.2.8 Spatial Analysis

"Spatial Analysis"

By *Crystal Fodrey*

pp. 133–135

If you are asked to conduct an analysis of a space on campus, begin by touring the grounds and buildings on the University of Arizona campus with a critical eye, looking for a location that exhibits an inequality or that has some sort of impact on its occupants. You could, for example, pick a building on campus and analyze how accessible it is for someone in a wheelchair. How difficult might it be for such an individual to get into the front door of the building without assistance and make it to a room on the second floor? What does the level of accessibility say about inclusion and exclusion? Alternatively, you could observe the outdoor green spaces on campus and analyze the different ways people use these areas. How do green spaces facilitate student interactions? How does the spatial arrangement of a lecture hall affect how students or instructors interact with other people in the room? How does the space reflect certain power dynamics?

Our campus has limitless potential for spatial analysis because any location where people have individual and/or collective experiences can be read as a text worthy of interpretation. One popular space for collective experiences at UA is Arizona Stadium. To analyze the stadium—or any other space—we can consider some of the following questions:

- What was the space designed for? How do people actually use the space?

- How does the architectural design of the space impact who uses the space and how people use the space?

- What elements of the space are restrictive? What elements are creative?

- Who is allowed to speak and move about in the space, and who is not?

- What does the space say about what is valued by the people who inhabit the space?

- How does the space divide power among the groups or individuals who occupy it?

- To what extent do the discourses and everyday practices of that space question or confirm the status quo in society?

- What is the significance of all or some of the above? The answer to this question could become your thesis.

Photo by Eli Szabady

Photo by Brad Hensley

How you analyze the space depends to some degree on your perspective:

Example one: A football player might focus more on the field and the types of interactions and power relations that the field facilitates among teammates, between players and coaches, and between players on different teams. From this perspective, the field could be analyzed as a gendered space to which only referees and young men with a high level of athletic ability can gain access during the game. When someone enters the field who does not belong, teams or individuals suffer consequences in the form of personal injury or referee-imposed penalty.

Example two: A cheerleader might analyze the sideline, focusing on it as both a repressive space that restricts movement and a creative space that allows for free expression during the game.

Example three: The majority of us best know the perspective of a fan in the bleachers. From this vantage point, the stadium as a whole becomes a transformative space. People who might not otherwise interact with each other find common ground as they root for the Wildcats. They wear the same colors in support of the team, they know the same cheers, and they share the same traditions and values that are characteristic of UA football culture. Conversely, fans supporting opposing teams find themselves at odds with one another when each person believes that his or her team is superior and believes that their side will win. The energy of the space—created by shouts of praise and disgust—inspires most in attendance to act rowdier and more carefree than they would act at home, at school, or at work. Ultimately, the decisions and actions of the players on the field determine how the fans will react, which shows that the players—and the football itself—hold most of the power in this space.

This analysis of Arizona Stadium is a general one that could be developed with specifics from any given game. The focus of the analysis could even change if, for example, a game takes place during a heavy rainstorm and many fans seek shelter near the concession stands or leave the stadium to finish watching the game elsewhere. Your experience in any given space at any given time can provide you with details for an interesting spatial analysis so long as you approach the space with an open mind. Always make sure to keep track of your observations.

8.2.9 Analysis of a Literacy Experience: The Literacy Narrative

The Literacy Narrative assignment asks you to analyze your acquisition and use of language and writing. Sharing and reflecting on your own story is a way for you to examine how your social and cultural experiences with language and composing have influenced you as a person both inside and outside of the classroom. For this assignment, you will write a first-person narrative in which you analyze how a personal experience has influenced the ways you think, read, write, and live in the world. Al Harahap's section will help you to think about what literacy means and about your multiple literacies.

8.2.9.1 What Is Literacy?

When we talk about literacy or being literate, we usually think about literacy as "the ability to read and write." We might even think that literacy is as simple as 1) being literate, or being able to read and write, or 2) being illiterate, not being able to read and write. However, this simplistic distinction does not adequately capture the range of abilities that we have when it comes to using language for various purposes. We are not divided into two distinct and separate groups of those who can and those who cannot read and write. Rather, when we think of literacy skills, we should consider how well one acquires and uses language along a continuous spectrum. Someone who is a great public speaker may be considered highly literate in the world of politics, while a successful web designer could be considered highly literate in writing for online spaces. Place these two people in the realm of creative writing, and they may flounder.

"What Is Literacy?" and "Identify Your Literacies" activity

By Al Harahap

pp. 135–136

LEARNING ACTIVITY:
Identify Your Literacies

2.C

2.E

2.F

As you begin to think about your multiple literacies, remember that literacy is not simply "the ability to read and write." Instead, think about the range of skills in regards to language or writing that you have acquired over the years and how those abilities have defined who you are as a person.

1. **Think about Your Past:** Consider the early and developmental literacy skills that you acquired growing up and continue to develop throughout your life. Have you heard any stories about your first attempts to speak or communicate with others? How did you learn to read? How did you learn to write? What languages do you speak, and in what ways did you come to learn them? "Languages" could also include informal speech patterns, regional expressions, and slang. How do you use these languages differently and in different contexts? What kinds of texts are you comfortable with reading or comprehending? What kinds of texts are you comfortable with writing or composing? These may include anything from the alphanumeric, to the visual, to the digital. Be specific—even the literacy skills used when reading newspapers and magazines, or writing emails, texting, and using social media, can be very different from one another.

2. **Consider Your Literacy in Specific Communities:** Another way to identify your repertoire of literacies is by thinking about the communities you belong to. For example, being part of a band may have allowed you to hone your skills in reading sheet music or writing poetic language for music lyrics, while being active on a social media site such as *Facebook* or *Twitter* may give you the skills to be concise and take in a lot of different information in bits and pieces. Consider the multiple communities to which you belong. What kinds of different languages do you use in these communities? Here, we are not just considering national and ethnic languages, such as Arabic or Gaelic, but very specific subsets that have unique or unusual lingo and usage, such as African American Vernacular English, casual French, business Hindi, video gamer Japanese, l33t speak, and so on. How do you interact with different texts and different languages in these communities?

3. **Remember Your Academic Literacy:** Now that you have a deeper understanding of literacy as a multifaceted concept in your life, consider how you will develop and describe your academic literacy. What would you consider academic literacy? What kinds of reading, writing, and other language skills are necessary for success in college? How might you transfer certain skills you have gained from existing literacies to help you succeed in college?

8.2.9.2 Literacy Narrative as a Genre

One way to think about genre is as a category with definable characteristics or language patterns. Point of view, word choice, length, and structure are a few such characteristics and patterns that your instructor may ask you to consider. If you haven't written a literacy narrative before, it may be helpful to pay attention to the patterns of language that characterize this genre. As you read through examples of literacy narratives assigned by your instructor, look for aspects of the language that affect how you read the piece, especially strategies that are repeated. You'll find choices that work in literacy narratives but might not be appropriate in other writing projects you complete during your academic career. It's a useful practice to start looking for recurring patterns in language across various writing situations. As you think about how the strategies are working in the narratives, you can imagine what strategies you might want to use when you write your own.

The following list contains just a few of the language patterns that characterize literacy narratives. As you read, fill in the chart so that you have many strategies that you can choose from when telling your story.

Before you start writing your own narrative, reread your instructor's assignment sheet and think about your purpose as a writer. You can then decide which strategies to use.

> "Literacy Narrative as a Genre"
>
> *By Rachel Buck*
>
> pp. 137–138

Pattern	List examples of the strategy from a text	What does the strategy accomplish in the text?	How will this strategy help you in achieving your purpose in writing your narrative?
First-Person Voice (Using "I")		Connects you to your writing and also connects you to your reader. This is your story.	
Descriptive Language		Helps readers imagine the scene you are describing; engages them in your story.	
Dialogue		Can be effective in developing the other characters in your narrative by reflecting their speech patterns; it can enhance the humor or the seriousness of a situation.	
Introductory Paragraphs		Authors introduce themselves and their story to readers and set the tone of the essay.	
Reflections about Language		Authors often weave reflections throughout their stories in order to draw connections to social aspects of literacy and language use.	

LEARNING ACTIVITY:
Timeline of Major Literacy Experiences

Before you start writing your Literacy Narrative, use the following chart to map out memories of your own literacy experiences. Refer to the questions in the "What Is Literacy?" section on page 135 if you are having trouble thinking of ideas.

Timeline of Major Literacy Events

	Childhood	Young Adult	College and Beyond
Literacy at Home			
Literacy at School			
Literacy in the Community			

8.3 Strategies for Synthesizing Ideas

As you locate and analyze individual sources or pieces of data, you can start to put your sources in conversation with each other. Consider the following questions to help you synthesize the many perspectives of your chosen topic:

- What **stakeholder** does each source or piece of data represent?

- Which writers or data appear to agree or hold similar views on the issue? How are their arguments similar?

- Which writers or pieces of data are positioned against each other? In what ways do their arguments differ, and why?

- Are any writers using similar rhetorical strategies in making their arguments?

- Are there informational or conceptual gaps in one source that are being covered in another source or piece of data?

Read more about "Synthesizing Sources" under "Integrating Sources" within "Research" in Writer's Help 2.0.

At this point, it might help you to visualize the conversation that is taking place around your chosen research question. Consider making a drawing, like idea mapping in the next section, to help you organize your sources and map out the connections between/among your sources. Consider points/rhetorical strategies of similarity and difference. You might also make lists of each source's points and ideas and draw connecting lines between similar ideas and similar rhetorical strategies.

8.3.1 Idea/Cluster Mapping

Idea mapping, also called webbing or clustering, can help with both analysis and synthesis activities. Idea mapping visually represents how the ideas in a single, or across multiple, text(s) are related to both the main point(s) and each other. An idea map emphasizes the interconnectedness of ideas and can reveal different information than a traditional written outline. Notice that the map on the next page shows how different parts of Stephen Crane's story, "The Snake," relate to each other.

To cluster map,

1. Place a key word at the center of a piece of paper and circle it.

2. Begin to make conceptual connections by adding new words, circling them, and drawing lines between them and the original key word. As you draw visual links among related ideas, consider what idea or fact links those ideas, and write down terms or details that form those links.

3. Continue attaching words and phrases to any of the circles on the diagram.

When you are done, your page will look like a web filled with bubbles. Your webbing will represent a map of concepts and relations that are relevant to your topic. This conceptual mapping can be useful if you are a visual learner who sometimes gets lost trying to find the right word for an idea. After clustering, you will have some important ideas written down and you will be able to better articulate the connections among those ideas.

You can use the web or cluster to review a text and make initial claims by following various paths represented in the map. Based on the example diagram, you could create an outline by filling in the connections between the circled ideas. Many of the words in the following paragraph are the same words that are circled in the cluster, showing one way you might incorporate these ideas into a more linear prose format:

> "The Snake" is about a contest of will. The story examines the will to fight and the will to survive. The story shows how the contest of will is motivated or complicated by instinct and emotions like rage and fear, and how this

contest of will is tied to human history. It also has more social or political connections like war. There is clearly a contest between humans and animals in the story, but where does the dog fit in? Rover seems more aligned with the man than the snake. What does this say about history and evolution? Everything is brought together in an act of violence when the man kills the snake.

Idea Map of Stephen Crane's "The Snake"

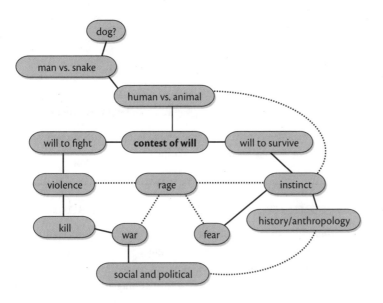

You can also use idea mapping to analyze multiple texts or sources of information. The following idea map demonstrates how someone understands the connections across multiple sources and the perspectives they take.

Idea Map of Stakeholders

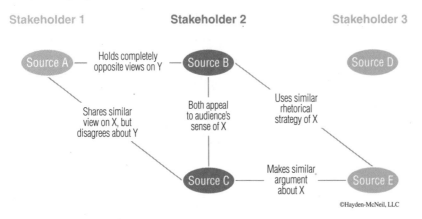

LEARNING ACTIVITY:
Map to Synthesize Research

Creating a mind or cluster map of your topic(s) is a great way to help synthesize what you have learned. You can make your mind map by drawing, using post-its, or an application like any of the following: MS Word Smart Art, MindMeister, Mindomo, Lovely Charts, Maptini, Popplet, Gliffy, Cacoo, Webspiration, SpicyNodes, Coggle, and/or LucidChart.

1. Begin by writing your topic in the middle of the page and circling it.

2. Based on your research, create additional circles of information that contain smaller topics within that larger field.

3. From those smaller circles, make even smaller circles and connect specific texts (authors and/or titles) to the circles/topics/sub-topics.

4. Don't be afraid to draw lines connecting one circle and/or one resource to another. It's ok if it's messy! (Doodling can also help you generate ideas.)

5. Take a look at the connections you've made and write a topic sentence about the connections between those topics.

8.3.2 Systematic Comparison of Information

Once you find more than four or five sources or pieces of information, it can be difficult to keep track of the ways you might compare and contrast the information found in each. Sometimes it is useful to systematically compare and contrast the different sources or pieces of information. Consider using a table or chart to divide up the work. You might also just need to slow down and focus on topics you need to inspect across all your different sources and data.

LEARNING ACTIVITY:
Synthesize in a Spreadsheet

1. Without looking at your sources, data, or other information, identify 2–5 themes that develop over multiple sources (not necessarily all of them).

2. Create a table in a Word, Excel, or Google Doc or Spreadsheet. Look at the table on the following page as a possible example.

3. Input your theme ideas into the final columns in the spreadsheet.

4. Fill out a row for each source you have. Do not just mark yes/no that the source discusses this theme; instead, include brief notes on how the source discusses the theme, including what reasons and evidence it uses.

	Full Bibliographic Citation	Summary	How/why authoritative/ credible	How/why help answer the research question	Theoretical Framework	Research Methodology	Research Idea/ Concept/Theme #1	Research Idea/ Concept/Theme #2	Research Idea/ Concept/Theme #3
Source #1									
Source #2									
Source #3									

LEARNING ACTIVITY:
Make Targeted Connections

Sometimes it is overwhelming to compare, contrast, and synthesize all of the primary and secondary data you have collected. Try starting small.

1. Identify one specific piece of primary data or one specific secondary source.

2. Systematically compare and contrast (note similarities and differences of) that individual piece with all similar pieces (all the other data or all the other secondary sources from your research).

For example, pick one of your scholarly articles. Identify all of the similarities and differences between it and your other articles. Points you might compare include:

*   **Author:** Do the authors of your sources share similar credentials (e.g., academic with PhD, expert based on experience, etc.)? In what ways do their credentials differ?

*   **Argument:** Do the pieces argue for the same general idea/thesis? Do they differ on some or all points?

*   **Reasons:** What reasons do the sources use? What sub-issues do the sources cover? Some sources may use different reasons to support the same thesis.

*   **Evidence:** What types of evidence do the articles use?

*   **Publication process:** When, where, and how were the sources published?

8.3.3 Sketching, Drawing, and Other Visualizations

There are other techniques for organizing your notes and making meaning besides writing words on a page. After you annotate a text, it may be helpful to create a visual representation sketched by hand or to use the drawing function on a computer program like Microsoft Word or PowerPoint. The aesthetic value is not important, so stick figures, graphs, Venn diagrams, or any other method that works for you can be effective.

You may want to try this instead of, or in addition to, other organizational tools. Try it now by quickly sketching a representation of a reading assignment.

Some potential ideas:

- After reading an argumentative piece, you can sketch "how it is" according to the writer, and then "how it could be."

- You might want to draw a storyboard or comic strip of a narrative (like "The Snake"). What plot elements or details make it to your drawings? Why might they be significant?

- When comparing multiple texts, try to show how they are alike and how they are different.

Take time to discuss your visualizations with a classmate or in a small group. You can use your drawing as support for your explanation of the text, and you can also use the opportunity to ask for clarification about the work of your peers. What are some similarities or differences in your depictions? Think about how other people's visualizations can support or complicate your impression of the text.

Using Evidence to Make Arguments

CHAPTER

9

(continued)

9.1 Evidence and Arguments: An Overview

In **analysis**, an **author** provides **evidence** by explaining how a given element of a **text** relates to its overall message or **purpose**. Let's say that you're **rhetorically analyzing** a children's book. It may not be sufficient to say that the author uses rhymes and conclude that this **rhetorical strategy** helps him effectively reach his **audience** of children. You should locate specific examples that show the use of rhyme in the text and then be able to explain how and why these particular rhymes connect the author with his young audience. In what way does he connect with the children? Is he connecting with them like a teacher might connect with students? Like parents connect with their children? What purpose do the rhymes serve? How does this relate to the overall message or purpose of the whole book?

Similarly, an author who wishes to address an audience about a **controversial** issue will need to show how information from **primary** data and/or **secondary sources** supports their position on that issue. Imagine that you want to **argue** that housing killer whales in marine parks negatively affects the health of these creatures. Arguing this position with evidence would require you, first, to define what constitutes a negative health effect in killer whales. You would then need to identify and describe specific instances of killer whales that have suffered these or similar effects as a result of being kept in marine parks. Here, as before, the evidence that you gather and your ability to fully explain how it supports your position can determine whether or not your audience is persuaded to accept your case.

While the previous chapter presented strategies for closely analyzing a single text, this chapter considers how authors support ideas and positions with evidence from multiple types of **sources** and data. In the following sections, you will learn how to:

- Develop a **thesis** that makes an original contribution to an ongoing conversation.

- Distinguish between different types of evidence, such as statistics, surveys, and anecdotes.

- Incorporate evidence at the sentence and **paragraph** levels.

- Organize an argument.

- Use personal experience as evidence in an argument.

LEARNING ACTIVITY:
Conduct Mini-Class Debate

- Students are divided into 4 groups.

    - Instructor gives selection of topics
    - Instructor determines which groups are pro and con
    - Speakers are allowed to use their notes during debates
    - Members are encouraged to take notes

- Each set of students is given a specific topic they must research thoroughly.

    - Groups conduct research using multiple sources to support their position
    - Connect the information collected to experiences or other related texts
    - **Synthesize** information from multiple sources in order to draw conclusions
    - As a group, evaluate effectiveness of sources, making sure that evidence clearly supports their position and speaks to their intended audience

- On debate day each group member should be assigned a debate position.

    - 1st speaker—1 minute to speak—opening speaker presents position
    - 2nd speaker—1–2 minutes to speak—presents empirical evidence that justifies position
    - 3rd speaker (crossfire)—2–3 minutes—engages in a lively discussion with the opponent, and balances opinion with evidence
    - 4th speakers (optional crossfire)—2 minutes—this is a whole group discussion (argument)
    - 5th speaker—1 minute—final words/summation of position/argument

Note: Because debaters do not take formal turns during Crossfires, these sequences tend to create a great deal of tension. Debaters might have a tendency to go off track.

9.2 Theses, Claims, and Reasons

As you construct an argument, remember that there are already a significant number of existing arguments with which you will be engaging. You might even say that you are entering an ongoing conversation on the **topic**. To ensure that your contribution to the topic is focused and organized, you might start by developing a solid **thesis** statement (some may also call a thesis statement a **claim**). A thesis makes a contribution to that conversation in the form of an *arguable* claim with supporting **reasons** and evidence. A thesis or claim does not merely present a well-known fact but is a statement open to debate.

> Read more about "Formulating a Working Thesis" under "Constructing Arguments" within "Critical Thinking and Argument" in *Writer's Help 2.0.*

In the following sample thesis, the arguable claims are marked in blue.

Using "Indian" mascots demonstrates that contemporary U.S. society has an inadequate understanding of both the history of Native Americans and their continued presence as active members in local and national communities; therefore, these "mascots" should be challenged, and people living outside of these communities should work to increase their understanding of Native American history and contemporary life.

This example shows that the thesis of the paper can include a series of reasons that must be further developed. This particular thesis sets up a problem that exists and then proposes a specific solution. A thesis may also serve to:

Example Thesis
Statements

By Kenneth Walker

pp. 148–149

- **Correct false impressions**

  If you believe the topic you are arguing has somehow been misrepresented or misconstrued, the following types of thesis statements can be useful.

  Model: Although many believe **X**, a careful examination suggests **Q** and **Z**.

  Sample: Although **credit card companies appear to offer special services to college students**, evidence suggests that these companies aim to exploit students' inexperience with buying on credit and often charge students comparatively high interest rates while **offering limited benefits**.

- **Fill a gap**

  If you believe that certain information or perspectives have been neglected from the topic you are arguing, these claim statements are particularly effective.

  Model: Although many people talk about **X**, many people miss the importance of **Q** and **Z**.

  Sample: Although many people talk about **financially inexperienced students being exploited by credit card companies**, people neglect the fact that **these students are legal adults** and, therefore, **should be capable of making their own decisions and dealing with the consequences**.

- **Argue through extension**

  This thesis often takes a qualified position toward the conversation by invoking the arguments of others while demonstrating the writer has something new or important to say that will bring the conversation to a different level.

  Model: I agree with people who argue **X**, but it is also important to extend/refine/limit their ideas with **Q** and **Z**.[1]

---

1 Adapted from Stuart Greene and April Lidinsky's "Developing a Working Thesis: Three Models" in *From Inquiry to Academic Writing: A Practical Guide*.

Sample: Although I agree that **all adults, including college students, should be held accountable for their financial decisions**, it is also important to consider that **many college students are just learning about financial responsibility**, and **credit card companies should be required to educate inexperienced customers on how credit and credit cards work**.

It is common in an academic essay to state one's thesis or claim directly and near the beginning. In other **genres** of writing, a thesis may be stated later or not at all, leaving readers to infer the author's primary reason(s). No matter the genre of writing, you should ensure that your audience can recognize your thesis and primary reasons.

9.2.1 Supporting Reasons

To develop an argument, you will need supporting **reasons** with sufficient evidence that help support your central argument. Closely examine your thesis and consider what information your audience will need to understand your perspective. It is often useful to re-read your thesis with these questions in mind: "How so?" or "In what way?"

Consider the thesis regarding the use of "Indian" mascots from the previous section. This thesis suggests that U.S. society has an "inadequate understanding" of Native American life. The development of supporting reasons can help to validate this point. In this example, one might ask: How do "Indian" mascots demonstrate a lack of understanding? The answer to this question becomes a supporting reason.

Supporting Reason 1

Using names such as "Indians," "Savages," or "Seminoles" as mascots demonstrates an ignorance of the historical realities experienced by indigenous peoples of North America.

Supporting Reason 2

"Indian" mascots freeze representations of Native Americans in time from a specific perspective; they are always "braves," "savages," and "warriors," rather than real people experiencing everyday life.

The sample thesis also suggests that these mascots should be challenged. To develop a supporting reason in response to this primary reason, one might ask, "In what way?" or "Why?" Answers to these questions become supporting reasons.

Supporting Reason 3

State legislators have a responsibility to protect the cultures of Native American citizens.

When making a reason, it is also important to consider the counter reasons that could be raised by either the primary, secondary, or even tertiary audiences. Think about the various stakeholders in a controversy and consider who might disagree with all or some of your argument and why. Identifying and responding to potential counterarguments can help you build your **ethos** as a well-informed participant in the debate. Acknowledging that not everyone will agree with you also shows that you understand the complexity of the issue and that you have listened to other perspectives.

In the mascot example, some members of your audience might point out potentially high costs (financial and in public opinion) of changing the mascots. If this student argues that Native American mascots demonstrate an ignorance of historical realities and damage the perception of a culture and its people, she might want to address how the potential costs of changing mascots would be worthwhile.

9.3 Evidence

It is important to make sure that you have a strong thesis and solid supporting reasons as you continue through the analysis process, but it is also important to remember that all of your reasons and arguments should connect to some form of evidence. Your ability to connect evidence to your main reasons will dictate the effectiveness of your argument. Evidence can come in various forms, so it would be to your benefit to keep your audience in mind as you select and incorporate pieces of evidence to argue your reasons.

> Read more about evidence in "Identifying Toulmin's Elements of an Argument" under "Analyzing Arguments" within "Critical Thinking and Argument" in *Writer's Help 2.0.*

9.3.1 Types of Evidence

As you build your argument, ask yourself which types of evidence might be the most influential towards your audience. For example, does your audience expect compelling anecdotes? Or do they prefer strong statistical evidence? It may be necessary to vary forms of evidence in order to maintain reader interest.

The following is a list defining varieties of evidence. As you go through this list, mark the items that might make for good evidence in your own argument.

- **Bulleted lists of information:** Bulleted lists provide quick accessible facts, statistics, and examples to bolster a reason.

- **Facts or statistics presented in charts, graphs, and tables:** Like bulleted lists, graphical representations of information allow audiences to take in a great deal of information quickly and efficiently. Graphs and charts can also show relationships between different types of information.

- **A public opinion poll or survey:** You can find reliable public opinion polls in your research, or you can conduct your own. Polls and surveys can offer a grassroots perspective for your argument, but they often work best when paired with other types of evidence. When offering findings from a poll or survey, be sure to acknowledge the limitations of your findings. Interviewing 100 UA students may seem sufficient, but not when you consider that this campus has almost 40,000 students with a large variety of backgrounds and experiences. In addition to making sure the sample size is adequate, it is also important to ensure that the population you are sampling is appropriate to the reason you are making. For example, if you are conducting a poll on the reasons why retention rates at UA are lower for out-of-state students than for students from within the state of Arizona, you would want to make sure that the students you interview represent those populations proportionately.

- **Quotations:** You can use quotations to demonstrate the scope of your research and establish your **credibility**, to add to the emotional appeal of your argument by using a particularly charged bit of language from another writer, or to draw on an authority in the matter at hand. The best time to use a quotation is when the source uses particularly precise, specific, or unique language. Quotes should usually be contextualized by your own writing, but in **visual** arguments (like an infographic) it can be effective to list a quote by itself.

- **Stories or anecdotes from individuals affected by the issue at hand:** Stories and anecdotes can add a personal quality to arguments that are otherwise steeped in facts and statistics. It is especially helpful to include stories from individuals who have been directly impacted by the controversy you are discussing. Think of how often politicians will bring in an "average Joe" to show how a specific policy might influence people's lives. Stories and anecdotes are also a useful way to include the perspective of others without appropriating their **voice**.

- **References to commonly known cultural sources:** Referencing a popular or familiar cultural source, such as a film or television show that your audience is likely to be familiar with, can help you establish rapport with your readers or viewers. Think of this as sharing an inside joke, but be careful; like inside jokes, cultural references risk excluding people who might not be familiar with the text you are referencing. This is especially true of sacred texts such as the Bible and Koran, whose interpretations vary according to the religious, cultural, and additional backgrounds of readers. Other examples of cultural sources include poetry, song lyrics, and idioms.

- **Images:** Images can elicit a quick emotional response in audience members, and they can help to illustrate points that have also been made textually or verbally. In multimedia presentations, images can be paired with most of the other types of evidence on this list.

- **Color, font typeface, style, and size (style and format):** Each of these choices can help make a document more visually appealing, but they can also invoke emotional responses from audiences. For example, consider what you might think if you saw the word EARTH written in large green letters versus what you might think if you saw **EARTH** in large red letters. In addition, you can use font typeface choices to help establish your relationship with the audience. Think of the different feelings evoked by **Comic Sans**, which is playful and found frequently in comic strips, and by **Century**, which is formal and found most often in newspapers.

- **Sounds and music:** Sounds can draw an audience into a presentation by evoking a particular mood. Audio stimulation can be soothing, exciting, or impart a sense of danger or fear. To get an idea of how important sound can be in audience response, try watching a scene from your favorite scary movie with the sound turned off. Is it as suspenseful without the music helping to generate tension?

- **Spaces and places:** Where you choose to make your argument is just as important as how you convey it. The kind of space you choose for your argument will determine the range of your audience and, often, how your argument will be contextualized.

LEARNING ACTIVITY:
Identify Evidence

1. Generate a list of the types of evidence that are acceptable to your instructor, for your assignment, and in your field or discipline. Some examples might include: primary data collected from research, secondary data shared in publications about other research, expert opinions, theory describing how something works, etc.

2. Look at all the data and secondary sources you have collected for this project.

3. Categorize the information you have by the list of evidence you generated.

4. Address the following questions: Are you missing any types of evidence? How/why might that type of evidence be important for your project (or not)?

9.3.2 Using Evidence

Once you have defined and selected the evidence to help build your argument, you might consider the ways in which you will incorporate the evidence into your writing. Remember, your purpose is to build a convincing case for your audience. You should not assume that the audience will automatically see the connections based off of the evidence you include and your main reasons. Instead, guide your audience with strategies like **signal phrases** and anchors in order to make sure that they can follow the reasons you're making, and they can understand how the reasons are connected to pieces of evidence.

Consider the following example that illustrates possible steps in incorporating **paraphrases** and quotations as forms of evidence. When incorporating evidence into your argument, there are two to three components you should include:

Read more about "Integrating Sources" within "Research" in *Writer's Help 2.0*.

1. introduce the evidence (story, fact, paraphrase, quotation, etc.)

2. if evidence comes from a secondary source, cite the source

3. connect the evidence to your argument.

9.3.2.1 Introduce

- Use a "signal phrase" or "author/source tag" to refer to the author, source, or piece of data before incorporating the actual paraphrase or quotation.

- Use a complete sentence followed by a colon to anchor a direct quotation. Note that the "anchor" sentence must logically introduce the idea expressed in the quote.

Note: When using evidence from another source, you'll need to check the guidelines for the specific requirements of your formatting style (e.g., APA, MLA, Chicago, etc.).

9.3.2.2 Cite

In any writing situation, incorporating outside sources demonstrates an active and informed engagement with the text, issue, or idea. Effectively incorporating outside sources can help strengthen your credibility, or ethos, and can provide evidence for the argument you are making. However, in order to maintain your credibility, you need to be able to introduce and **cite** other writers' ideas correctly. If you do not correctly credit and cite your sources, it may seem as though you are trying to "steal" a source's ideas, and this may cause your readers to mistrust you. In addition, the University of Arizona prohibits any form of plagiarism, and the consequences for committing plagiarism can be severe. See the end of this section for descriptions of different forms of plagiarism.

If you are using evidence from another source or text, you need to include an in-text citation. By signaling to your readers the name(s) of the author(s) or source associated with your paraphrase or quotation, you have done part of the work of documenting your source—but there are a few more steps to ensure your citation is complete.

- When page numbers are available, reference them in parentheses.

- If you choose *not* to include a signal phrase, the author/source name must be included in the parentheses along with the page number.

- If quoting directly, make sure to use quotation marks!

- If paraphrasing, make sure it is clear where your ideas begin and end and where the paraphrase begins and ends. If paraphrasing, make sure to use your own words.

Note: The guidelines for the specific requirements of your formatting style can be found in *Writer's Help 2.0*. APA format used below.

Examples:

1. Glenn (1994) argues that "when the delivery of purposeful silence is considered a strategic choice, its presence resonates with meaning and intention, just like that of the spoken word" (p. 282).

2. Silence is often associated with passiveness; however, Glenn (1994) argues that silence can be active and rhetorically productive: "[W]hen the delivery of purposeful silence is considered a strategic choice, its presence resonates with meaning and intention, just like that of the spoken word" (p. 282).

3. Although silence is often associated with passiveness, "when the delivery of purposeful silence is considered a strategic choice, its presence resonates with meaning and intention, just like that of the spoken word" (Glenn, 1994, p. 282).

"Writing with Integrity: Intentional vs. Unintentional Plagiarism "

By Emma Rose Miller

pp. 154–155

9.3.2.3 Writing with Integrity: Intentional vs. Unintentional Plagiarism

Plagiarism involves taking credit for someone else's work or ideas without giving proper credit. Although plagiarism is not always intentional, the consequences for committing plagiarism are the same regardless of intention. The UA Code of Academic Integrity strictly prohibits any form of cheating, plagiarism, or fabrication. Unfortunately, many students make honest mistakes and plagiarize without intending to because they do not understand the conventions of academic citation or fail to see that their actions are academically unethical.

Read more about "Acknowledging Sources and Avoiding Plagiarism" within "Research" in *Writer's Help 2.0*.

The following chart outlines some common forms of plagiarism—some of which might seem surprising. Admittedly, it is sometimes hard to know when to cite a source in your paper and when you do not need to. The general rule is: if you had to look it up somewhere, you should cite it. For example, you may want to mention in your paper that about a half million people live in Tucson. You know that fact because it is an approximate figure that people just happen to know. It is common knowledge, and, in this case, there is no need to cite a source. However, if you are writing a paper on the fluctuating population of Tucson and you use statistics from the U.S. Census Bureau or the City of Tucson's website to offer precise figures for the population between 2001 and 2010, you should cite the source that provided the information.

Intentional Plagiarism		Unintentional Plagiarism
Using someone else's work (or essay examples from websites) as your own	Submitting the same work for multiple classes without instructor consent	Assuming borrowed information is "common knowledge"
Paying someone else to write your paper for you	Quoting without using quotation marks	
	Incorporating sources without proper citations	

9.3.2.4 Connect

Finally, the paraphrase/quotation needs to clearly connect to the argument or main point of the **paragraph**. It's the writer's job to make sure the audience understands how the paraphrase/quotation supports the argument/main point. Instead of assuming that your reader will understand the connection, it is best to write a separate sentence that explains the connection between the piece of evidence and the reason. Write this connecting sentence in your first draft; have reviewers help you decide whether or not it is explicitly needed.

LEARNING ACTIVITY:
Insert Evidence

1. Use one of the templates below to draft a sentence that includes the 3 parts every quotation or paraphrase should include:

    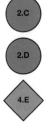

    - According to **[insert author/source name]**, **[insert paraphrase or quotation] [insert page number]**.

    - In their **[insert copyright year of source]** study, **[insert author/ source name]** found **[insert paraphrase or quotation][insert page number]**.

    - **[insert author/source name]** argues/explores/notes/examines **[insert paraphrase or quotation][insert page number]**.

2. Now, take one of your paraphrases or quotations from above and follow up with a sentence or two that clearly connects it to your reason.

9.3.3 Vivid Description as Evidence

In *On Writing*, Stephen King describes writing as a form of "telepathy," a "meeting of the minds" in which an image is transmitted from one person to another. After providing an elaborate description of a strangely painted rabbit in a cage, King writes, "[W]e all see it. I didn't tell you. You didn't ask me. I never opened my mouth and you never opened yours. We're not even in the same year together, let alone the same room…except we are together. We're close" (106).[2] Vivid description and concrete details can bring people closer, creating a moment of telepathy in which an image or a concept travels from one mind to another. Or, as is the case in Dave Eggers' writing, description can carry personality, fostering a connection between author and audience. For example, when looking at San Francisco through Dave Eggers' eyes, the traffic over the Bay Bridge becomes "a string of Christmas lights being pulled slowly, steadily," and foggy mornings in Berkeley are "filmstrip white" (51).[3] His unique descriptions allow readers to experience the city in a new way.

Description becomes especially vivid when an author uses sensory detail to breathe life into places and personalities. For example, in her essay "Words of My Grandmother," UA student Rachel Park doesn't just tell the reader that she felt stuck inside as an eight year old. Instead, she compares herself to a butterfly in a collector's frame, "stuck, helpless, trapped, and only there because someone wanted me to be there…to gratify its owner with its beauty, and nothing more." Through the use of this **metaphor**, Rachel creates an emotional connection with her reader. Concrete and sensory details create living moments on the page, moving a reader to see, feel, or experience something differently.

Of course, it is important to keep in mind that there is a fine line between effective detail and overuse or filler. Figurative language (e.g., metaphors and **similes**) can enliven writing; however, if overdone, the details become roadblocks that interrupt the flow of the writing. Here are some revision tips to help bring your reader closer with vivid description.

1. **Include vivid sensory details.** "His hands were like sandpaper" is more interesting and entertaining than "his hands were dry." Always strive to connect to one or more of the reader's five senses (sound, sight, touch, smell, taste) when you use figurative language.

2. **Use discerning details.** Make sure your descriptive writing differentiates in a way that is informative. If you write, "the automobile has four tires, a steering wheel, and two bumpers," that does not help distinguish the car from any other your reader is likely to encounter. If, however, you describe a sedan with rusted paint, a broken back window, and stained upholstery, it creates a much more vivid and meaningful picture.

3. **Avoid vague adjectives such as "interesting," "amazing," "nice," "good," "bad," or "weird."** These words can mean very different things to different people. Your definition of weird might differ drastically, for instance, from someone else's definition of weird. If you feel a word with many possible meanings is appropriate, you should incorporate your specific understanding of that word into your discussion. In all other cases,

---

2 King, Stephen. *On Writing: A Memoir of the Craft*. New York: Scribner, 2000.
3 Eggers, Dave. *A Heartbreaking Work of Staggering Genius*. New York: Vintage, 2001.

aim for more precise adjectives such as "adventurous," "brash," "curious," "unfortunate," or "eccentric."

4. **Consider positive and negative connotations of details.** Adjectives and descriptions can be used strategically to influence your reader's attitude toward a person, object, or event. For example, the word "serene" used to describe a person's eyes will convey a more positive feeling than "calm," which is more neutral. Awareness of the **connotations** of words can help you guide readers to see the world from your point of view.

5. **Keep organized.** One easy mistake to make is to believe that reflective writing does not need a solid **structure**. In fact, descriptive writing needs to be extremely organized. For example, the order in which you offer details impacts how successful your descriptions will be: "The delicate silver, etched with flowers from your mother's garden antique spoon was so beautiful" is confusing, whereas, "The delicate silver spoon, etched with spring garden flowers, was a stunning antique" includes much of the same detail while remaining clear and accessible to the reader.

6. **Keep your purpose in mind.** Remember that you are translating an experience onto the page and not giving a news report. Instead of trying to give your readers a sequential rendering of events, spend time thinking about which aspects of your idea need more description. Should you spend more time describing what it was like to have your mom read to you in bed as a child? Should you pare down on that one scene from your ninth-grade literature classroom and instead **summarize** it in a sentence? Keep in mind that your readers will assume that highly descriptive language is emphasizing an important moment in a **narrative**, so it should be used strategically and mindfully.

LEARNING ACTIVITY:
Writing Vivid Description

Now try your hand at writing vivid description.

- First, find one sentence from a draft of your personal or reflective essay that you would like to revise.

- Next, eliminate any weak or vague words, decide if anything sounds redundant or unnecessary, and remove any problematic language from the sentence. Rewrite the sentence.

- Now that your sentence is grammatically streamlined, go back through and insert strong, descriptive adjectives and clear, appropriate verbs. Rewrite the sentence one final time.

- Lastly, describe the major revisions you did to this sentence and how you could make similar changes in your draft.

9.3.3.1 Experience as Evidence in the Literacy Narrative

Some types of evidence mentioned earlier that provide unique perspectives for analysis are stories and narratives. These types of evidence are based off of the experiential; they recognize that there is value in people's experiences, and those experiences offer important points that can connect with arguable reasons. As discussed in the previous chapter, some foundations writing courses like to begin the semester by having students write **literacy narratives** that ask students to think critically about their histories with writing and **literacy**. The following learning activity continues the discussion on the literacy narrative and offers suggestions for utilizing narratives as evidence in making arguments.

LEARNING ACTIVITY:
Analyze and Synthesize Your Literacy Experience

1.A

2.A

2.C

2.F

"Analyze and Synthesize Your Literacy Experience"

By Sonia Arellano, Kate Chaterdon, and Katie Silvester

pp. 158–159

In order to get started, you will want to choose an experience that has significant meaning for you, as well as one that will allow you to write an interesting narrative.

One of the most important things to remember when writing your literacy narrative is to avoid telling your entire history with literacy in the span of your essay. Instead, try to focus on only one or two important experiences listed on your timeline, and elaborate on what those experiences mean to you and why they are significant. This will ultimately make for a much better essay.

For example, writer Sandra Cisneros explains how being the only girl in her family affected her relationship to literacy:[4]

> "I was/am the only daughter and _only_ a daughter. Being an only daughter in a family of six sons forced me by circumstance to spend a lot of time by myself because my brothers felt it beneath them to play with a girl in public. But that aloneness, that loneliness, was good for a would-be writer—it allowed me time to think and think, to imagine, to read and prepare myself." (89)

Cisneros explains to her reader that because she had to spend a lot of time alone, she developed the skills necessary to become a successful, published writer. Your story may not only explain how you came to be a great writer but could also explain how your experiences have caused you to struggle with reading or writing.

After considering your lived, literate experiences, you might still be unsure how to analyze those events in order to make a statement about what literacy is and does. Developing some questions around the way literacy operates in your

---

4 Cisneros, Sandra. "Only Daughter." *Families in Later Life: Connections and Transitions*. Ed. Alexis Walkes, Margaret Manoogian-O'Dell, Lori A. McGrew, and Diana L. G. White. Thousand Oaks, LA: Pine Forge, 2001. 89–91.

narrative and answering those questions in your paper will help you draw out the greater significance of your particular experience.

The following questions are designed to help you start thinking reflectively and analytically about your literacy narrative:

- How do/did others engage in literacy around you, now and when you were a child? In what ways are your approaches to literacy similar to or different from the practice of those around you?
- What inspired you to choose a particular experience for your narrative, rather than some other literacy event? Do you associate this experience with some feeling, place, special person/people, challenge, or accomplishment? Why?
- What makes your literacy experience unique or different from others? Perhaps someone close to you taught you a special technique for strumming the guitar, or you learned to draw by imitating your favorite animators. Maybe you learned to read by being read to by a parent, or perhaps you prefer expressing yourself through text messages rather than emails or letters?
- What family or community (group) literacy practices came before, during, or after the event you describe?
- In what ways did the events surrounding this experience change you? What can you see about the experience now that you could not see then?
- What could an audience, such as parents, college students, children, instructors, or aspiring writers learn from this experience?
- How has your experience affected your attitudes toward reading, writing, and communicating today? What are the implications of your attitudes toward reading and writing? In what ways might your attitudes serve you well in college? In what ways might they get in your way?
- How do you think your life experiences, cultural affiliations, race, gender, and/or religion have influenced your chosen literacy experience and your attitudes toward reading and writing? How have the following **contexts** influenced your experience: other languages, language or educational policies, traditions, beliefs about literacy, etc.?
- In what ways is your experience similar to or different from the experiences of the published authors whose stories you have read in class? What are the reasons for these similarities and/or differences?

LEARNING ACTIVITY:
Provide Details in Literacy Narratives

Identify one moment/scene in your outline for your Literacy Narrative. Fully write that moment/scene. Be sure to use the various strategies for writing a vivid description. After writing a paragraph or two, include another paragraph that reflects on your writing. Discuss how you completed at least four of the six following strategies:

1.B

1.E

3.C

3.F

- include vivid sensory details,
- use discerning details,
- avoid vague adjectives,
- consider positive and negative connotations,
- keep organized, and
- keep your purpose in mind.

In your reflection be sure to refer to specific words, phrases, and/or sentences in your moment/scene. Share and discuss your writing with others. In what ways were you successful in providing detail in your writing? In what ways might you revise to include more detail?

Read more about "Organizing an Argument" under "Constructing Arguments" within "Critical Thinking and Argument" in *Writer's Help 2.0*.

9.4 Argument Arrangement

This chapter has highlighted the importance of establishing main theses or claims and supporting reasons that are then reinforced with various types of evidence. This next section discusses strategies for the arrangement and organization of an argument. As mentioned earlier, your task as a writer is to make sure the audience can follow the connections you are making, and a majority of that depends on the way in which that evidence is presented.

The arrangement of ideas and the connections between them have a significant impact on the effectiveness of a text. Many of us are familiar with organizational methods for popular narratives: start with the introduction to characters, setting, and a problem; lead up to a climactic action; and then wind it all down to a satisfying conclusion. However, this organizational pattern does not necessarily work for all stories. You also probably won't find this **format** in academic texts, and it doesn't apply to most visual texts, either. So if there is no single, one-size-fits-all organizational method, and your instructor does not have a specific structure in mind, how should you organize your writing?

The key to a "well-organized" text is that it is purposeful in its presentation of ideas and effective for the audience. Just as a traveler is guided by signs or guideposts, it is the structure of a text that tells readers where they have been, where they are now, and where they are going. To construct a purposefully organized essay, consider the following questions about the placement of your sentences and paragraphs:

- Why is this idea, sentence, or paragraph in this particular position?

- How does each idea relate to the content before and after it?

- What happens to the argument or the momentum if this idea, sentence, or paragraph is moved?

- What will the audience expect to see here? Should I meet their expectations, or is there a reason for not doing so?

Although we think of paragraphs as a way to present individual points, it is important to show readers how the points connect with each other and with the thesis. For this reason, a paragraph needs to relate to the paragraphs before and after it so that the essay moves smoothly from one idea to the next related idea. Sentences should also build upon each other and appear in a logical order. Effective transitions can help the reader understand how sentences and ideas relate to each other.

Here are some tips to evaluate the effectiveness of your overall organizational method:

- Do a "reverse outline."

- Cut up your essay and rearrange the pieces. This is especially helpful if you are a visual or kinesthetic learner, or you feel stuck in an organizational pattern and can't find a way out.

- Read your essay aloud. Listen for the gaps, the places where you lose interest, or the places where ideas feel random or confusing.

- Listen to someone else reading your essay out loud and position yourself as the audience. Does the reader stumble at any point? Do you lose interest as they are reading? Do you sense a "jump" in ideas?

- Draw connections between your ideas. Underline terms or ideas that are repeated to find ideas that are related.

LEARNING ACTIVITY:
Scratch and Citation Outlines for Organization

1. Creating a scratch outline is a very informal construction of your paper's main topics in a rough order of how you plan to put them in the paper. This helps you visualize how the flow of the paper will go from one topic to the next.

   Example: hip hop and technology

   - Early hip hop history
   - Economics of the culture
   - Turntables
   - Synthesizers
   - Sampling
   - Autotune

2. The scratch outline is great for just giving yourself a rough idea of what you plan on talking about in your paper from paragraph to paragraph.

3. Next we will turn this scratch outline into a citation outline using the research that you have done up to this point.

4. The citation outline includes notes about the articles that you found and where they will fit into your paper based on the topics from your scratch outline. It should look something like this:

Example: hip hop and technology

- Early hip hop history
  - Rose, 1994
  - Gray, 1995
  - Reynolds, 2002
  - Johnson, 1998
  - Dyson, 2004
- Economics of the culture
  - Rose, 1994
  - Davies, 1995
  - O'Neill, 1997

- Turntables
  - Miller, 1996
  - Davies, 1995
- Synthesizers
  - Miller, 1996
  - Reynolds, 2002
- Sampling
  - Rose, 1994
  - Miller, 1996
  - Davies, 1995
- Autotune
  - Smith, 2013

5. As you can see, having overlap among the categories is completely fine. It's all about considering where the articles you have looked at fit into your outline based on how you have broken down your paper's topics.

LEARNING ACTIVITY:
Review Paragraph Construction and Organization

Conduct a paragraph analysis of one of your drafts. You might use a commenting feature in a digital document (such as MS Word or Google Docs) or a pen/pencil on a paper copy. Using the "Developing Paragraphs" section under the "Writing Processes" section in *Writer's Help 2.0*, analyze how well each paragraph

- focuses on a main point or idea (writing unified paragraphs)
- develops the main point (developing paragraphs with supporting details)
- organizes itself internally (following patterns of development)
- makes itself coherent (making paragraphs coherent)
- Transitions with both the paragraph before and after (linking paragraphs together)

Write a concise but detailed reflection on this exercise by explaining what you learned overall about the strengths and weaknesses of your document's paragraphs. Share that reflection with your classmates, and discuss trends you notice in your paragraph construction and organization.

Read more about "Developing Paragraphs" within "Writing Processes" in *Writer's Help 2.0*.

9.4.1 Ways and Means of Transitions

Writing is fundamentally about building communicative relationships for specific times, purposes, places, and people. Transitional words and phrases play a key role in the kinds of relationships writers co-create with readers.

"Ways and Means of Transitions"

By Devon R. Kehler

pp. 163–164

Transitions act as connectors between thoughts. The very word transition is derived from a Latin word meaning to "go across." Transitions in writing are like bridges that provide readers passage across your thoughts. They link ideas across sentences, paragraphs, and pages. To determine when and where transitions are needed, writers need to repeatedly ask, "What kinds of connections and relationships am I trying to build?" The chart below offers common kinds of transitions:

Kinds, Purposes, and Examples of Transitional Words/Phrases					
What kind of connection are you trying to build?	**Comparison** (used for bringing different things together)	**Repetition** (used for reminding readers what's been said)	**Summary** (used for signaling a synthesis or conclusion)	**Sequence** (used for giving a sense of order or time)	**Addition** (used for explanation and support)
What words or phrases can help build this type of connection?	Whereas Meanwhile Although Though However	As I have said As I have shown As noted earlier In brief Returning to	Consequently As a result Therefore In conclusion Finally	Following this Simultaneously Previously Subsequently First, second…	For example Again Further Moreover In addition

Note: Many transitional words and phrases serve multiple transitional purposes.

Sometimes your organizational options are limited by constraints such as assignment guidelines or genre conventions. For instance, in the genre of business letters, the audience will probably expect the body of the letter to begin with a greeting such as "Dear" or "To whom it may concern." Consider genre, your purpose, and your audience's expectations as you structure your writing.

Consider these ways to create "flow" or connect ideas:

- Use transition words to connect related ideas or to shift from one topic to another.

- "Forecast" the content that will follow. Sometimes a forecast might be written in the form of a concluding sentence in a paragraph that leads into the next idea. However, you should connect this forecast to the material in the current paragraph so it does not feel like an abrupt break or diversion.

- Use "pointing terms" such as "this" to help you move from an illustration to an explanation or from one idea to the next. For example, "this example shows" or "this idea is further complicated by...." Make sure to always follow the word "this" with a noun or noun (nominal) phrase so that your reader can clearly see your point of reference.

PART IV:
REFLECTION AND
REVISION

Introducing Reflection and Revision

10.1 Goal 3: Reflection and Revision

*Reflection and Revision: Understand **composing** processes as flexible and collaborative, drawing upon multiple strategies and informed by reflection.*

Writers need to develop flexible composing processes that can be adapted to different **contexts** and tasks. All writers also benefit from **feedback**. This means writing doesn't happen in one night. To foster an awareness of your composing processes, writing classes ask you to reflect on your writing. Through reflection you make explicit connections between what you did to complete a project and how well you responded to **audience** needs, **genre** conventions, and expectations of a context. You gain awareness of how to write effectively for differing contexts. Reflection and revision are each multifaceted tasks that require a sense of responsibility on your part as a writer and the ability to reflect on one's own thinking in order to identify multiple strategies to undertake writing and research.

Take the five-**paragraph** essay as an example. What happens when you start to reflect on the five-paragraph essay? You've learned that an introductory paragraph should end with a **thesis** statement, which will name the three points to be discussed in the body paragraphs. Each body paragraph develops one point. The conclusion reiterates your thesis. When you begin to reflect on the rules of a five-paragraph theme, what do you find? Why is a thesis required as the last sentence in the opening paragraph? Why do you include three supporting points rather than two or four? In many ways, the five-paragraph theme is a strategy for focusing ideas and organizing them. Yet the five-paragraph template also implies inflexibility. If you call it a five-paragraph essay, then you expect five paragraphs. It's as if five is the magic number for good writing. That's not flexible. That's rigid.

While some argue the five-paragraph essay is not a real genre outside of school, there are aspects of it that adapt to other writing contexts. For example, introductions, body paragraph, and conclusions are used in other genres as well. Introductions can have multiple paragraphs. Some effective genres have a single body paragraph. Some genres typically include a thesis at the end, as part of the conclusion, following an inductive analysis of **evidence**. But these variations still include some kind of introduction, body, and conclusion. Rather than writing five paragraphs for every assignment, you should adapt aspects of the organizing pattern (an introduction, a body, and a conclusion) to suit the context, **purpose**, and audience. Reflection about the five-paragraph essay as an organizing pattern can help you adapt it to other academic contexts. To learn how to adapt and be flexible with these strategies, revision and reflection are necessary.

To meet Goal 3: Reflection and Revision, at the end of Foundations Writing, students will be able to:

A. adapt composing and **revision processes** for a variety of **technologies** and **modalities**.

B. produce multiple **revisions** on **global** and **local** levels.

C. suggest useful global and local revisions to other writers.

D. identify the **collaborative** and **social** aspects of **writing processes**.

E. evaluate and act on peer and instructor **feedback** to revise their **texts**.

F. **reflect** on their progress as **academic writers**.

> Read more about "Reviewing and Revising" as well as "Reflecting to Learn" within "Writing Processes" in *Writer's Help 2.0.*

10.2 Student Learning Outcomes: Descriptions and Key Terms

3.A: Adapt composing and revision processes for a variety of technologies and modalities.

Acts of writing are always relative to their situations. The expectations for writing in the university will change based off of the type of class, the type of instructor, and the type of assignment. With each situation comes a variety of possibilities in both the invention of the composition as well as what is possible with revision. Writers who adapt their composing and revising strategies to specific constraints of the writing situation place themselves in a position to create and write effectively.

Consider a six-page essay assigned three weeks from its due date versus a timed writing exam. For the six-page essay, you have more time and opportunities to meet with your instructor and peers to work through your ideas when you are in the initial invention stages. You also have the opportunity to consult with both the instructor and your peers during the various revision stages. The writing exam, however, places a constraint on time and will force you to handle both the invention and revision stages accordingly. You might not be able to consult with your instructor or peers during your drafting and revising stages, but you can still utilize an inventive strategy such as webbing or outlining to lay out your ideas, and you can plan your writing timeline out to include multiple moments of revision.

Writers will also want to consider the differences in writing technologies that are available for each situation. You could use a word processor for the six-page essay, in which case you have different revision options such as track changes, comments, or spell checking. The timed exam might be handwritten, which changes your options and potential approaches for both invention and revision; it is more difficult to revise a sentence you have written with a pen.

Through reflection, writers will begin to uncover and utilize the strategies and processes that best fit their situations, which can then lead to effective moments of composing.

Revision Processes: the strategies and practices in which writers review, reimagine, and reconceive their composition. These processes are revolving and recurring, and will be utilized throughout all points of the composing timeline.

Technologies: the materials and applications used by writers and readers throughout all stages of the composing and consumption process. Technologies greatly impact the options and possibilities presented to writers while also shaping the ways in which readers are able to engage with a text. All writing requires some form of technology, whether it be a pen, a pencil, or a word processing or image editing application on a computer. For this reason, technologies might be thought of as integral and inseparable parts of writing.

Modalities: the different types of **media** used in producing and publishing a text. Alphanumeric, **visual**, auditory, kinesthetic...all of these modes may be used, even mixed, to produce a text. Each mode includes its own affordances and constraints for both the **author** and audience in producing and consuming the text.

LEARNING ACTIVITY:
Reflect on Process

Think about the past 2–3 times you have produced a text (consider both academic and non-academic compositions). Compare and contrast your **rhetorical situations**, composing processes, as well as the technologies and modalities you engaged. How and why were the specific modalities, composing processes, and technologies appropriate for the specific situation?

	Rhetorical situation (purpose, audience, context, genre, etc.)	*Modalities* of, and used to produce, the final text.	Composing and revision *processes*/steps	*Technologies* used to produce the text
Situation #1 (school)				
Situation #2 (professional)				
Situation #3 (social or civic)				

3.B: Produce multiple revisions on global and local levels.

Have you ever watched a science fiction movie that had wonderful makeup and special effects, but the plot made no sense? That is similar to having a beautifully written document that does not meet the rhetorical situation; correct **grammar** and spelling do not help if the document does not do what it needs to.

Obviously the makeup on an alien impacts the story: does the alien look friendly or scary? Smaller details can greatly impact the overall meaning of a text. These differences between the content or organization of a text and its surface elements might be described as global concerns versus local concerns, both of which are important at different stages of the workshopping process.

Global Revisions: revisions focused on making changes to the content or organization of a text. Making global revisions might mean adding or subtracting details or evidence. It might mean rearranging the order and presentation of points, reviewing the text's purpose, or considering the **audience**'s wants and needs. Global revisions are sometimes also referred to as Higher Order Concerns (HOCs).

Local Revisions: revisions focused on surface features such as grammar, spelling, and **mechanics**. These details have an impact on the text as a whole, but they should be reviewed in later stages of the production process. Local revisions are sometimes referred to as Lower Order Concerns (LOCs).

LEARNING ACTIVITY:
Distinguish between Global and Local Revisions

Reflect on changes to a text suggested by a friend or former teacher. Briefly describe the suggestions made and whether they were of global or local concern.

LEARNING ACTIVITY:
Describe Local Impacting Global

Global and local concerns are not separate from one another; word choice can radically change the meaning of a text. For example, in a horror story, what would be the difference between a character being *terrified* rather than *stricken*? Compare and contrast both the connotative and denotative definitions of the words. Try finding images that might represent the differences between each term.

3.C: Suggest useful global and local revisions to other writers.

Since writers benefit from understanding how a reader engages with their text, learning to provide useful feedback is fundamental to a writing class. In foundations writing, you will read your peers' writing, offering advice on how to address global revisions and local revisions. The process of giving and receiving feedback will help you understand composing **rhetorically**. It will help you understand qualities that make a piece of writing effective for a given audience and situation. A former foundations writing student, Christina Stephens, explains,

> **"It is very helpful to have someone else's opinions and/or ideas during the revising stage, especially if you are all writing on the same topic."**

Feedback geared toward global-level revision addresses the big picture—examining how well content and **structure** of a project supports the writer's purpose. In other words, global comments evaluate how well the piece develops in response to a rhetorical situation. When writing global comments, you should:

- discuss whether or not the lines of **reasoning** and evidence adequately support the **claim** or **thesis**.

- suggest holistic changes such as eliminating paragraphs, adding paragraphs, or moving paragraphs around.

- comment on how well the organizing pattern supports the writer's central point, audience expectations, and the context for writing.

- comment on transitions between ideas, especially between paragraphs. It means identifying what's working and what's not working.

The purpose of local-level feedback is to help writers increase clarity and precision of meaning at the sentence level. In some instances, you comment on the internal organization of a paragraph to point out when sentences are unrelated to the purpose of a single paragraph or to rearrange sentences. You also comment on mechanics, sentence clarity, usage, word choice, or **documentation** style.

3.D: Identify the collaborative and social aspects of writing processes.

When you think of a writer, you probably imagine a person writing in isolation, such as Sandra Cisneros hunched over a keyboard, dictating notes to be transcribed for the lyrically poignant *The House on Mango Street*. Yet a writer in isolation is a partial story of writing that ignores the other part of the story—collaboration. People write every day, and we do so for social purposes. Indeed, any writing is addressed to a reader or a group of readers and, thusly, responds to a reader's social context; this is why writing classes privilege the role of readers. Technical writers produce documents to help mechanics work with different pieces of hardware or fix objects like planes, trains, and automobiles. Technical writers think about the circumstances in which their documents are needed and used.

Writing can be developed socially by providing feedback on different drafts and working in groups to develop ideas, construct claims and reasons, identify evidence, and complete other steps during the composing process. For example, the technical writers above usually get feedback from engineers working on the same project; they might also get feedback from potential audience members. Through these **collaborative writing process** activities, writers consider constraints and affordances of audience needs and contexts for reception, and they collaborate with each other during different stages of drafting and revision.

Some of the most popular family or childhood games mimic the social aspects of writing. If you ever played *I Spy*, you would have composed a series of clues to help players guess the object you spied or gathered information by asking questions of other players. When playing *I Spy*, how often did you repeat an effective clue or question that another player asked? You probably had at least one instance when you thought, "I would have asked a different question." Writing works similarly. You try out an idea to see if it is effective for your audience and for your purpose. When you become immersed in a conversation, you learn to adapt ideas

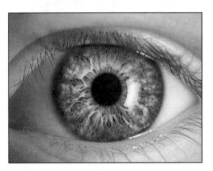

offered by others for your own purposes. In having readers engage your writing, you test different rhetorical choices for organization, evidence, and language expression. With each attempt, you identify which strategies most likely accomplish your objective. All of this is to say, writers do not usually write in isolation; they write more effectively when they use readers to guide them.

Collaborative Writing Processes: more than one person participates in the processes used to contribute to a final text. At minimum, many authors ask others to review their drafts before considering a piece of writing final. In many writing classes, this process is called peer review. However, individual authors may seek help from others at many points of the process. For example, many people talk through ideas before they set pen to paper or keyboard to screen. Others like to have a final set of eyes copy edit or proofread before finally submitting a text. Of course, collaborative writing might also describe teams of writers who collaborate during the whole process and are collectively considered *authors* of the final text.

Social Writing Processes: rather than working in a vacuum, during the process of generating ideas, planning your approach, and drafting, you as a writer are continually thinking about audience expectations. What has, or will be, going on near and around the intended audience when they go to consume your text? Every step of writing involves evaluating limitations and affordances of the social context and its readers.

> Read more about "Working with Others" within "Writing Processes" in *Writer's Help 2.0*.

3.E: Evaluate and act on peer and instructor feedback to revise their texts.

Whether you receive feedback before you finally submit or publish a text, or after, you will need to process it so that you continue to improve as a writer. In writing classes you are sure to receive lots of feedback from both your classmates as well as your instructors. Mature writers know that they do not have to accept and follow everyone's feedback; instead, you will need to learn to evaluate feedback and incorporate what makes most sense for you and the specific rhetorical situation.

Peer reviews may take place in either the classroom, conference room, digital collaboration environment, or the individual's own personal space. At this point in time, the writer takes the suggestions for improvement and considers applying any necessary changes to their own work. They also may consider what they learned from reviewing their peer's work and apply that to their own project in process. When evaluating the advice and suggestions your in-process paper receives, keep in mind that this is a fresh new outlook. It is not a judgment call, but rather a new way of looking at your work from another angle—a new way that prompts *re-vision*. Peer evaluations or reviews are meant to encourage writers to step away from their own writing in order to gain perspective.

Don't forget you are also responsible for reflecting upon, and learning from, feedback that you receive after submitting a final version of a project. Whether or not you have the opportunity to revise that particular text, you must still carefully consider the feedback from your audience, especially your instructor.

Feedback: comments provided about a piece of writing. Think of feedback as tangible evidence of a reader's experience with your writing. There is no better mechanism for testing whether or not you are communicating effectively. While you can read your own writing to identify global and local level revision, readers offer an account different from your own. Good commenting practices depend on reading closely and carefully in order to offer specific comments.

LEARNING ACTIVITY: Start a Writer's Diary

Grab a small notebook or open a new word processing document on your computer. On the first page, list the types of revision suggestions that others have given to you in the past. Try to think about at least 3–5 different projects. Are there any trends or themes, similar types of revision suggestions? If so, circle, highlight, or otherwise mark those suggestions in some manner. At the top of the next few pages, write the general names of the projects you'll be writing in your upcoming course (or just write something like "ENGL101 Project #1" and "ENGL101 Project #2"...).

As you complete each project, keep track of the types of revisions that your peers, instructors, and other mentors gave you during and after the writing process. Try to identify themes as you add comments and suggestions. At the end of the course, take a moment to reflect upon what strategies you should continue to work on in future writing projects.

3.F: Reflect on their progress as academic writers.

Reflection is imperative to your overall progress as a writer and learner. Through reflection you take the time to review what you have done so that you learn from your past to improve activities in the future. While reflecting on your writing, you should focus on both strengths and weaknesses. You assess your writing critically and plan for future improvements. You also take the time to celebrate. Writing isn't easy; finishing a competent essay is an important accomplishment and worth a little victory dance.

Reflect: the act of thinking about current and past actions in order to explore significance, make meaning, or connect to other ideas, concepts, and experiences. Writers and learners reflect so that they might build on prior experiences to respond to new and challenging contexts. Reflecting is looking backwards to help you continue moving forward in a more productive manner.

CHAPTER

Reviewing and Revision

11

11.1 Reviewing and Revision: An Overview

Writing includes the recurring processes of invention, drafting, and revising. Revision is an ongoing process that is often collaborative in nature. It requires you to be open and willing to accept **feedback** from your instructor and peers, which can be difficult when you have already spent significant time writing.

Your success in foundations writing as well as in future writing situations will depend, in part, on your willingness to revisit or "re-envision" your writing and attempt to see it from the perspective of another reader. It may be difficult to see areas for improvement in your own work; therefore, seeking this feedback from your peers and instructor is an invaluable tool for identifying the strengths of your writing and potential areas for improvement. There are many reasons for giving and receiving feedback, but here are a couple for your consideration:

> Read more about "Reviewing and Revising" within "Writing Processes" in *Writer's Help 2.0.*

- The feedback that you give and receive will offer a fresh perspective on a draft. Writers are often too close to their own work to imagine it taking any other shape. Because they already understand what they are trying to say, they can have trouble locating areas that need more clarification. Outside readers can offer a new perspective on what does and does not make sense to them.

- The process of giving and receiving feedback will help you understand the **rhetorical** characteristics of composition, particularly the qualities that make a piece of writing effective for a given audience and situation.

- The process of reviewing your own drafts, providing feedback on your peers' drafts, and evaluating the feedback you receive from other readers will help you develop your skills as a writer. This process will help you learn how to make critical choices about the revisions you need to incorporate in order to best serve the **purpose** of your essay.

Because every writer has a unique approach to writing, part of the challenge of writing is finding a revision process that suits you. Here is some advice about the revision process from former UA foundations writing students:

- **Do Not Procrastinate:** "I think the main reason I was successful in first-year writing was that I always finished drafting my papers a few days before they were due. This helped lift all the stress off my heart. Then, I would reread my papers over and over again. Every time I reread my paper, I made changes in the **text**. I was not a great writer by any means, but being ahead of time helped me succeed."—Nick Vaughn

- **Read Aloud to Revise:** "I find it very useful to read each draft of my essay out loud before turning in the final draft. That way I can listen to certain phrases that might not make sense and paragraphs that do not flow." —Bethany Bell

- **Recognize that Writing Is a Process:** "I always thought writing draft after draft of a paper, and the whole revising process, was a huge waste of my time. I'd never written first drafts, second drafts, or final drafts. I would just sit down at a computer and write, and I would turn in whatever came out. This year, I was forced to go through the whole drafting process. We were required to not only turn in our first draft, second draft, and final draft; we had to do assignments that showed the research we were doing and what we thought of it. To an experienced procrastinator such as myself, this was hell. However, what resulted from this process really impressed me. All the papers I had ever written could have been so much better. This shows that revising and rewriting are not pointless efforts of teachers to make their students work hard to no end. They actually help. That is probably the most valuable lesson I have learned about writing this year."—Katherine Byrnes

- **Be Prepared for Peer Review:** "Peer review is an excellent tool for improving essays. However, if an adequate rough draft is not presented to reviewers, then useful feedback cannot be expected."—Britt Burridge

- **Give Constructive Criticism during Peer Review:** "When writing peer edits, really dig deep into their paper. Do not just look for the obvious, because they are writing a peer edit for you as well. Think what would be useful for you."—Rebecca Peterson

- **Be Prepared for Instructor Conferences:** "It is very important when you go into your conference with your teacher that you have a strong thesis and a good sense of direction for your paper. It helped me very much to receive advice from my teacher because I had a good start and knew what I wanted to do, thus my teacher was able to give me good advice to refine my ideas. I know that you can fall into the trap of knowing that it is still a couple of weeks from being due, so why start it early? It really makes a difference in getting strong feedback."—Richard Karasch

As this advice demonstrates, revision takes many forms and can be useful in many ways. This chapter will provide you with a foundation for revision and peer review strategies.

11.2 Practicing Global and Local Revision

This section focuses on suggestions and practices that help in both the **global** and **local** stages of revisions. You might refer to Chapter 10 for in-depth definitions for these stages of revision. An important aspect about both stages that you should remember is that they are always rhetorical and dependent on context. The following section will remind you to always consider your audience, your purpose, and the overall situation as you work through revisions.

11.2.1 Suggestions for Global Revisions

Making global revisions requires you to reread your essay with a focus on the **rhetorical situation**. At this stage in the revision process, you will want to revisit the assignment guidelines provided by your instructor to make sure that your essay or project fulfills the necessary requirements. Revising your draft should include an evaluation of how well your specific choices align with your intended **purpose**, **audience**, and the **context** of your writing.

The following questions will be helpful as you evaluate your draft. Keep in mind that global changes based on your answer to one question may impact the rest of your essay. For this reason, it is important to return to these questions throughout the revision process.

Purpose:

- What do I hope to achieve with this essay? Am I trying to persuade the reader of something? Inform them of a particular perspective? Lead them to take specific action? How will they know what my goals are?

- Am I making an **argument** or merely stating the obvious?

- Are my ideas developed enough to achieve my purpose? Do I progress through my argument carefully, patiently, and with enough detail? Am I supporting my ideas with appropriate **evidence**?

After answering these questions, you might find that you need to refocus your ideas, collect more information, rearrange sentences or paragraphs, cut unnecessary or confusing information, add more details, or make clearer moves and transitions.

Audience:

- Who, specifically, is going to be reading this essay? Who am I trying to reach with my argument? (My instructor, my classmates, members of my academic community, members of the local community, etc.)

- What are their values and expectations? Am I mindful and respectful of those values and expectations in my writing?

- What assumptions am I making about my audience's knowledge of the **topic**? How much background information or context should I provide for them without insulting or ignoring their knowledge?

- What kind of language is suitable for this audience?

- What **tone** should I use with my audience? Do I use this tone consistently throughout my draft?

Context:

* What are the **formatting** requirements of the assignment? Do I meet them?

* What are the content requirements for the assignment? Do I meet them?

* Does my draft reflect knowledge and content discussed in class in addition to my own ideas and **voice**?

Remembering your rhetorical situation as you review your draft will help you make purposeful global revisions.

11.2.2 Suggestions for Local Revisions

Once you have effectively addressed your draft's global revisions, you are ready to start local revisions. Paying careful attention to issues occurring at the local level allows you to communicate effectively through your writing and enhance audience understanding.

> While focusing on local revisions, consider reviewing "The Top Twenty" in *Writer's Help* 2.0.

The following list includes some stylistic elements you might consider when performing local revisions. Please see the course handbook for more discussion on local revisions:

* **Wordiness:** Unnecessary words can take all the energy out of a sentence. Practice expressing your ideas concisely. See how many unnecessary words you can eliminate from your writing.

* **Tense Usage:** Be consistent with your verb tenses as unnecessary changes in verb tenses could confuse readers. While you do not need to write your entire essay in a single tense, make sure that if you do change between the present and the past or future tense, there is a logical reason to do so.

* **Passive and Active Voice:** Pay attention to your usage of passive and active voice. In your essays for foundations writing, consider the impact that active verbs might have (such as *achieve, demonstrate, suggest,* and *consider*), compared to their passive counterparts: *is achieved by, is demonstrated by, is suggested by, is considered by*.

* **Variety:** One of the best marks of effective writing is variety. By varying the types of sentence structures, paragraph structures, vocabulary, and punctuation that you use, you can help your reader stay focused and engaged. Look for repeated sentence structures, words, **punctuation**, and phrases, and experiment until you have included more variety and fluidity in your writing.

It is important to remember that local revisions are also rhetorical. Paying attention to your audience and your purpose will help you in aspects such as word choice and level of **formality**.

11.3 Effective Peer Reviewing

11.3.1 Tips for Successful Workshopping

"Tips for Successful Workshopping"

By Laura Gronewold

pp. 182–184

Every writer needs a reviewer. Even the best writers create multiple drafts. During this revising process, the writer collaborates with other editors and writers so that a number of people contribute to the final, polished product. That is one reason authors thank so many people in the acknowledgments at the beginning of books. Think of your peers as collaborators working to produce the best essay possible. You can learn a lot about what to revise after several pairs of eyes have seen your work.

11.3.1.1 Discussion about Your Peer's Essay during the In-Class Workshop

When you come to class, you will need to be ready to discuss your classmates' writing. Think about the ways you have talked as a class about the essays, fiction, poetry, and/or films you have read or viewed. When you talk as a class, you are not making judgments about the writer, but you are making assessments about the writing. The same goes for a workshop. Your goal is to offer "constructive criticism" or advice that serves a useful purpose. You want to keep your comments specific to the text your peer has produced so that the author will have concrete suggestions for improving and reorganizing her or his draft.

During an in-class workshop, your instructor will be present, listening and potentially participating with the group. Your instructor may help guide the workshop with questions, comments, and ideas, but the heart of any workshop's success is you and your classmates. Remember that the goal of the workshop is not only to give your classmates feedback, but also to train yourself to make these same assessments of your own writing.

11.3.1.2 Advice for the Writer

Come to the workshop prepared to receive a critique of your work. Even if you feel that your draft is well written and has a clear argument, remember that your classmates can give you constructive criticism that will help make it even better. Bring an open mind to your workshops so that you can really listen to what ideas your classmates offer to improve your draft.

- Listen quietly to the discussion of your work when it is happening.

- Try to think of feedback as a response to the current stage of your writing, not as a judgment of your talent or ability as a writer.

- Take notes! You should have a page of specific notes that you can refer to when you revise your paper.

- After listening, ask questions so that you are clear on the feedback your classmates have offered. At the end of the discussion, voice any additional concerns or questions about your essay.

Once you have received feedback, try to wait a few hours before revising your essay. This will give you some distance from your writing and will help you to more fully consider the comments from your workshop partners.

As you revise, think about the different comments from your readers. Do they all say that you need a more focused **thesis** statement? If everyone agrees, it is likely, though not certain, that this issue will remain a problem for your teacher or an intended audience. However, if only one student comments about your paragraph breaks, then you will need to assess whether or not you want to implement this revision. Remember, this is your essay, so you will need to decide which comments you will accept and reject based on your intentions and the effect you want to achieve.

11.3.1.3 Advice for the Reader

Your job as a reader is to carefully assess your classmates' drafts so that you can give them detailed feedback about their essay. Giving written (and verbal) feedback is another **genre** of writing, and it requires practice and skill. Even if you feel like you are not the best writer in class, your feedback during workshop is very important! If you are not clear about why a paragraph exists in another student's essay, for example, mention your confusion during peer review—even if you aren't sure how to "fix" it. During the workshop, you, the author, and any other peer reviewers can collaboratively figure out how to address the issue.

As you review your peers' drafts:

- Read the writing as closely and carefully as possible.

- Consider the writer's intentions and the assignment guidelines, and provide feedback addressing particular concerns or sections of text.

- Read the essay at least twice.

- Write specific suggestions for revision on each page as you are reading.

At the end of the essay, offer your overall reflections about the argument, the organization, the tone, and the **style**. Don't be afraid to state the obvious. Details that are noticeable to most readers may have become difficult for the writer to see if she has put many hours into a draft. Sometimes just restating what you think the writer is trying to do can help her know if the writing is effective.

11.3.1.4 Giving Written Feedback

Your goal when you review your workshop partners' drafts should be to write specific comments and questions that the writer can understand later, even if you are not there to explain them. Marginal comments such as "good!" or "???" are vague and will not clearly help the writer make revisions. Therefore, when you are reviewing a peer's work, consider the kind of feedback you would like to receive and strive to be constructive in your comments. If you are struggling to write meaningful and detailed comments of your own, consider using some of the sentence starters listed in the chart on the following page.

Compliments	Constructive Criticism
• You got my attention here by… • This example is great because… • I like the way you use…in order to… • I like this sentence/paragraph because… • This approach is effective because…	• Here I expected…instead of … • You need more evidence to support your claim that… • You might consider adding… • What about…? There are other perspectives on this topic including… • I had to read this sentence twice because… • This paragraph needs more…

LEARNING ACTIVITY:
Construct Critical Feedback

You may find it helpful to use the following questions to guide you when giving feedback on a peer's paper. Note that some assignments and writing situations may not utilize each of these elements or may not include them in this order. Use your understanding of the assignment prompt to determine how much weight to place on each element.

Introduction: As the reader, your job is to make suggestions for how the writer can make her or his introductory paragraph specific and interesting. Does the introductory paragraph establish the theme or idea of the essay? Is the introduction focused, or does it jump around and confuse the reader? Does the introduction offer the basic facts about the topic (short summary of a **text**, brief overview of a political issue, etc.) to help orient the reader? Think about how you might help the writer restrict the summary to the points in the text that are most relevant to the central argument.

1. **Thesis Statement:** Does the author have a precise thesis statement (or central claim) that articulates a specific opinion or argument about a topic? Your job is to provide suggestions to the writer that could help make the topic more focused and include a supportable, **debatable** opinion. If the thesis statement already includes an opinion, is it phrased in a way that makes you interested in reading the rest of the essay?

2. **Summary and Analysis:** Does the author have too much summary of the text or too much vague information about a research topic? How can the writer move beyond offering only summary to develop a specific line of argument regarding the text or topic under consideration? How can the writer incorporate **quotations**, examples, or other forms of evidence to support her claims? Mark places where the writer is doing a great job making specific claims and using supporting evidence, but also make note of where analysis can be strengthened.

3. **Use of Evidence:** Does the writer support **claims** with evidence? Does the kind of evidence—quotes, anecdotes, summary, outside research, personal experience, etc.—match the expectations of the assignment? Point out where the evidence is especially effective, where you think more evidence is needed, or where a different kind of evidence might better support the claim.

4. **Use of Sources:** Does the writer integrate **sources** appropriately in the essay? Does the writer make it clear to the reader when another text is being quoted? Do you ever have any questions about the original source for a quotation or an idea (especially if it is an idea that is **paraphrased**)? Your job is to help the writer establish **credibility** and ensure that all of the sources are utilized effectively.

5. **Organization:** Does the organization of the essay support the purpose? Should any paragraphs be moved around, expanded, or deleted? See the "Reverse Outlining" learning activity later in this chapter for strategies to test the effectiveness of organization.

6. **Transitions:** Does the author have smooth transition phrases between the paragraphs and sentences? See section 9.4.1, "Ways and Means of Transitions" for more about transitions.

7. **Conclusion:** Does the conclusion leave you with a new idea or concept to consider? Does it do more than simply restate what has already been argued?

11.3.2 Alternative Approaches and Suggestions for Workshopping

In order to really benefit from a writing workshop, you will need to do several things. First, come to the workshop prepared. This means that you need to submit your best draft, at that point in the process, for feedback. Second, come to the workshop with an open mind. Instead of trying to defend your essay, listen carefully and thoughtfully to your peers when they give you feedback. Ask questions about their suggestions. Take some time to think through your options. Remember, you do not have to make all the changes your peers or instructor suggest, but you do want to give careful consideration to their feedback. Third, give helpful, specific, constructive feedback to your peers. Although it is nice to tell your peers what you like about their essays, this is only helpful if you explain your opinion in detail and let them know why you like it. Here you will see some examples of not very helpful, somewhat helpful, and very helpful workshop comments.

Not Very Helpful

"I really like this paper!"

This is friendly, but provides no concrete suggestions for the writer.

"Well, I'm just not that into poetry, so I couldn't get into your paper."

This comment is about the reader, not the paper. It does not provide any suggestions for revision.

"You use way too many commas."

Even if this critique is correct, it does not specify where commas are unnecessary. Local suggestions are most helpful on drafts that have already been revised for global concerns.

Somewhat Helpful

"I really like your first body paragraph, but after that you kind of lose me."

This comment identifies strong and weak areas but does not tell the writer what makes them strong or weak.

"You assume that I already know what this poem is about and that I think it is a great poem. Since I do not know anything about the poem, I feel lost when I read this paper."

This honest reaction identifies the assumptions made in the draft. It might also identify an opportunity for global revision, if the assignment requires the writer to assume that the reader is unfamiliar with the poem.

"In this sentence, the commas actually make it harder to understand. Maybe you should take them out."

This local editing comment effectively identifies a problem sentence, connects the idea (or the content) to the **form**, and provides a specific suggestion.

Very Helpful

"I really like this paragraph because you choose an interesting example from the text and in the last sentence you show how this paragraph supports the thesis. Maybe you could do this more in your other body paragraphs."

This comment identifies what makes the paragraph strong and gives the writer specific suggestions for improving the weaker paragraphs.

"If you gave a little bit of summary and background at the beginning of the paper, it would really help me to understand what's going on, because I've never read the poem before. You could also connect your argument about racism in this poem to a recent event, which would help people who do not know much about poetry to be more interested in your overall argument."

This comment expands the second "Somewhat Helpful" comment by providing specific suggestions for revision.

"In this sentence, the commas actually make it harder to understand. You could take them out. In the next sentence, you have an unnecessary comma again, but the sentence is also a run-on. Try making this into two separate sentences, which would make it easier to understand and would give the paragraph more variety."

This local revision identifies specific problems, provides specific suggestions, and addresses both clarity and style.

You should also consider the impact that your comments might have on the writer. Peer reviewing places both writers and readers in a very open and vulnerable position, and in those moments some minor miscommunication can lead to major misunderstandings. (This does not mean that you should avoid suggesting changes, but it does mean that you want to be aware of how you are communicating with your partner.) It is also important to remember that, as a peer reviewer, you do not have to agree with the arguments of a draft. Rather, you should focus on your ability to understand the logic (language and structure) presented by the writer. Try to comment and give feedback on the effects of the writing, and try to avoid comments that deal directly with the writer.

LEARNING ACTIVITY:
Peer Review in VoiceThread

"Peer Review in VoiceThread"

By Ayda Fontecha

pp. 187–188

VoiceThread is a useful and flexible technology that helps students peer review each other's writing without having to be in the same physical space. Subsequently, students can respond to feedback or comment on points that were not clear for their peers. This continuous dialogue enables students to be more aware of their audience.

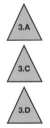

Steps to peer review using VoiceThread:

Step 1: Log on to D2L and select your foundations writing course. Highlight the UA tools feature and select VoiceThread.

Step 2: Create a new VoiceThread.

Step 3: Upload your peer's writing: Make sure you have access to your peer's writing, and then select the plus sign that says "add media" to upload the document.

Step 4: Give your VoiceThread a title. For example, "your classmate's name Peer Review" and then select save. The first page of your partner's writing is going to show as the first slide. There are arrows towards the bottom of the screen that allow you to move back and forth between slides.

Step 5: Start peer reviewing your partner's writing piece. There are two options for peer review:

A.   Record audio comment: Select the plus sign inside the speech bubble in the middle of the screen and select the microphone. Make sure your microphone is not muted. A square dialogue will pop up asking you to allow the application to use your microphone. Select "allow" and begin recording. There is a pen next to the stop button at the bottom of the screen that you can use while you are talking that allows you to underline the sentences you are talking about or point to specific words in the text. As you underline sentences or words with the pen, the previous underlined sentences disappear from your screen; however, when your partner receives your feedback he/she will be able to see everything you did. When you are done with your peer review select the "stop recording" button. You can select it at any time and record again if necessary.

B.   Type a command: Follow the same steps as above, but instead of clicking the microphone, select the "abc" icon. There is a square that pops up and you can type your feedback for your partner. Save your text when you are finished. You can see your initials or your picture on the left side of the screen. If you hover your cursor over the picture, you can see your comments and make any additional changes.

Step 6: Share your peer review with your partner. On the left side of the screen there are three bars next to the title of the VoiceThread. Select them to get a link that you will be able to share with your peer.

11.4 Receiving and Making Sense of Comments

Writing is a social act, and the process of peer review provides an example of that social dynamic. The process of peer review extends beyond simply meeting and discussing drafts. A writer's ability to respond critically to her feedback can directly impact how successful a project might be in achieving its purpose. The following sections deal with that crucial point in the peer-reviewing process: how to make sense of and critically respond to comments from peers and instructors.

11.4.1 Managing Feedback

Once you receive written and oral comments from your peers and instructor, it is time for you to decide which comments and suggestions to use. Reading feedback on your work can be intimidating, as it is easy to become attached to your writing and take comments personally. Remember, the comments are reflections on the draft in its current stage and not a reflection of the writer. Here is some advice to help you manage feedback:

- Read through all the comments from all the reviewers before making any decisions.

- Watch for patterns in the responses you receive. If three out of four readers suggest you expand a certain point, chances are good that future readers would want you to say more about it, too.

- Look for global issues such as focus and organization that need attention before you attend to local problems such as **grammar** and word choice. You will waste your time if you fix sentences that you decide to delete later on. However, it is useful to note habitual errors so that when you generate new material, you don't continue to make the same mistakes.

- Always keep an open mind as you read comments. Try to see it from the reviewer's point of view. Did you leave out important information or explanation that would solve the problem?

- If you really think a comment is questionable, ask other readers what they think. Sometimes you will decide not to take action on a suggestion or comment.

- If you have a specific concern that is not included in the feedback you get from your readers or you want more feedback in general, do not be afraid to ask people for specific advice. A workshop is a partnership, and it is your responsibility to ask the questions that you would like answered.

- Think critically about all comments and then make the revisions you think are most important for the purpose and scope of your work. You are the writer and you make the final decisions.

"Construct a Cover Letter"
By Maria Conti
pp. 189–190

LEARNING ACTIVITY:
Construct a Cover Letter

Purpose: You will reflect on your approaches to writing and your writing processes to help you become a more effective writer.

Audience: You are writing to your composition instructor so that they can better tailor their feedback for your future papers or projects to areas that will be most helpful to you. You are also writing for yourself, as you will be able to think through which processes and strategies have been the most successful and effective for you.

Task: Metacognition, or thinking about our approaches to a given task, helps us to improve at almost any activity. Writing is no exception. Take some time to reflect on the revision and editing changes you made to this paper or project, assess its strengths and weaknesses, and critically consider your overall approach. You will also be asked to provide some direction for your instructor's feedback comments.

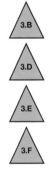

3.B

3.D

3.E

3.F

1. **Global revisions**

   List **all** the *specific* global changes that you made from the first draft to the final.

   - Be thorough here—for what section, what was it before, what change(s) did you make, and why did you make them?

2. **Local revisions**

   List **all** the *specific* local changes that you made from the first draft to the final.

   - Be thorough here—for what section, what was it before, what change(s) did you make, and why did you make them?

3. Writing is a collaborative, meaning-making activity. After each change that you mention in #1 and #2, indicate in parentheses which changes were prompted by the peer review like this (**P**), which were prompted by me as your instructor (**I**), and which were the result of a Writing Center consultation, if applicable (**W**). Feel free to skip letter categories that don't apply to you.

   Note: Make these letter markings in #1 and #2 of this Cover Letter, not in the paper or project itself.

4. Which parts of your paper or project do you feel are the strongest? Why?

5. No piece of writing is perfect or ever truly final. If you had more time to return to this paper or project, which parts would you work on or strengthen? Why?

6. Think back to earlier major papers or projects of this course or any similar writing-intensive course.

   - Describe the major feedback comments you received from the instructor.

   - Do you feel any of these areas have improved for this paper or project? If so, describe which areas and why.

   - Did you do anything differently to make that happen?

   - If you're not sure if these areas have improved, or if you don't think they have improved much (this is a valid response, since the two assignments may be very different), just name the area and provide some context for your perspective.

LEARNING ACTIVITY:
Outline in Reverse

If you are interested in determining how well your essay addresses your intended argument, you might want to consider doing a "reverse outline" of your essay. In a reverse outline, you go back through your draft and re-create an outline based on what you actually see in your writing—not on what you imagined or hoped to see. This is a very useful exercise either for working through complicated texts or for revising your own essays.

To create a reverse outline of your essay, complete the following steps:

1. In the left-hand margin, write down the topic of each paragraph by using as few words as possible. If you cannot sum up the main point of your paragraph in just a few words, you might need to revisit the intention of the paragraph.

2. Then, in the right-hand margin, write a quick assessment of why the paragraph is necessary to enhance the argument.

3. Reconstruct your new outline and compare it to any original outlines or brainstorming work you did to see how your argument changed as you wrote your essay. Here, you can determine whether or not you need to add new information, cut redundant information, or rearrange existing information.

11.4.2 Approaching Instructor Feedback

From The University of Arizona Writing Instructors to Our Students

As part of the ongoing revision process, you will receive feedback from your instructors, sometimes during conferences, and most often after you submit your final draft for a grade. The following statement aims to help you make sense of how instructors generate written responses to your writing and how they hope you will use these responses. Though there is often a relationship between the instructor's comments and the letter grade you will ultimately earn in the class, this message encourages you to use both the grades and the comments as tools for improving your writing throughout the semester and beyond.

1. We would like you to understand that our comments are part of the teaching and learning process. We write comments not just to evaluate your essay, but to help you see how the lessons about writing from class emerge in your writing. One way to better understand the purpose of our comments is to participate actively in class and carefully read the assignment sheet, rubric, and any other assignment materials your instructor distributes. These are the ways we communicate with you ahead of time about what we are looking for in your writing.

2. We would like you to know that we intend our comments to be constructive. We value your ideas and want to learn from you and hope that you will use our comments to learn from us as well.

3. We would like you to approach each essay not as an independent unit, but as a brief moment in your overall development as a writer. Our comments are meant to be useful to you in this assignment and your future writing.

4. We would like you to accept responsibility for using our comments in the revision process. We also expect you to share your strengths as a writer in commenting on your peers' papers.

5. We would like you to understand that comments are both descriptive and evaluative. Writing a letter grade is perhaps the least interesting thing we do as writing instructors. Take the time to reread the entire essay alongside our comments to understand the grade in context. We invite you to use our comments as an opportunity to talk further about your writing.

Written by UA instructors Roseanne Carlo, Anne-Marie Hall, Faith Kurtyka, Rachel Lewis, Jessica Shumake, and Cassie Wright in collaboration with Professor Nancy Sommers, former director of Harvard University's Expository Writing Program.

CHAPTER

12

Reflecting

12.1 Reflective Writing: An Overview

> "Reflective writing helps you to grow as a writer and a thinker. Intellectually, you push your ideas further and your work develops."—Amanda Fahey, UA Student

Reflection is a form of writing that focuses on the writer herself as the main subject of a work, giving structure and meaning to her experience based on insight gained with the passing of time. Whether writing a reflective end-of-semester essay, **freewriting** to help you brainstorm for a particular assignment, or composing a discussion post, blog, or journal entry, you will produce some form of reflective writing in your foundations writing courses. These kinds of reflection will help to prepare you for the kinds of reflective writing you may be expected to practice beyond the university, such as an employee self-evaluation or statement of purpose.

Your writing instructor may ask you to reflect on something you have read, an activity you have completed, an event or experience outside of the classroom, or your semester experiences in the course. Alternatively, you may be asked to write an essay in which you use a **text** you have read as a **context** for talking about your experiences as a writer. These are all examples of prompts that lead to reflective writing: the theme of this chapter.

> Read more about "Reflecting to Learn" within "Writing Processes" in *Writer's Help 2.0*.

Reflective writing, like the **academic writing** you have composed in this course, is a process—one that calls on your skills in **rhetoric** and research and requires an openness to the sometimes "messy" process of getting from an idea to a final product. In this chapter, you identify a **purpose** and **audience** for your writing, consider your **ethos** as a writer, and see that the concepts of **analysis** can be applied to reflective writing.

12.2 Approaches to Reflective Writing

In the course of the semester, your instructor may ask you to write one or more reflective essays on how your understanding of reading and writing has developed through one or more projects for the course. While the assignment parameters will vary, it is important to remember that this type of analysis should focus on process—the writing process, the process of becoming a writer, the peer-review process, the revision process, the editing process, or another process. A reflective analysis of this kind focuses on your experiences producing texts, a topic on which only you can provide unique insights.

Discussing your own writing can be difficult because many of the strategies that you used for a particular assignment might have been compulsory (your instructor required you to do something) or unconscious (you just did something because you always have). However, the reflective process asks you to think critically about what you did and why you did it. Why do you think your instructor asked you to do something in the writing process? Was it useful? Why or why not? Why did you choose to revise a paper the way that you did? What worked and what did not work?

Consider investigating the following topics to start generating ideas for a reflective essay:

- your assumptions and ideas about writing before completing a particular assignment, or series of assignments, and how these assumptions were reinforced or challenged

- the most important lessons you have learned as both a reader and a writer as a result of completing one or more assignments

- the ways you generated ideas, narrowed down **topics**, and worked on **thesis** statements

- the peer-review process, including feedback you offered and **feedback** you received

- individual or group conferences with your instructor

- the discussions you had about your paper(s) with people who were not in your class

- how you approached the revision process for one or more essays

- your understanding of reading and writing in one or more **genres**

- how a particular kind of writing you practiced fits into your life now and how it may fit into your major and future career

- what you would do differently if you were to take one or both of your first-year writing courses again

Once you have generated some ideas, you will want to find a common thread between your reflections so that you can write a cohesive and focused essay. Remember to always read your instructor's assignment sheet carefully so that you can adequately meet the expectations for this assignment. The following topics and questions might help you focus your reflections and develop a thesis statement for your reflective essay:

- **Compare past and present writing experiences:** Did your experiences writing a particular paper challenge or reinforce the ideas you held previously? Has your writing or process undergone a dramatic change as a result of completing one or more assignments?

- **Reflect on strengths and weaknesses:** If you did not gain as much from a particular project as you had hoped, what are the possible reasons for that and what might you do differently the next time? What are some of your strengths as a writer? How did you practice or improve on your abilities through a particular writing assignment or assignments?

- **Focus on course objectives:** Think about the course objectives listed in your syllabus as you consider your success in the class. What course objectives did you meet? What objectives are you still working on?

- Return to the "Reflect on Your Writing Processes" activity from Chapter 2 (p. 18). Has your perception of yourself as a writer changed since you started your foundations writing course?

Reflective writing provides you with an excellent opportunity to analyze yourself as a writer, noting your own strengths within the larger scope of the writing project, the course, or your ongoing development as a writer. Keep in mind that addressing disappointments or even failures can also help you gauge what you have learned and how you can continue to develop your writing abilities.

12.3 Reflection Processes

The previous section introduces many questions and ideas to help you begin the process of reflection. As you begin to narrow your ideas and prepare to write your essay, you'll also want to consider the **rhetorical situation** for your assignment.

12.3.1 Audience and Purpose for Reflective Writing

Like all writing, starting a reflective writing project involves establishing an awareness of your audience and **purpose**. In other words, the reflective writing process is intricately linked to the **rhetorical situation** as discussed in Chapters 4 and 5.

The left column in the following table shows how one UA student, Christopher Tursi, might have identified the rhetorical situation for an end-of-semester reflective essay. Use the right side to generate ideas about the rhetorical situation of your upcoming assignment.

Sample Student Answers	Your Essay
What topic do I want to discuss with my readers? What do I want them to understand about the topic? *I want to explain the ways I have grown as a writer over the course of my first semester. Looking back I realize that my first essay was mostly summary not analysis, and I want to show my reader that I understand what would make it better.*	**What topic do I want to discuss with my readers? What do I want them to understand about the topic?**
Who is my primary audience? Who is my secondary audience? *My primary audience is my instructor. He read the first essay and will be reading and grading this one. My secondary audience is my classmates because I'll be discussing this with them.*	**Who is my primary audience? Who is my secondary audience?**

Sample Student Answers	Your Essay
What do my audiences already know or believe about the topic? *Well, they already know me and my writing, and they have already seen my first essay. My instructor and my classmates also know the strategies that we have focused on this semester, so I should really highlight those.*	**What do my audiences already know or believe about the topic?**
How will I organize and develop my ideas to make them convincing to these readers? *Because my main audience is my instructor, I'll want to show specific aspects of the original and explain exactly how I would change it. Since we have talked so much about analysis and using evidence in class, I'll make sure to take specific examples from my essay and explain clearly how I would improve them.*	**How will I organize and develop my ideas to make them convincing to these readers?**

Once you have a central purpose and primary audience in mind, you can shape the content and the overall presentation of your writing accordingly. For example, as a writer you get to shape the **voice** or voices that emerge in your writing. Having a voice in writing does not mean that you strive to transfer your speaking voice onto the page. Instead, your goal is to construct voice(s) in your writing to create an **ethos**, a sense of **character** or **credibility**, that suits your purpose. Just as credible **sources** are important in a research essay, the voice and ethos that you create are fundamental to the success of reflective essays. The relationship you build with your audience and their perception of you will depend on your rhetorical choices.

Let's look at an example of how Christopher builds a relationship with his audience within the first few sentences of his essay. His ethos plays an important role in making an **argument** about an assignment he disliked because he could easily come across as unmotivated, bitter, or even whiny, especially to his teacher. As you read Christopher's opening few sentences, note the specific details, **tone** of voice, and sentence construction that he uses to create his ethos:

> *It is impossible to enjoy every essay that you are assigned in school. There will always be at least one that you hate writing and the resulting essay will reflect that. A reader can feel your disdain for the paper. That was the problem I had with essay two.*

Following up on student writing:

- What kind of relationship is Christopher trying to create with his audience?

- In what ways do his choices reflect an understanding of his rhetorical situation (the purpose, audience, and context of his writing)?

- Can you think of ways this opening could be improved?

- How does his use of the second person ("you") impact the relationship between reader and writer?

Thinking about the ethos you want to create in your writing can help shape your choices as you begin drafting. Here are questions to consider as you plan your writing:

- What kind of relationship do you want to create with your audience(s)?

- What choices can you make in your writing to earn your audience's trust or encourage them to view you in a certain way? Consider diction, content, **structure**, and **style**.

12.3.2 Drafting

Though there are many ways to approach this assignment, a reflective essay should do the following:

- Analyze your writing process in terms of the experiences, writing assignments, or the concepts you have learned. You are not merely offering a report on the class. You are demonstrating how your writing or your view of writing has been affected by what you have learned or experienced through your composition class.

- Provide concrete examples from your own writing (either **quotes** from your writing or rich descriptions of your writing process) as **evidence**. For help with integrating quotes, see *Writers Help 2.0*.

- Explain why you made certain choices (not just "it was on the assignment sheet"), and evaluate whether those choices were effective.

- Write about your experiences during the process of producing your text. What steps did you take? How did you get feedback from others? How often did you revise? What type of feedback did you expect? Did you gain anything from reading your peer's work? What prompted major and minor revisions?

- Use vocabulary words and concepts from your writing course. For example, if you explain that you revised something, name what sort of revision it was (**local, global**, stylistic, and so on). Use *Writer's Help 2.0* and the glossary terms from this book to help you discuss writing concepts more precisely.

- Write to engage your reader. As a reflection is a more personal genre of writing, it may be appropriate to use more evocative language. You might consider using anecdotes and descriptive language to more fully immerse your reader in the world of your **narrative** (see "Writing Vivid Description" in Chapter 9).

12.3.3 Reflective Thesis Statement

Your thesis for a reflective essay should focus on a particular assignment, experience, or concept of writing and help you to organize your thoughts. In the following sample, Christopher decides to focus his reflection on one particular assignment that he struggled to compose and knew he needed to revise in specific ways. The following excerpt is from the introduction to his end-of-semester reflective essay:

> While I was writing the assigned paper, I knew it was bad. I wrote sentences poorer than I thought possible for me, but I had to push out ideas I didn't fully believe in anyways in order to try and receive credit for this monster I was creating. I couldn't even make the designated amount of words; I was so unmotivated. Moreover, I was coming off a fantastic essay-one that I backed with my entire heart. I hated myself more and more with every word and every sentence I put into this essay-two. That is how I knew this was the one I needed to revise. My essay-two needed to be revamped from beginning to end by rewriting the introduction, including more complete ideas in my body paragraphs, and to fill my conclusion with the requirements needed like a summary of the main argument and an answer to the reader's "So what?" question.

Following up on student writing:

- What is Christopher's thesis? If you were in a peer review with Christopher, how might you suggest he revise his thesis?

- Where does Christopher's language and syntax seem more informal or casual? How do these choices impact his tone and his relationship with the subject matter? How does his diction affect his audience?

- Where do you expect Christopher's essay to go from here?

12.3.4 Evidence in Reflective Writing

To effectively analyze a particular experience, or your growth as a writer over the course of the semester, it is important to include proper evidence to support your **claims**. The following list—while certainly not exclusive—represents some of the ways you can include evidence in personal or reflective writing:

- Anecdotes or stories

- Quotes or **paraphrases** from your own writing and/or sources such as this book, *Writer's Help 2.0*, a class handout, or PowerPoint

- Dialogue (perhaps part of a conversation you had with your instructor or peers during office hours, peer review, or class discussion)

- Comparison and contrast of early and later drafts of an essay

The following paragraph comes from a reflective essay written by Ashley, a student in English 101. Here Ashley compares early and later drafts of her Profile essay in order to argue that revising this assignment helped her to achieve SLO 1.E:

> Changing the point of view of the essay to first person displays one of the learning outcomes [1.E] in Rhetorical Awareness that is "develop facility in responding to a variety of writing contexts calling for purposeful shifts in structure, medium, design, level of formality, tone, and/or voice." Changing the point of view of the essay from third to first person seems to go along with some of these like level of formality, tone and voice. I feel like altering these things improved the voice of my paper because I was able to put more of myself into it. In order for me to achieve this learning outcome, I had to understand the reason why I changed the point of view to first person and there are two main reasons for it: to engage my audience more and to make my writing stronger. Since I could not use words like "I" and "me", I found myself relating things to people in general. This made me feel like no real connection to this essay was shown. Redesigning to first person allowed me to revise things to relate them to myself and my own personal experience with the interview. This shift in tone and voice helped to make my paper more personal and conversational, which will attract my audience more.

Ashley explains her choice to change the essay's point of view, first, by *describing* her use of third person in the original essay: "I found myself relating things to people in general." She then provides a specific **reason** why her original approach was ineffective: "This made me feel no real connection to this essay." Ashley proceeds to describe her shift from third to first person in the revised essay: "Redesigning to first person allowed me to revise things to relate them to myself and my own personal experience with the interview." Finally, she provides a reason why this was a better approach than in the first version of the essay: "it helped to make my paper more personal and conversational, which will attract my audience more." With this statement, Ashley proves that the shift in voice from first to third person was purposeful, fulfilling SLO E under Goal

1: **Rhetorical Awareness**: "Develop facility in responding to a variety of writing contexts calling for purposeful shifts in structure, medium, design, level of formality, tone, and/or voice."

As in other writing assignments, make sure to properly introduce your evidence with a **signal phrase** or other cue for your reader. If appropriate, also explain how your evidence connects to the claims(s) you are making. Chapter 9 contains tips on integrating quotes and evidence.

12.3.5 Focus on Writing

As you revise your reflective essay, keep in mind the goals of this genre of writing, especially when you are asked to reflect on your writing:

- Did you demonstrate an ability to think about your writing and yourself as a writer?

- Did you provide **analysis** of your experiences, writing assignments, or the concepts you have learned?

- Did you provide concrete examples from your own writing (either quotes from your writing or rich descriptions of your writing process)?

- Did you explain why you made certain choices and whether those choices were effective?

- Did you use specific terms and concepts related to writing and the writing process?

- Did your reflection demonstrate a mastery of the skills you have learned in your writing course (including a heightened awareness of diction, **grammar**, rhetoric, analysis, etc.)?

LEARNING ACTIVITY:
Reflect on Process

When you finish an essay or major writing project, take a few minutes to write about the process. What steps did you take to complete the project? Did you research? Did you use an outline? Did you procrastinate? Did your peers give you important suggestions? How many times did you revise the project? What did you focus on each time?

Identify the aspects of the writing process that were the most helpful and be prepared to use similar strategies on your next effort. Additionally, note the aspects of the process that didn't work as well so that you can use more effective strategies in the future.

12.4 Habits of Mind

Successful writers and reflectors share similar practices or habits. Three professional organizations dedicated to writing, the Council of Writing Program Administrators, the National Council of Teachers of English, and the National Writing Project, co-authored a list of practices, or habits of mind, that are necessary for successful writers:

- **Curiosity**—the desire to know more about the world.

- **Openness**—the willingness to consider new ways of being and thinking in the world.

- **Engagement**—a sense of investment and involvement in learning.

- **Creativity**—the ability to use novel approaches for generating, investigating, and representing ideas.

- **Persistence**—the ability to sustain interest in and attention to short- and long-term projects.

- **Responsibility**—the ability to take ownership of one's actions and understand the consequences of those actions for oneself and others.

- **Flexibility**—the ability to adapt to situations, expectations, or demands.

- **Metacognition**—the ability to reflect on one's own thinking as well as on the individual and cultural processes used to structure knowledge.[1]

LEARNING ACTIVITY:
Reflect on Habit of Mind

3.F

After you have completed a major writing project in one of your courses, consider reflecting with these questions:

- In what ways did your personal or reflective writing engage these habits of mind?

- What challenges did you face in your personal or reflective writing assignment?

- What did you learn about yourself in this assignment? What did you learn about your writing process?

- How can you use the skills and strategies you learned in this chapter in other writing situations?

---

1 Council of Writing Program Administrators, National Council of Teachers of English, and National Writing Project. *Framework for Success in Postsecondary Writing, 2011.* Council of Writing Program Administrators, wpacouncil.org/files/framework-for-success-postsecondary-writing.pdf.

PART V:
CONVENTIONS

CHAPTER

Introducing Conventions

13

(continued)

13.1 Goal 4: Conventions

*Conventions: Understand conventions as related to **purpose**, **audience**, and **genre**, including such areas as **mechanics**, usage, **citation** practices, as well as **structure**, **style**, graphics, and **design**.*

Why are conventions important? The use of conventions shows that the writer understands the expectations of a genre within a specific **context**. When a **text** uses common conventions, it also makes it easier for readers because the text includes the **forms**, content, and **rhetorical strategies** that they expect to find.

Naturally there are different conventions for different genres. For your science papers you may be expected to write "objectively" without using the word *I*. For your English papers, you might be expected to write about your personal experiences and use the word *I*. Thus you can assume that there are differences based on the task at hand, including purpose, audience, and genre. Certainly, some features of **grammar**, mechanics, and citation practices remain constant across college assignments (such as ending a sentence with a period), but many features will vary depending on purpose and genre.

Why are conventions important? It is important to be aware of which conventions are relatively constant across contexts and also of which conventions might vary across genres and settings. When writing a résumé or fellowship proposal, for example, formal editing is very important; when writing a text message to a friend, it is not.

With time, experience, and close attention, you will gradually gain a sense of which conventions are appropriate and expected for different genres and situations.

Read more about "Language Variety" within "Language" in *Writer's Help 2.0.*

To meet Goal 4: Conventions, students will be able to do the following at the end of the Foundations Writing sequence:

A.   follow appropriate **conventions** for **grammar**, **punctuation**, and spelling, through practice in composing and revising.

B.   reflect on why genre conventions for structure, **paragraphing**, **tone**, and **mechanics** vary.

C.   identify and effectively use variations in genre conventions, including **formats** and/or **design** features.

D.   demonstrate familiarity with the concepts of **intellectual property** (such as **fair use** and **copyright**) that motivate **documentation** conventions.

E.   apply **citation** conventions systematically in their own work.

13.2 Student Learning Outcomes: Descriptions and Key Terms

4.A: Follow appropriate conventions for grammar, punctuation, and spelling, through practice in composing and revising.

By now you may have taken English classes where SWE (Standard Written English) was part of the expectation for writing. If not, foundations writing courses are a prime moment to review standard conventions. Many students think grammar is hard, but it's just a set of rules. You will have access to *Writer's Help 2.0* to help you. You may find the occasional rule hard to interpret, so be sure to ask your instructor to help you. Like grammar, punctuation is a set of rules. If you adhere to basic punctuation rules, you are attempting to make your reading legible to your audience.

LEARNING ACTIVITY:
Compare "Standards" of Written English

Read both "Preparing to meet expectations for U.S. academic writing" (in Writing Processes > Expectations for College Writing) and "Language Variety" (in Language) in *Writer's Help 2.0*. How "standard" is Standard Written English? Why is it important to understand what some people consider U.S. academic English? Why is it important to understand there are a variety of English "languages" and "styles"?

When composing, you might consider using all available tools, strategies, and technologies to your advantage. If you're writing in *Microsoft Word*, chances are that the program will catch most of your misspellings. (But, will it catch American or British spellings of certain words? What are your settings in the software application?) It's much more difficult to catch wrong words; do you need *their*, *there*, or *they're*? For that you need to edit your work carefully, perhaps with the help of extra readers. For example, suppose you wrote *effect*, which is usually a noun meaning the result of something, but you really wanted the verb *affect*, meaning to have an impact on something. Spell check won't tell you that you selected the wrong word because it's not misspelled. Human eyes and a critical mind are needed to discover this kind of error.

In class you will probably workshop your essays. During the early stages of workshopping, you should concentrate on the content of your writing: your message. During the final stage of workshopping, you may have time for editing. At that very last stage, it's helpful to have your classmates look over grammar and mechanics. They might be able to spot problems you couldn't see yourself. Indeed it's often hard to find the inconsistencies in your own work. The trick is to take time for careful editing before you submit your final draft. One way to help yourself find the inconsistencies in your own writing is to give your draft a "rest"—get away from it for a day or two—so that you can come back to it with fresh eyes. Writing is such a complex task that you shouldn't expect to do everything in one step. Instead give yourself the luxury of writing multiple drafts. Finish your essay and revise the content. Then tackle the editing. Finally, check your citations. Then re-read one more time.

> Read more about "Grammar" and "Punctuation" in *Writer's Help 2.0.*

> Consider adding the results of this activity to your Writer's Diary from the Learning Activity "Start a Writer's Diary" (Chapter 10, SLO 3.E).

Conventions: an agreed-upon way to do things. Conventions relate both to **global** issues like topics, content, organization, and design as well as **local** issues like grammar and mechanics. The specific **rhetorical situation** (purpose, audience, **topic**, genre, etc.) will help identify what set of conventions are appropriate for a given text.

Grammar: rules that govern sentence and word construction such as subject-verb agreement, verb tense, word form, and pluralization.

Punctuation: symbols used to help organize written text and provide meaning to words, phrases, and sentences.

LEARNING ACTIVITY:
Identify Your Writing Trends

4.A

What two or three conventions of grammar, punctuation, and spelling do you tend to have difficulty with in your own writing? After identifying two or three specific conventions that are challenging for you, find sections in *Writer's Help 2.0* identified with each convention. Try revising a current or recent writing project focusing on these conventions.

4.B: Reflect on why genre conventions for structure, paragraphing, tone, and mechanics vary.

4.B

Different texts have different jobs and are therefore constructed differently. While most texts still follow rules for grammar and perhaps mechanics, many other features will vary from genre to genre. For example, newspaper writing is done quickly because what's most important is the very latest news. Newspaper articles are purposefully written in short paragraphs—sometimes a paragraph consists of only one sentence. Sometimes the sentences aren't even complete.

Instead they are purposefully cut to affect readers in a certain way, such as to grab their attention. Tone is another feature that varies from text to text. Some texts are written to be as objective as possible, so the tone may be neutral or even bland. Other texts use tones that are purposefully sarcastic or humorous. **Authors** use their understanding of the rhetorical situation (purpose, audience, topic, genre, etc.) to help understand what is expected for a given genre.

Paragraphs: larger units within an alphanumerically written text that are usually composed of three or more sentences. Paragraphs usually focus on a specific sub-topic, line of **reasoning**, or explication of a piece of **evidence**.

Mechanics: capitalization, **punctuation**, spelling, and other conventions that convert oral language to written text.

LEARNING ACTIVITY:
Analyze How Genres Differ

Using a search engine, find examples of a

- save-the-date card,

- a wedding invitation, and

- a wedding announcement.

What are the most visible differences related to content, structure, paragraphing, tone, and mechanics? How do these differences better support the rhetorical situations (purpose, audience, topic, and context) of each genre?

> Read more about "Developing Paragraphs" in Writing Processes and "Mechanics" in *Writer's Help* 2.0.

LEARNING ACTIVITY:
Recognize Appropriate Conventions

Find 2–4 texts you have written relatively recently (consider pulling from both academic writing as well as other texts you may have produced at work or on social media). How do the rhetorical situations (purpose, audience, topic, context, genre, etc.) differ for the texts? What are the expected conventions for each of those rhetorical situations? Identify one or two expected conventions that are similar across the texts. Identify one or two expected conventions that are different.

4.C: Identify and effectively use variations in genre conventions, including formats and/or design features.

As mentioned previously, different texts have different jobs. This is why genre conventions, such as **format** and features of design, vary. Even texts focused on the same topic but written for different audiences or professional contexts will have different approaches to format and design. Think about how many application forms are designed to allow the applicant and then reader to easily identify different sections of the document. Resumes are designed in the same way; readers who are looking at large numbers of resumes at the same time need to be able to easily find relevant information.

As another example, newspaper articles are purposefully written in short paragraphs. Another feature of design is news headlines. They are purposefully short and are designed in larger font and in bold. Depending on its prominence, a newspaper article will include an image or photograph to accompany the story and headline. Often a news story will reference professional research related to the news story. An empirical study published in a **scholarly** journal about the same topic, however, will follow vastly different conventions for format and design. Design will include multiple sections, research questions, methodology, results, analysis, and discussion. Data will be presented **visually** in tables, graphs, or figures.

Format: the organization and arrangement of a text. Format usually focuses a bit more on the organization and function of a document; however, it is also concerned with design.

Design: the look and format of a text. Design usually focuses a bit more on the visual aesthetics of a document; however, it is also concerned with format and function.

LEARNING ACTIVITY:
Analyze Format and Design

Using a search engine, find examples of a

- condolences card,

- a funeral announcement, and

- an obituary.

What are the most visible differences related to content, structure, paragraphing, and design? How do these differences better support the rhetorical situations (purpose, audience, topic, and context) of each genre?

4.D: Demonstrate familiarity with the concepts of intellectual property (such as fair use and copyright) that motivate documentation conventions.

Common understandings of intellectual property are not static. What would be academically and legally considered intellectual property or appropriate use of another's words or ideas depends on a number of variables. Are you writing for an academic situation, such as a class research project, or publically blogging for your own interest? Are you researching and writing about background that is considered common knowledge for your professor or others reading it? Are you not sure if the information you are referencing is common knowledge? In what country (context) are you writing and publishing? The motivations and expectations for some documentation conventions are different in academic classes versus public domains. The audience can also affect documentation expectations, since you need to cite **sources**, even common knowledge sources, when it will help the reader find you credible.

Citations are also important on an ethical level. Although views around the world differ, in the U.S., professionals believe very strongly in the power of intellectual property or ownership. Therefore, texts are viewed as belonging to the writer, and the writer should be given credit for those words and ideas when they are used elsewhere. When you write texts that incorporate the words or ideas of others, it is therefore extremely important to document those words and ideas. Whether you are **summarizing**, **paraphrasing**, or **quoting**, you are expected to give credit to the authors.

Although citations of outside information used in academic papers, movies, and songs are sometimes ignored or even invisible, that information is still required. Academic papers always have *works cited* or *references* lists. Movies have end-of-film credits for a variety of things like music or clips of other visual media used in the film. Material packaging, or digital meta-data, connected to songs usually includes documentation information, especially if the song was written by someone other than the performer. Think of citations and documentation as a way for the reader to follow a thread back to an original text.

Universities and other academic organizations outline the expectations for students to give credit to others for words and ideas that they use. At the University of Arizona, this is outlined on the Dean of Student's website in the *UA Code of Academic Integrity*.

Intellectual Property: "something (such as an idea, invention, or process) that comes from a person's mind" (*Merriam-Webster Dictionary*). When thinking and writing your own work that may draw on ideas from another person, it is important to recognize and note when you are using that other person's idea or words.

Fair Use: a United States federal policy that allows several considerations for when intellectual property can be used *without* explicit permission, including how much of the work is being used and whether it is for nonprofit educational purposes. Two guidelines that are most likely to apply to your academic use of intellectual property are:

1. if using smaller pieces of a larger text in class projects or presentations (that will not be shared with anyone beyond participants in the class), cite the texts in the format required by your instructor;

2. if using images or large chunks of work from sources in projects or pre-sentations that will be presented publicly or online, choose images in the public domain or with Creative Common license, gain permissions from the authors, or use less than 10% of the work. In all cases, cite the works you quoted, referenced, or used in your project.

Copyright: a legal protection that authors or creators can seek to limit the ways that others can use their work. Creative Common licenses are a type of copyright license; some are quite restrictive and others allow authors to use the Creative Commons licensed text in any way as long as the author is attributed.

Documentation: any method of telling the reader that the idea, work, or image is from someone else. Documentation typically happens in two places in **academic writing**:

1. in the text, such as with an introductory phrase or a parenthetical citation; and

2. in a reference page, usually found at the end of the paper or document.

In multimedia works, the location of documentation should be visible, although where it appears needs to fit the work.

LEARNING ACTIVITY:
Compare Documentation Patterns

4.D

Go into the Pew Research Center (http://www.pewresearch.org/) and select a topic.

*   Find an article about the topic hosted on the Pew Research website.

*   Find a news article on the same topic.

*   Go to the library's **databases** and find an article from a scholarly journal on the same topic.

| Read more about "Acknowledging Sources, Avoiding Plagiarism" within "Research" in *Writer's Help 2.0*. |

Compare how each of these articles cites information from outside sources. How much information do they give about the outside source? How is that information presented?

4.E: Apply citation conventions systematically in their own work.

4.E

In the best possible situation, readers are so interested in the sources you used in your essay that they want to find the texts you used as soon as possible and read every word. Hence your paper needs to include a direct trail so that readers understand where the information is coming from and how to trace it back to the original sources. For writers to maintain **credibility**, readers must be able to find this information quickly and easily, so writers must cite their sources in a conventional manner.

In **academic writing**, credit to other authors is given through citations using a documentation style system, such as MLA or APA (there are numerous other citation systems; be sure to check with your instructor what style you will follow in a given course). Within your text, in the in-text citation, you may provide the author's name and a page number (MLA), an author's name and date (APA), or a footnote or endnote number (CMS). At the end of your paper, you will also include a Works Cited (MLA) or References (APA) list to provide the full information about the sources that you used; these lists allow your readers to locate the original sources if necessary.

Citation: the method used to document when an author is referencing or using information from another text. Most **academic writing** citations require that authors use a specific citation style. Style guides are usually associated with specific disciplines like MLA (Modern Language Association), APA (American Psychological Association), or CMS (Chicago Manual of Style—regularly used by historians).

> Read more about "Documentation" in *Writer's Help 2.0.*

Chapter 13: Introducing Conventions

Glossary

Academic writing: Writing that follows discipline-specific style guidelines and genre conventions and may incorporate academic research to support arguments and/or observations.

Alliteration: The repetition of consonant sounds in a sequence of words. For example, "Peter Piper picked a peck of pickled peppers."

Allusion: An indirect reference, often to a person, event, statement, theme, or work. Allusions enrich meaning through the connotations they carry, or the associations that they evoke in a reader's mind. For example, authors may allude to a historic event by mentioning its name or to a play by Shakespeare by using similar language in their writing.

Analysis: The act of explaining how and why a written or visual text does something and whether or not it does so effectively. Analysis goes beyond summary/description; summary/description explains what is happening with a topic, while analysis explains how and why something is happening. Analysis is the act of breaking a text into parts and examining how those parts create a message and affect a reader's or viewer's response. Analytical statements reveal a careful consideration of the text beyond just its main point and open up a space for dialogue.

Angle: In visual analysis, the vantage point from which the viewer is seeing the image. An angle can be high or low and can be exaggerated for a pronounced effect.

Annotated bibliography: Alphabetical lists of topic-related sources in MLA format, each with a summary paragraph.

Annotation: The process of writing notes and comments about a text. These notes can include first impressions, questions, summaries, associations, strategies used, analysis, and more.

Appropriateness: The relevance of the source for our writing situation.

Argument: The overall claim that your essay makes. An essay's argument should be summarized in its thesis statement. Arguments must be debatable, meaning that they must make a claim that a reasonable person could object to.

Assonance: Repeated or similar vowel sounds in words in close proximity. Assonance contributes to the rhythm and music of language, most notably in poetry. Can include words with end rhymes and internal rhymes.

Atmosphere: The general feeling created for the reader or audience by a text. Atmosphere is usually accomplished through descriptive language, setting, and imagery.

Audience: The person or people who are reading, listening to, or viewing a text. An author targets an intended audience by using strategies that will be particularly effective for that person or people. An audience might be a primary audience (the person for whom the text is generated) or a secondary audience (the person who has an interest in the topic because that person is connected to/interested in the speaker, the primary audience, or the topic).

Author/Speaker: In a rhetorical situation, the author/speaker is the person or people seeking to communicate a specific message.

Balance: In visual analysis, the "visual weight" of crowded or attention-grabbing items in the image. For example, an image with most of its important focal points on one side of the image could be described as off-balance and weighted to the left.

Blogging: Compiled from the two terms "web" and "logging," blogging refers to personal or reflective writing that is published online. Blogs can have very limited or very broad audiences, and they can cover virtually any area of interest.

Character: The summation of moral and mental qualities of a person. Character is often used to build credibility. Usually a subjective evaluation of what constitutes a "strong character" depends upon the audience's (or evaluator's) values.

Citation: The method used to document when an author is referencing or using information from another text. Most academic writing citations require that authors use a specific citation style. Style guides are usually associated with specific disciplines like MLA (Modern Language Association), APA (American Psychological Association), or CMS (Chicago Manual of Style—regularly used by historians).

Claim: Assertions made in support of the argument a writer is advocating. An essay's thesis is often referred to as its "primary claim."

Cliché: An expression used so often that it has become hackneyed and lost its original impact. For example, "since the beginning of time," and "throughout history" are both clichés.

Close reading: Focusing attention on the aspects of a text that seem most important. Close reading involves first scanning a text to get a basic sense of the text and its purpose. Then you should read more closely for content and meaning, considering how the text is constructed. In addition, you should consider your reactions to the text. Finally, you should review the text and your responses to form some general conclusions.

Collaborative writing processes: An understanding that more than one person participates in the processes used to contribute to the creation of a text.

Composing practices: The strategies and processes for producing texts. Just like reading, the steps of writing will depend on the elements of the rhetorical situation like the genre, purpose, audience, and context. As you begin composing, you might need to brainstorm some ideas, collect some information, then begin a draft of your essay, get feedback, and delete an entire section and start again, re-read articles to polish a line of reasoning, brainstorm ideas for a different section, and edit again before you turn in a final draft.

Connotations: The associations evoked by a word beyond its literal meaning. Connotations can be unique to a particular individual. For instance, a victim of near-drowning may associate water with terror.

Context: The circumstances surrounding the creation and reception of a text. For example, the personal associations of readers, the biographical backgrounds of writers, related historical events, and political purposes can all contribute to a text's context. The best contexts to study are those that illuminate the meanings and uses of the text.

Contrast: Strong juxtapositions of opposites, such as light and dark, depressing and cheerful, rigid and soft, frantic and calm, etc.

Controversy: A contentious social issue that has a larger relevance for a society and those living within it.

Copyright: A legal protection that authors or creators can use to seek to limit the ways that others can use their work. Creative Common licenses are a type of copyright license; some are quite restrictive and others allow authors to use the Creative Commons licensed text in any way as long as the author is attributed.

Counterclaim: An argument presented in opposition to the argument a text is making. When making a claim, it's important to consider the counterclaims that might arise against your own arguments.

Credibility: How trustworthy or reliable a source is for an author's purpose. You might consider the identity of the source's author, who published it, where and when it was published, the target audience for the source, and the timeliness and relevance of the information.

Database: An electronic collection of a wide variety of resources, such as newspapers, magazines, and scholarly journals that have been compiled electronically and are searchable by keyword, author, title, subject, and more. Examples of databases include Academic Search Complete, JSTOR, and ProQuest.

Debatable topics: Appropriate topics for a researched argument. Debatable topics must fulfill two criteria. First, they have to stimulate some sort of argument or disagreement, meaning they go beyond reporting the "facts." Second, debatable topics are issues that other researchers have investigated enough for you to be able to locate sufficient resources to inform your understanding of the topic.

Design: The visual layout and presentation of information in a document. This includes the relationships among visual elements, such as images and graphics, and textual elements. The purpose of design is to enhance visual appeal and readability.

Discourse community: A group of people who share a specific set of writing and speaking practices, as well as specialized vocabulary that is understood by members of the group.

Documentation: Any method of telling the reader that the idea, work, or image is from someone else.

Dominance: In visual analysis, the first thing that your eye is drawn to in an image is the dominant part of that image.

Ethos: A rhetorical strategy in which a writer/speaker attempts to build credibility and character in a text.

Evidence: specific pieces of information or data used to support a reason that then supports a larger claim. Evidence can be from either primary or secondary data.

Fair Use: United States federal policy that allows several considerations for when intellectual property can be used *without* explicit permission, including how much of the work is being used and whether it is for nonprofit educational purposes.

Feedback: Comments provided about a piece of writing that can act as tangible evidence of a reader's experience with your writing.

Figurative language: Language that employs one or more figures of speech, such as metaphor, simile, synecdoche, or personification.

First-person: Narration strategy that relies on the personal pronouns "I" and "we." The **first-person point of view** is usually considered to be more subjective and often used in autobiographical and personal writing.

Focus: In visual analysis, refers to whether a section of the image is clear (in focus) or blurry (out of focus).

Foreshadowing: The technique of introducing material into a narrative that prepares the reader for future events or revelations. Examples of foreshadowing could include mentioning a gun early in the narrative that will later shoot someone, or implying that a character is threatening through suggestive language before his actions become villainous.

Form: The patterns and structure associated with a specific genre of writing. For example, in poetry, patterns such as rhythm, rhyme, meter, repeated words and images, line breaks, stanza breaks, spatial organization on the page, and more create the form of a poem.

Format: The organization and arrangement of a text. Format usually focuses a bit more on the organization and function of a document; however, it is also concerned with design.

Formality: Observance of the rules or conventions that govern a particular genre or medium of communication. For example, the use of contractions ("We're," "Haven't," "It'll") is common in casual conversation but discouraged in the writing of some academic disciplines.

Framing: In visual analysis, what is included in the field of the image (what is visible to the viewer) and what is not included. For example, an artist can frame his or her image to only show part of an item and therefore call attention to it.

Freewriting: A prewriting technique designed to help a writer develop ideas. Freewriting involves designating a set amount of time (e.g., fifteen minutes), and writing whatever comes to your mind, without pausing or rereading, until the set amount of time has expired.

Gender criticism: Rhetorically analyzing a text in terms of gender involves examining the ways that a text seeks to reinforce, challenge, or disrupt systems of inequality based on gender.

Gender performance: Behavior that performs femininity or masculinity in culturally appropriate ways, such as wearing a skirt and high heels to emphasize femininity.

Genre: Categories that group texts based on their audience, purpose, content, and form. As a writer, understanding the genre of a text will help you in knowing the expectations and conventions surrounding that text and will help in distinguishing the **rhetorical options** that are available. As a reader, the ability to identify a text's genre will give hints to its purpose and will also provide an appropriate framework to aid in comprehension.

Global revisions: Revisions focused on making changes to the content or organization of a text. Also may be referred to as Higher Order Concerns (HOCs).

Grammar: Rules that govern sentence and word construction such as subject-verb agreement, verb tense, word form, and pluralization.

Hyperbole: Employing deliberate, emphatic exaggeration, sometimes intended for ironic effect. Saying something is "the very best in the world" could be a hyperbolic statement. The opposite of this is understatement.

Idea mapping: As a method of organizing analysis, a visual representation of how the ideas in a text are related to both the main point(s) and each other. An idea map emphasizes the interconnectedness of ideas. This is also called "webbing" or "clustering."

Identification: A rhetorical strategy in which an author/speaker works to identify with the members of an audience by pointing out the qualities, characteristics, assumptions, beliefs, and goals that they share with one another. It's important to keep in mind that identification does not mean "sameness," and an author/speaker must define and explain the importance of any type of identification he or she establishes with the audience.

Ideology: Ideology involves the beliefs that people hold, the prominent ideas that tell us what should be, must be, or what seems normal. Sometimes called "cultural values" when in reference to a popular or widely held belief. For example, the idea of democracy in the United States is an ideology—it assumes that everyone should have a voice and that everyone's voice should be equal. Other ideologies include capitalism, socialism, and education.

Ideological criticism: A strategy for rhetorical analysis that examines the ways that an author/speaker uses language to reinforce, challenge, or modify an audience's ideological understanding of the world.

Inquiry: The process of investigating a question or series of questions about a topic of interest.

Intellectual property: "Something (such as an idea, invention, or process) that comes from a person's mind" (*Merriam-Webster Dictionary*). When thinking and writing your own work that may draw on ideas from another person, it is important to recognize and note when you are using that other person's idea or words.

Irony (ironic): A contradiction or incongruity between appearance or expectation and reality. This could be the difference between what people say and what they actually mean, between what appears to be true and what actually is true, or between what someone expects to happen and what actually happens. This is often subtly comic or tongue-in-cheek.

Literacy: Generally refers to the ability to understand a system of language. Literacy usually refers to the competent understanding and use of written language, including abilities in reading and writing. However, literacy can also refer to one's level of knowledge of a particular culture (cultural literacy).

Literacy narrative: A personal narrative that focuses on an event or events in the author's acquisition of literacy. Literacy narratives can explore a specific, significant experience with writing, reading, and/or language, or they can discuss how writing, reading, and/or language have played a role in the author's past experience.

Local revisions: Revisions focused on surface features such as grammar, spelling, and mechanics. May be referred to as Lower Order Concerns (LOCs).

Logical fallacies: Arguments in a text that are questionable or invalid because they rest on faulty logic. Logical fallacies may be persuasive even if they are not logically valid.

Logos: A rhetorical strategy in which a writer/speaker appeals to an audience by making logical arguments. The most basic analysis of logos considers whether claims are developed using inductive or deductive reasoning. Analyzing the logical fallacies in an argument is another way to consider a text's logos.

Mechanics: Capitalization, punctuation, spelling, and other conventions that convert oral language to written text.

Medium: The form or material through which communication takes place or is finally delivered. For instance, an alphabetic print document communicates information differently than a painted mural. Audiences will therefore read and interpret a print document differently than a mural.

Metaphor: Associates two distinct things without using a connective word such as "like" or "as." "That child is a mouse" is a metaphor.

Modalities: The different types of media used in producing and publishing a text.

Narrative: Can refer to any story that describes events or experiences, whether fictional or factual. Thus newspaper articles that describe recent events or novels that describe a character's journey follow a narrative structure. When you are telling a group of friends about your most recent camping trip, you are telling a narrative as well.

Paraphrase: Presentation of another's thoughts or ideas in your own language. Unlike a summary, it usually includes the same level of detail as the original text. Paraphrases help the audience better understand the original text and why it is important to the author's argument. You should cite page numbers for the sections of text you are paraphrasing.

Paragraphs: Larger units within an alphanumerically written text that are usually composed of three or more sentences. Paragraphs usually focus on a specific sub-topic, line of reasoning, or explication of a piece of evidence.

Pathos: A rhetorical strategy in which a writer/speaker appeals to an audience's emotions in order to move the audience toward the author's position.

Persona: Refers to the ability to present yourself differently according to different situations.

Personal writing: A nonfiction genre of writing that focuses on the writer's personal experience(s) as the main subject of the work. Reflective writing is a kind of personal writing.

Personification: Involves giving human characteristics to anything nonhuman. For example, "Father Time" is a personification.

Point of view: The vantage point from which a narrative is told, either first-person, third-person, or second-person. First-person narratives are told by a narrator who refers to himself or herself as "I" and is often a part of the action. Third-person narrators can either be omniscient, all-knowing and reliable, or limited, restricted to a single character at a time. Second-person narrators speak directly to the reader as "you."

Popular source: A text written for a public audience rather than for an audience of experts. You may think of a popular source as a text written by a non-expert (or occasionally by an expert) for a broad audience of non-experts.

Prewriting: The stage of composition that generally involves thinking about your writing situation, exploring possible topics to write about, choosing a topic, generating ideas about the topic, researching the topic, and outlining the essay.

Primary research: Any type of research where writers directly interrogate the object of study and collect new data for themselves. If researching flowers, the researcher will observe or experiment with flowers. If researching student's attitudes about required general education courses, the researcher will ask students. Much primary research is completed outside of the classroom, library, or office; it requires that researchers go out into the field.

Primary source: This term is used to refer to original materials on which other research is based. Primary sources are often the result of primary research, where the writer gathers firsthand information directly him or herself through observation, experimentation, interviews, or other research methods.

Punctuation: Symbols used to help organize written text and provide meaning to words, phrases, and sentences.

Purpose: Refers to the reason and objective for writing. As a writer, your purpose, usually determined before you begin writing, can be as varied as persuading an audience to change his/her opinion on an issue, to do something, or to feel a certain way. Your purpose can also be to report facts and information, to entertain a reader, or to simply express your feelings, as you would in a diary. Much writing has more than just one purpose.

Quality: The accuracy and reliability of the information contained in a source. One way to assess a source's quality is to determine whether it was self-published (without the input of an editor or editorial team) or published via a media company (with the assistance and input of an editor or editorial team).

Quotation: Uses the exact words from a writer's original source, with no changes in language or punctuation. You may quote an entire sentence or a part of a sentence, depending on what is most useful for your writing purpose. Quotations must always be cited.

Reading practices: The strategies and processes for consuming texts. Think of a *practice* as a loosely defined step—you might start with pre-reading questions, summarize a section of a text, underline terms, re-read another section, skim a section, write connections in the margins, and underline passages to use as quotes in a response paper. These different strategies can help you achieve your purposes as you read a text.

Reason: A statement or idea that supports your thesis.

Reflect: The act of thinking about current and past actions in order to explore significance, make meaning, or connect to other ideas, concepts, and experiences.

Reflective writing: A kind of personal writing that focuses on a writer's responses to a particular experience or text.

Research methods: The means by which a writer acquires information and data about a subject of interest. Researchers may be asked to articulate specific methods they used to collect, manage, and analyze data.

Revision processes: The strategies and practices in which writers review, reimagine, and reconceive their composition. These processes are revolving and recurring, and will be utilized throughout all points of the composing timeline.

Rhetor: Refers to any person who is using rhetoric.

Rhetoric (rhetorical): Any type of communication that seeks to move an audience toward a specific position, understanding, or action.

Rhetorical analysis: An analysis of how writers and speakers use language in particular situations to achieve predetermined goals. Rhetorical analysis involves evaluating the effectiveness of a speaker/author's rhetorical strategies.

Rhetorical awareness/Rhetorical knowledge: An author's awareness of the choices available for communicating effectively with audiences. Authors make different choices depending on the audiences they desire to reach and the purposes they hope to achieve in particular circumstances. Awareness of these factors will enable you to discern why and how a particular text was produced. Your rhetorical knowledge as a reader can in turn help you to discern the *rhetorical situation*—the audience, context, and purpose—for your own writing, and to decide upon the strategies that you will employ to achieve your purposes.

Rhetorical options: The features that an author selects from when communicating with an audience. Rhetorical options include strategies and appeals, and they can range from choices in words and designs in a text to the actual medium in which that text is presented. In any writing situation, an author has multiple rhetorical options available to choose from, and each option may impact a primary or secondary audience in various ways.

Glossary

Rhetorical situation: A communication event in which the author/speaker attempts to communicate some message to an audience for a specific purpose and within a specific context.

Rhetorical strategies: The rhetorical methods an author uses to construct a text, develop ideas, and persuade an audience.

Rubric: A tool that your instructor may use to grade essays. It often resembles a chart with rows for categories of writing criteria and columns that describe achievement levels. These columns usually progress from the highest level of achievement on the left to the lowest level on the right.

Scale: In visual analysis, the size of objects within an image. If all objects seem to be of a normal size, then the scale of the image is natural. If some seem larger or smaller than normal, the scale of the image could be exaggerated.

Scholarly source: A text written for an audience with specialized knowledge about a particular subject. You might think of a scholarly source as a text written by an expert for an audience of experts in a given field.

Second-person: Narration strategy that directly addresses the reader, using the pronoun "you." Second-person point of view is usually used to instruct the reader or to demand the reader's attention. Often used in business and technical writing. An informal substitution for a general subject ("you want" instead of "one wants"). Sometimes discouraged in academic writing.

Secondary audience: The readers of a text that are not the author's primary focus. This audience has access to the text but is not the principal audience for which the text was designed. They may have different values or backgrounds than the primary audience and so may react differently to the text. Sometimes, they are simply a wider or broader audience than the addressee of a text.

Secondary research: Any type of research where the writer discovers information about the specific topic generated by other writers/researchers.

Secondary source: Sources that comment on and have a direct relationship to the primary text. Some common examples of secondary sources are an analysis of a literary text, a critique of a painting or photograph, a movie review, or an opinion about an interview.

Secondary text: Sources used to enable or extend an analysis of a primary text. Secondary texts may not comment directly on the primary text.

Signal phrase: Words that identify the original speaker your text is borrowing from. Signal phrases make it clear that you're borrowing from someone else's ideas. Example signal phrases include "As Author L writes," "According to Author L," and "Author L argues."

Simile: Compares two distinct things by using words such as "like" or "as." "That child is like a cyclone" is a simile.

Sources: The people, places, or texts that provide information (research and evidence) for your use.

Student Learning Goals: A category of knowledge or ability that students will gain in foundations writing. Everything you do in your class, from discussion of assigned readings to major projects, is designed to help you meet one or more of these Goals and their associated Student Learning Outcomes.

Student Learning Outcomes: A specific knowledge or ability that students will gain from an articulated learning situation.

Structure: The arrangement and organization of your writing and the relation of each part to the whole.

Style: Refers to specific traits in a written work, including elements such as word choice, sentence/paragraph structure, sentence/paragraph ordering, or genre conventions. When instructors grade an essay for "style," they are often looking for a combination of the conventions of academic writing and comfortable, readable diction/sentence structure.

Summary: An abbreviated version of a longer text—your statement of what you see to be the major points of a text using your own words. Summaries usually include the who, what, why, when, where, and how of a given text. A summary can be one sentence long, one paragraph long, or one page long, depending on the length of the text and your purpose as a writer.

Symbolism: The sustained use of symbols to represent or suggest other things or ideas. For example, you could say that an author "uses symbols of nature" to evoke certain associations for the reader.

Synecdoche: A part of something used to represent the whole, such as referring to a car as "wheels."

Synthesize: To combine or put sources of information into conversation as a way to develop understanding or a new meaning. A writer who synthesizes primary data and secondary sources compares and contrasts information looking for trends, themes, similarities, and differences. Synthesized information should move from having separate pieces to a more fused whole (or something new).

Technologies: The materials and applications used by writers and readers throughout all stages of the composing and consumption process.

Text: In analysis, any artifact or object that you analyze—whether written or visual. In your first-year writing courses, you'll be dealing with a variety of texts. For example, a text might refer to a book, a newspaper article, a short story, a poem, a speech, a movie, a picture, a video game, a person, an event, a space, a place, and so on.

Glossary

Thesis: An *arguable* claim with supporting reasons and evidence. A thesis makes a contribution to an ongoing conversion. It does not merely present a well-known fact but is a statement open to debate.

Third-person: Narration strategy that uses pronouns such as "he," "she," "it," and "they." Third-person point of view does not address readers directly but rather relies on an outside, impersonal narrator. The most common point of view in academic and formal writing.

Tone: As a textual strategy, this is an author's attitude toward the reader, audience, or subject matter. An author's tone can be optimistic, morbid, humorous, excited, etc. As a writing strategy, tone refers to the attitude that you, the writer, develop toward your own audience.

Topic: In a researched essay, a topic is a general area of inquiry, the overall subject of your essay. A topic is not an argument; rather, it's the more general subject about which your essay argues.

Topic sentence: One sentence that states the main point of the paragraph. Sometimes, the topic sentence is the first sentence of your paragraph. Regardless of where it is placed, every paragraph should include a topic sentence, while other sentences in the paragraph develop, illustrate, or define the idea in that topic sentence.

Visual: A graphic, image, or other type of text that is perceived through the audience's optical sense. Visual texts may be used as specific pieces of evidence in an argument. For example, presenting quantitative data in tables or charts usually makes them more easily understood to an audience.

Visual rhetoric: A form of communication in which visual elements create meanings and arguments.

Voice: The style used to convey an individual author's, or character's, personality. Voice is usually composed of the amalgamation of the rhetorical choices in formality, tone, word choice, sentence style, etc.

About the Editors

Christopher Brown is a PhD student in Rhetoric, Composition, and the Teaching of English. He has taught first-year writing, technical writing, and profes-

sional writing at the University of Arizona. His research considers how composition teachers can draw on students' deeply held beliefs to encourage and facilitate critical thinking. In addition to studying and teaching, Chris enjoys hiking in the desert and exploring botanical gardens.

Eric House is a PhD student in Rhetoric, Composition, and the Teaching of English. He has taught first-year writing and

technical writing at the University of Arizona and serves as a co-chair on the Writing Program's Difference & Inequality Committee. His research is focused on uncovering connections between hip-hop and the teaching of composition. Outside of the classroom you can find Eric attempting (and often failing) to relive his glory days on the basketball court, or blending in with the crowd at a local hip-hop show.

About the Editors